On Psychothe

The Whurr Psychotherapy Series seeks to publish selected works of foremost experts in the fields of counselling and psychotherapy. Each volume features the best of a key figure's work, bringing together papers that have been published widely in the professional literature. In this way the work of leading counsellors and psychotherapists is made accessible in single volumes.

Windy Dryden
Series Editor

Titles in the Psychotherapy Series

Person-centred Counselling: Therapeutic and Spiritual Dimensions
Brian Thorne

Reason and Therapeutic Change
Windy Dryden

The Essential Arnold Lazarus
Edited by Windy Dryden

Breakthroughs and Integration in Psychotherapy
John Rowan

From Medicine to Psychotherapy
Mark Aveline

On Psychotherapy
Petrūska Clarkson

On Psychotherapy

Petrūska Clarkson

Psychotherapy Series

Series Editor: Windy Dryden

Whurr Publishers
London

First published 1993 by
Whurr Publishers Ltd
19b Compton Terrace, London N1 2UN, England

British Library Cataloguing in Publication Data
A catalogue record for this book is available from the British Library.

ISBN 1-870332-53-9

Photoset by Stephen Cary
Printed and bound in the UK by Athenaeum Press Ltd, Newcastle upon Tyne

Preface

The Book

My philosophical values have always been to encourage freedom of thought, excitement of exploration, emphasis on individuality and a reluctance to accept a single doctrine as an ultimate truth. At the heart of this orientation is the concept of individual responsibility for individual behaviour (whether conscious or unconscious), as well as responsibility towards others. So while striving for excellence of individual development, I attempt to encourage this within a framework of respect for the person and our shared common humanity, and the development of specialist, as well as integrative, skills and interests. Obviously such polarities are not always harmoniously reconciled at any one moment for all time. The enquiry is to be valued as well as the attempt in an atmosphere of mutual respect, all the while knowing that at some times one aspect of a polarity will be in ascendance. At other times the natural balancing effect of enantodromia will have something to contribute to the continuing process of the evolution of our ideas, practice and ideals. We have learned from our planetary and individual histories that what seemed like incontrovertible truths at one time may later need changing or substantial revising. However painful, uncomfortable (or seductively easy) this process of change, revolution and re-evaluation may seem at times, we are committed to discovery rather than certainty. This reflects the striving for authenticity in a therapeutic relationship which, transferential or not, seeks to affirm the unique individuality of every person rather than seeking to fit the person to a theory.

This book brings together a small selection of some of my major papers, published and as yet unpublished.

It is divided into five sections: professional orientation; cornerstones of psychotherapy – the relationship, change, commonality and difference; transference and countertransference in psychotherapy and supervision; systemic integrative psychotherapy; and a look to the future in terms of emerging new perspectives.

The material concerns many different moments of illumination, perhaps contradictory, if not complementary, visions of the work of psychotherapy and psychological counselling. I hope that I will already have changed again by the time you read about these moments. Certain themes among these papers are recurrently evident – the interest in professional overlap areas and boundary-making processes, the interplay between the individual and the collective, the importance of relationship, the particular relationship of the couple, the nature of change and change processes, the nature and celebration of healing and creativity, the notion of integration as based on common truths between apparently divergent or even contradictory points of view on reality, the transference–countertransference field related to the relationship between therapist and client, a preoccupation with the intriguing results of modern science, a fascination with how culture and literature can mirror or activate creative or empathic responses, the discomfort of multiple truths, the eternal quest of investigation and open-mindedness, in the end, eventually there is left only the mystery.

Because this is a collection of papers written for different audiences at different times, terms used may vary between chapters. For example, I may sometimes be speaking exclusively of psychotherapy, whereas the counsellor or counselling psychologist may equally well find the material useful. Reader are advised to hold their own areas of interest as a high focus throughout reading this book, and to interpret or translate according to their own profession and/or orientation, whatever seems of interest and usefulness to them. Anyone who is interested in contributing to some of these cross-translations is very welcome to get in touch with me. Some people have already engaged in such work, for example, Jennifer Mackewn (1991) has re-interpreted and extended the transference/countertransference material for gestalt psychotherapists, and Patricia Shaw has done extensive work on applying the outcomes of psychotherapy material to the outcomes of organisational interventions in management development.

The first section, on professional orientation, concentrates on delineating counselling, psychotherapy, psychology (clinical and counselling) and applied psychology. The ongoing confusion between different spheres of activity by helping professionals under an array of different titles exacerbates what is already a painful situation to ordinary people in need of help, and potentially impedes those who are in a position to refer them. There are sometimes reports of well-functioning individuals who set out to find someone to help them with a circumscribed problem such as a lack of interest in sex with a marital partner, and then, having entered, for example, five-times-weekly psychoanalysis or psychotherapy, may end up several years later with a sense of having been misled or misinformed. In organisations, the confusion surrounding people's understanding of the term 'counselling' in relation to popular appreciation of other terms such as 'psychotherapy', 'psychiatry', 'psychology', may seriously contaminate the well-intentioned provision of employee counselling services.

One of the reasons for writing this section is to contribute to the formulation of a well-defined professional identity for counselling psychologists and counsellors in general, including employee counsellors. An important implication of defining the domain of counselling is that guidelines can begin to be drawn up to enable referral agencies, professionals, and members of the public, to distinguish between different kinds of service provision, so that needs and resources can be more accurately aligned, including employee counselling services.

The second section concerns the cornerstones of psychotherapy as I see it now. These are relationship, change, difference and commonality. I find these themes common across most, if not all, of the psychotherapies I have studied, and recurrent in the work of both theoreticians and clinicians of a wide variety of persuasions. Whichever language (transactional analysis, psychodynamic, gestalt, existential, or ordinary English) I am using to discuss these seems less important than the fact that they all address central concerns in counselling and psychotherapy. The most important of these for me at the moment is the necessity to understand and use the multiplicity of psychotherapeutic relationships available within the helping relationship.

The chapter on a multiplicity of psychotherapeutic relationships (Chapter 2) distinguishes, theoretically and by means of clinical examples, dreams and kinship metaphors, between five different kinds of psychotherapeutic relationship which may potentially be available for constructive use in psychotherapy. These are: the working alliance; the transferential/countertransferential relationship; the reparative/developmentally needed relationship; the person-to-person relationship; and the transpersonal relationship. These five modalities can act as an integrative framework for different traditions (or approaches) of psychotherapy notwithstanding apparently irreconcilable schisms or popular stereotypes.

Chapter 3 considers outcomes of psychotherapy. It was originally submitted for a transactional analysis audience and won the 1989 European Association of Transactional Analysis Award for Contribution to Theory, Brussels, 1990. However, people from a variety of persuasions, including organisational consultants who did not know any transactional analysis, have found it useful and generalisable in a variety of different fields and idioms.

In this chapter, five possible outcomes of psychotherapy are identified: script cure, making progress, casualty, disillusionment and 'counterscript cure'. Each of these 'faces of change' is discussed in systematic terms with its own frame of reference, including idiosyncratic motivations for seeking/avoiding future changes, characteristic response patterns and differing capacities in managing distress. Each is associated with an archetypal or mythological image which may aid the psychotherapist in distinguishing, defining and recognising the five types of outcome so that he or she can facilitate life script changes which are genuine, stable under stress, and provide a fertile and resilient ground for future growth.

Chapter 4 is about metanoia – a process of transformation. Metanoia is presented as a unifying concept for describing change in life and in psychotherapy. The major circumstances under which metanoia occurs are reviewed, as well as its commonly occurring features, in order to broaden the perspective of the transactional analyst. Material drawn from clinical casework, literature, film and anecdotal sources is presented to illustrate the concept.

This chapter defines *metanoia* (a concept referring to the *turning point* in life and in psychotherapy), reviews the major circumstances under which it occurs, and indicates its commonly occurring features. The aim is to place psychotherapy in a wider context and perhaps broaden the consciousness of psychotherapists to adjacent fields of human enquiry and endeavour. Transactional analysis is one of many psychotherapies which have a particular interest in conditions that bring about change. Closer study of the elements of metanoia or turning points of different kinds can contribute to the learning, understanding and perhaps the clinical practice of transactional analysts. This chapter is, however, intended as an overall map of the territory and not as a detailed study of each of the individual circumstances and features.

The next chapter (Chapter 5) pursues the theme of what can and cannot be changed, and applies it to couples therapy with occasional references to much larger systems such as nations.

This chapter outlines a particular conceptual framework or working tool which individuals, couples and couples therapists have found useful in exploring the meaning of love and separateness, increasing the opportunities for love in couples relationships and reducing the potential for war in the intimacy zone. Three categories of difference between partners are outlined as an example, both of specific couples therapy work in the microcosm, and of the relationships of nations in the macrocosm.

The ideas in this chapter are designed to evoke questioning of what the psychotherapist can and cannot hope to facilitate, and what the couple realistically can or cannot hope to achieve, in couples counselling or therapy. Exploring the feasibility or likelihood of effective therapeutic action towards different therapeutic goals can sometimes prevent disillusionment and despair. Clarifying the kind of goals and achievability or morality of certain desired changes in couplehood seems to me vitally important, and sometimes a neglected aspect of couples work. Disagreement about the categories of difference I put forward here is to be welcomed and explored between the partners and the therapist. Such disagreement can be used to enrich the viability and usefulness of this contribution to the resources of the couples therapist.

The next chapter (6), Individuality and Commonality in Gestalt, is of particular interest to gestalt therapists and organisational consultants, but it also specifically concerns the creative evolutionary force, Physis, which I believe to be common to all growthful and healing endeavour, whether in education, pastoral care, organisations or concerns with the future of our planet.

This chapter explores a field perspective on gestalt, which acknowledges both its historical antecedents in early Greek philosophy, as well as the theoretical adjacents from which Perls, Hefferline and Goodman drew in order to create gestalt therapy in the 1950s. It is postulated that, as gestalt itself is a growing, changing organism, it is organismally healthy for it to be both proactive and reactive towards changing national and international developments, in terms of gestalt therapy in particular and psychotherapy in general, as we move towards the next century. The important polarities of individuality and commonality are explored, and it is suggested that creative growth or holistic evolution between these can be mediated by a third force, which Heraclitus called 'Physis'.

Physis, as conceived by the pre-Socratics, is the creative life force that strives for increased wholeness and increased perfection through evolutionary processes of growth and change.

> We are part of an Order, a cosmos, which we see to be infinitely above our comprehension.... But in the rest of the world, we can see a moving Purpose. It is Physis, the word which the Romans unfortunately translated 'Nature', but which means 'growing' or 'the way things grow' – almost what we call Evolution.
>
> (Murray, 1955, p. 215)

This is seen as identical with the generalised creative life force which is particularly characteristic of gestalt therapy and derives particularly from the legacy of Smuts, whom Perls acknowledged as a major influence on his work.

I believe that this Physis is the name people have been looking for in describing the life force; it is equivalent to Bergson's *élan vital* (1965).We need to reintroduce ourselves to Physis, the life force of which we are the servants in psychotherapy. I believe it is the task of psychotherapists and educators to allow people to get back in touch with that inner force.

The third section concerns a specific approach to integration called systemic integrative psychotherapy. The first chapter here (Chapter 7) is an early applied clinical paper called Systemic Integrative Psychotherapy with a Bereaved Girl and was co-authored by Roland Evans, a probationary clinical psychologist at the time, and Charlotte Sills, then a bereavement counsellor – both of whom were then in supervision with me.

This chapter describes brief focused therapy with a traumatised girl whose symptoms in response to her mother's horrible suicide served to stabilise and fixate the bereaved family in order to avoid and deny the loss of the mother. The therapists' decision to combine individual work with the child and family therapy is highlighted. An account is given of the interventions used to reduce the girl's phobic symptoms, pre-empt the possible development of incest and allow the family to start grieving normally. Within a systems framework based on integrating cathexis material with the racket system, a number of different approaches were used, including transactional analysis, gestalt, behavioural techniques and bereavement counselling.

The next chapter (8) concerns systemic integrative psychotherapy. This includes contributions from Phil Lapworth of major explanatory diagrams, and the case study, showing how he applied the model to a particular client. The chapter incorporates the seven-level model, which I developed and have taught since 1975. I also had the benefit of recent editorial input from James Low. As in psychoanalysis and psychotherapy generally, there is an impressive variety of integrative psychotherapy trainings (Norcross et al., 1986). Models for integrative psychotherapy training can be thrown into relief in terms of two arguably opposite positions: (1) integration from the beginning of psychotherapy training; and (2) integration after training in one or more 'pure' forms of psychotherapy has been completed. Proponents of the first view maintain that trainees who are educated in an integrative position from the beginning are better able to develop both academically and professionally, because they meet early on the required skills of intellectual questioning and tolerance for other perspectives. Proponents of the second view contend that integrative activities are the fruits of maturity and experience, which can be better done if solid foundations have been built in singular approaches that emotionally provide a sense of early security and later disillusionment, as the practitioner experiences the practical and theoretical limitations of any one particular system. At metanoia we have opted for both.

So, although insight, analysis and understanding are highly valued, these ultimately serve the processes of individual transformation and collective evolution. Difference can be delightful and communication and respectful cooperation are probably the desired climate for learning, growth and healing.

The fourth section concerns transference and countertransference in psychotherapy and supervision. Chapter 9 reviews both narrow and broad definitions of transference and countertransference and provides a map showing these definitions in terms of transactional analysis. It briefly differentiates four categories:

1. What the patient brings to the relationship (proactive transference).
2. What the psychotherapist brings (proactive countertransference or therapist transference – pathological).
3. What the psychotherapist reacts to in the patient (reactive countertransference – inductive).
4. What the patient reacts to as a result of what the psychotherapist brings (patient-countertransference or reactive transference).

Any of these may form the basis for facilitative or destructive psychotherapeutic outcomes.

Chapter 10 considers the management of transference and countertransference phenomena in transactional analysis – including Berne's original diagrams – in terms of crossed transactions. It is suggested that transference and countertransference (from both the patient's and the therapist's perspectives) function as an inseparable, systemic whole. The concept of parallel process is presented along with an analysis of these constituent parts of the interactional field in the therapeutic relationship. It is hypothesised that this interpersonal field is paralleled in the supervision process. It is further suggested that the mechanism for this replication is projective identification, conceived of as mutually interacting hypnotic inductions which occur out of awareness in the form of ulterior transactions.

Chapter 11 – New perspectives – attempts to draw together some of the most elusive, conceptual, and experiential threads which can inform counselling and psychotherapy as we head for the next century. I focus on changes in our conceptual environment, particularly postmodernism, and changes in our scientific context, particularly quantum dynamics and chaos theory. I also refer briefly to our changing world, drawing from experiences of the demolition of the Berlin Wall, the period after the release of Mandela in South Africa, and the so-called second Russian revolution to highlight some of the unanswered questions which face change agents of all kinds, including psychotherapists and organisational consultants in the future. Finally I come to some temporary conclusions or momentary punctuation marks. These, in some important ways, rest on the deconstruction of everything I have known so far, as well as an openness to 'beginner's mind', full to the brim of ignorance, humility, compassion, and incomprehension at the mystery of our existence and our strange profession. I gratefully acknowledge Vincent Keyter's editorial assistance and support in this chapter, and fittingly this volume ends with some poetic meditations.

The Author

When I was seven years old I decided to become a brain surgeon so that I could be a doctor of unhappy minds and 'make them better'. Several career decisions later, I started formal training and learning to be a clinical psychologist, a counsellor and then a psychotherapist. I had the deep and abiding hope that I could find understanding of the sadness and distress of human pain, learn the skills of helping people to free themselves from the shackles of their conditioning, their restricted beliefs and cultural limitations, and develop the necessary personal qualities which would transform my promising potential for healing into the genuine article. I studied Carl Rogers, went on encounter groups, did a Freudian analysis with a Tavistock trained analyst, learnt about changing organisational systems from American university teachers, worked in suicide prevention and in mental hospitals, advertising and universities; I had a brief and unhappy excursion with a Kleinian analyst, experienced and trained in gestalt, transactional analysis, bioenergetics, individual psychoanalysis, group psychotherapy, family therapy, sex therapy, suicide prevention and crisis counselling. These were not light studies – I gave several of these systems many years, an unstinting fortune in very hard-earned money, time and energy.

For all the years of academic study, I also worked for a living, as well as being extensively involved in voluntary work. This ranged from years of service on a telephone counselling team for the prevention of suicide, to a crisis clinic in mid-city Johannesburg. Here I first discovered the usefulness of gestalt in individual and family breakdown during the peak of the high drug seasons of the 1960s.

During the earliest days of multiracial humanistic psychology I met a medical student, the late Dr Brian Dobson, at a 10-day group event under a blanket where we just cried together for a substantial part of one of the first encounter groups to be held in South Africa. It was at this ecumenical centre – Wilgespruit – where my academic training in occupational psychology was also fleshed out with organisation development trainers from the USA who were getting involved with consulting for social and organisational change. Brian and I worked together at the Tara Mental Hospital in Johannesburg and Brian remained a true friend and an inspiring colleague.

I recruited another clinical psychologist, Maria Gilbert, to teach humanistic and existential psychology to both professionals and non-professionals with me. We had both attended a clinical psychology programme which was largely psychodynamic and existentially oriented. It is still my belief that psychological knowledge can and should be made available to ordinary people, who may be taught at school how to brush their teeth and how to use condoms, but do not get the affective education that can help them cope better, more creatively and compassionately, with failure, fear, disappointment, rejection and grief – their feelings and emotional bodies. Together we opened a private psychotherapy practice lecturing and teaching extensively on psychology, transactional analysis, existential psychology, gestalt and couples counselling.

In 1975, Sue Fish, as organiser of a local behavioural science study group, invited me to give a talk on humanistic psychology and some months later she joined our household. Besides training as a teacher, Sue had been the first student at Cape Town University to combine two full-time courses, a Bachelor of Social Science degree and a speech and drama diploma – the start of a vision to use enactment to help people change their lives.

I studied and studied, going from degree to degree, and eventually admitted to myself that my doctoral thesis in clinical psychology was an attempt to find the 'truth' about human unhappiness. I continued to hope that the real truth, the genuine key, was in the next book, in the next lecture I would attend, or the next experiential understanding carved from my own personal struggles with my inner demons. I loved, I married, eventually I created a family. I found a guru, said my mantra and meditated on the Buddha nature for many years. I travelled in search of teachers in Europe and North America (Whittaker, Esalen, Minuchin, Erickson's heirs). I studied at the Tavistock, the Institute of Group Analysis, and spent ten more years in Jungian analysis. This knowledge that change is possible (which has been honed on personal and collective experiences of oppression, poverty and injustice) is encapsulated in the name metanoia which means 'to change', 'to turn around' or 'a transformation of mind or character' (see Chapter 4). Although the metanoia Psychotherapy Training Institute had practically existed from my meeting with Brian in 1971 in South Africa, it was 1981 when I designed and started the first training courses in London. On 4 May 1985, at the house-warming, we formally named this dream-made-reality metanoia.

Training at metanoia is an ongoing interweaving of left hemisphere and right hemisphere, knowledge and experience, playfulness and seriousness, physicality and spirituality, individuality and commonality, flexibility and range. Individual trainees (from integrative supervision to person-centred counselling) will experience or influence the training programmes in a variety of directions. At some time it is hoped all will be touched by the poetic polarity of the therapeutic experience, as voiced by the existentialist, Marcel (1952):

> Life is achieved by resolving the tension in responsive feeling and creative activity, in which having is not eliminated but is assimilated to being, in which one and another become I and thou; in which science is integrated with metaphysics; in which autonomy (managing my own affairs) is tran-

> scended in liberty, which is participation; in which my body and the world with which it is consubstantial and which enlarges and multiplies its powers is the place in which I bear witness to Being; in which I work out my fidelity and my hope and keep myself open, fluid and ready to spend.
>
> (p. 66)

To me, change is the most exciting, interesting process in the whole world. To study, participate in and master the principles of personal and collective change has been a leitmotiv of my life's work, and this preoccupation is evident in this book. After many years of facilitating change in clients and trainees, and working in programmes that invited change in the wider community of South Africa, Sue and I left our home country at the end of 1976 after the Soweto school riot. We left South Africa because we could no longer live in a situation where our very existence caused guilt. We chose not to endanger our lives and liberty in fighting a struggle over land which we could hardly call our own; a heartfelt and heartbreaking decision. Our friend Brian said at the time, 'Maybe it's better to be a small fish in a clean pond than a big fish in a dirty pond'. Of course, cleanliness is also relative. We came to England with our education, energy, personality, but little cash and the despair of immigrants, and have unremittingly continued to work for social change; whether it be the mounting of an exhibition of drawings from Hiroshima survivors, the financial support of a black medical student in South Africa, planetary consciousness work or training and consulting services to social change institutions or the personal provision of bursaries for training and reduced fees for professional services. In all of this, I took support from the Franciscan prayer about changing what you can, accepting what you cannot change, and becoming wiser and more questioning about the difference.

Alongside full-time, regular employment, I began to rebuild my psychotherapy, supervision and consultancy practice and Sue extended her training from remedial educational and emotional work with children to adult psychotherapy. In 1978 Brian, now fully qualified, arrived from South Africa to join our household. We bought a small terraced house and all three continued to work in full-time employment. At the same time we each continued to build up clinical activities, and in 1987 Maria Gilbert and her son Matthew arrived to join the household and our professional community.

In 1987 metanoia moved to 13 North Common Road in Ealing, with many friends and trainees helping transplant both the effects and the flavour of metanoia, and the rooms in the institute were named after some of the major influences in our work – Freud, Reich, Alice Miller, Moreno, Perls, Rogers, Fairbairn, Berne, Jung. One room is named Dobson, in honour of Brian, the first medical director and the original psychiatrist in the core working team. However, metanoia is not the building in which we work – it is the spirit of all the people who have participated and contributed their share over the period. Currently metanoia offers a wide range of training courses: in transactional analysis, gestalt, integrative and systemic integrative psychotherapy, supervision, client-centred counselling, couples counselling and child psychotherapy, as well as training in organisational change and development, such as redundancy counselling, stress counselling and creative leadership in management. Continuing to run alongside these at the time of writing are clinical and consultancy practices. There is an active Education for Living programme which is the charity branch of metanoia, keeping psychological knowledge available to lay people who may want understanding, experience and skills which can help them live well and more fully, without necessarily being clients or trainees. It is not in receipt of donations and shoulders a heavy, varied professional contribution, including work on substantial research initiatives. For example, we have participated in what is probably the largest gestalt therapy research project in Britain, but are still in need of finance to process its results. Workshop topics include, for example, creative aggression, psychodrama, health and healing, sexuality, discovering your inner child, bereavement, workshops for children, communication skills and working in multi-cultural settings.

The organisation metanoia continues to grow, develop and change, sometimes in unpredictable directions, e.g. the institute training courses and charity are now amalgamating.

Graduates of metanoia have founded their own training centres all over the country. International metanoia *fellows* are using what they learnt here in places as diverse as New Zealand, Switzerland, South Africa, Russia, the former Yugoslavia and Turkey. Other graduates are choosing to work as staff as metanoia continues to evolve and, in so doing, experiments with devolving, embracing the idea that the situation is in eternal flux – knowledge that the only certainty in our changing world is more change.

The founder members, graduates and staff trainees of metanoia are also active in a comprehensive range of psychotherapy and consulting forums nationally and internationally. They have contributed to setting professional standards, working with colleagues from other institutes on committees and working parties, and developing an impetus for excellence in the various fields in which they work. In fact, metanoia is represented at the United Kingdom Council for Psychotherapy, and it is approved as a training and accrediting institute in transactional analysis both by the Institute of Transactional Analysis and by the European and International Transactional Analysis Associations, and its gestalt training by the Gestalt Psychotherapy Training Institute. The supervision training programme has achieved academic validation and the counselling course has been accredited by the British Association of Counselling.

Those at metanoia are familiar with the gestalt cycle in which life goes round (see Chapter 4). As Heraclitus wrote, 'The cycle is the compact experiential reconciliation of permanence and degeneration' (Guerriere, 1980, p. 88). What we know for sure is that metanoia will always be becoming different, whether bigger or smaller, more or less specialised, in evolution or revolution, appearing or even perhaps disappearing. The symbol for metanoia is an equilateral triangle, the Greek letter delta, meaning 'change'. Laing and Esterson (1972, p. 63) define metanoia as 'an enterprise of continual and continuing reappraisal and renewal, constantly bringing forth new experience with deepening understanding and wholeness'. I hope this for all of us, wherever we are located and wherever our hearts are leading.

I owe primary thanks to Windy Dryden who thought of this book, suggested the title and bore with me while I laboured seemingly endlessly on the last chapter. I also want to acknowledge with gratitude and affection the contribution of the co-authors of some of the collected papers – Michael Carroll, Phil Lapworth, Roland Evans and Charlotte Sills. To metanoia trainees, patients and clients I owe the deepest and most heartfelt acknowledgement for an enormous part in educating and calibrating me and my ideas, over the 20 or so years that I have been professionally engaged in the endeavour of healing human beings and human institutions. Without Rita Cremona, Lorraine Hill, Katherine Pierpoint, Camilla Sim and Lynda Townsend – editorial and academic administrative assistants *par excellence* – none of this would have been possible. Sue Fish and Margery Friedlander have been my severest critics and editors – I appreciate their input into my work and into my life.

References

BERGSON, H. (1965). *Creative Evolution.* London: Collier-Macmillan.

GUERRIERE, D. (1980). Physis, Sophia, Psyche. In: J. Sallis and K. Maly (Eds). *Heraclitean Fragments: A Companion Volume to the Heidegger/Fink Seminar on Heraclitus,* pp. 87–134. Tuscaloosa, AL: University of Alabama Press.

LAING, R.D. and ESTERSON, A. (1972). *Leaves of Spring.* Harmondsworth, Middx: Penguin.

MACKEWN, J. (1991) Transference and countertransference: A gestalt perspective. Unpublished paper delivered at metanoia.

MARCEL, G. (1952). *Metaphysical Journal.* (B. Wall, trans.).

MASLOW, A.H. (1963). *Toward a Psychology of Being.* Princeton, NJ: D. Van Nostrand.

MURRAY, G. (1955). *Five Stages of Greek Religion.* Garden City, NY: Doubleday Anchor.

NORCROSS, J.C. et al. (1986). Training integrative/eclectic psychotherapists. *International Journal of Eclectic Psychotherapy,* **5** (1), 71–94.

Contents

Part I
Professional Orientation

Chapter 1 Counselling, Psychotherapy, Psychology and Applied Psychology: The Same and Different

With Michael Carroll

Introduction

This chapter considers some of the factors involved in differentiating between counselling, psychotherapy, psychology, applied psychology and several allied fields. It is written for several reasons. One is to establish for counsellors, psychotherapists and counselling psychologists separate and valuable professional identities which have a place and domain of their own. Such an attempt can provide helpful guidelines for referral agencies, professionals, and members of the public to distinguish between different kinds of service provision, so that needs and resources can be more accurately aligned. Ignorance and confusion in themselves further perpetuate difficulties endemic to the most complex task of providing the best and most cost-effective help for individuals in emotional trouble, with the least long-term detrimental effects, and hopefully of most benefit in terms of improved psychological health.

Secondly, the ability to know where helping modalities overlap and where they differ can be a tremendous help to professionals themselves. It can establish boundaries, acknowledge strengths and limitations and afford a working relationship between them that fosters mutual respect rather than distrust. Professionalisation, accreditation and ethical sanctions can go some way towards reducing potential damage: they can also provide the first step towards professional identity and the ability to relate to other professionals from similar and different helping backgrounds.

There are three main approaches to considering the relationship between counselling, psychotherapy, psychology and applied psychology.

First, there are those who 'lump' them together and refuse to acknowledge any differences. They point dramatically to the client groups dealt with by each profession and hail the fact that counsellors see clients, psychotherapists see clients (but they call them patients) and counselling psychologists see clients (they call them both clients and patients) and that these clients do not differ substantially from one another. Domains held sacred by one profession are invaded without apology by another. Psychotherapists see clients in long-term therapy, some of whom are very disturbed and difficult people who may even have psychiatric histories and they work with transference and the unconscious. Such clients, traditionally, have been the work of the psychiatrist, the clinical psychologist or the psychotherapist.

The counsellor, on the other hand, often works in a college of higher education, can average six sessions a client and deals with crisis and developmental issues (was this not why the counsellor was born?). The counselling psychologist (a new breed on the British scene – soon to be born!) works in hospitals, organisations, mental health centres and all those areas once claimed by counsellors, psychotherapists and clinical psychologists. Why try to fabricate differences if all three approaches do much the same thing?

A second group 'splits' the groups and refuses to acknowledge many similarities. Counsellors, they claim, are low on theory, have no requirement for personal therapy in their training and work in the short term and with developmental issues. Counselling psychologists are psychologists who use counselling in their work, are high on theory and research and as yet are unsure about where they will end up or with what client groups they will specialise. Psychotherapists concentrate on personal therapy, use supervised client work, spend a long time as apprentices, and have deeply disturbed and long-term clients. However you view it, these are three different approaches to helping people and must be kept separate. Some view the differences in terms of specialisation, others in terms of training. Others again seem anxious about their 'power base' and that their areas of work, and client groups, might be stolen by rivals in the field. Was there a hint of this in the air when psychiatry once objected to clinical psychology as a new profession, in a way similar to how some regard the relationship between counselling and clinical psychology?

A third group talks about 'overlap' between the three: areas of similarity and areas of difference. Duffy (1990) recognises the areas in common and sees differences coming from 'intentionality', i.e. not what is done but how practitioners think of their work. This chapter belongs within that group and offers Figure 1.1 as a potentially helpful tool in guiding and demarcating the discussion areas between the overlapping fields of counselling, psychology and psychotherapy. It will form the basis for discussion in the rest of the chapter.

Figure 1.1 shows each area as distinct in itself, but relating to each of the other two areas, and indicates the inter-relationship between all three.

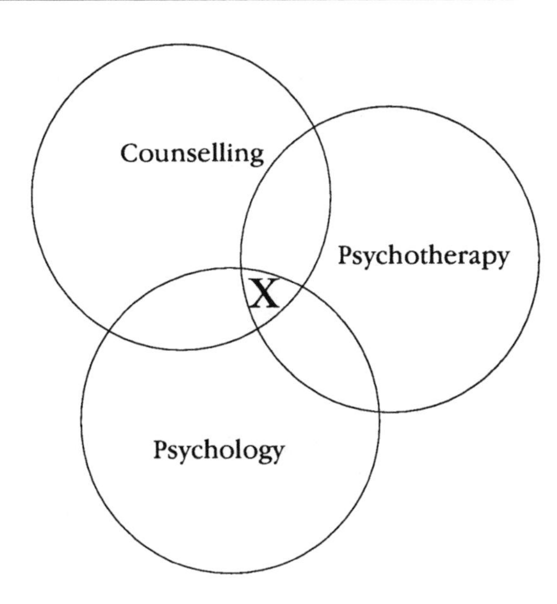

Figure 1.1. Venn diagram of the relationship between counselling, psychology and psychotherapy

The overlap area between counselling and psychotherapy represents the work of counselling professionals with advanced practice qualifications or the psychotherapist using counselling skills. The overlap area between psychotherapy and psychology represents psychotherapists with a psychology qualification or psychologists trained as psychotherapists. The overlap area between counselling and psychology represents counselling psychologists, that is, psychology graduates with counselling qualifications but no special training in psychotherapy. X marks the area of work that involves the work of psychology graduates who have training and experience in both counselling and psychotherapy. This may be the appropriate area for the profession of counselling psychology.

Each of the above will be examined in detail, that is, the counsellor, the psychotherapist and the counselling psychologist, and four areas noted where dialogue can take place between the three approaches.

Counsellor

The British Association for Counselling (BAC), founded in 1977, defines counselling as follows:

> Counselling is the skilled and principled use of relationship to facilitate self-knowledge, emotional acceptance and growth, and the optimal development of personal resources. The overall aim is to provide an opportunity to work towards living more satisfyingly and resourcefully. Counselling relationships will vary according to need but may be concerned with develop-

> mental issues, addressing and resolving specific problems, making decisions, coping with crisis, developing personal insights and knowledge, working through feelings of inner conflict or improving relationships with others.
>
> The counsellor's role is to facilitate the client's work in ways that respect the client's values, personal resources and capacity for self-determination.
>
> (British Association for Counselling, 1989, p. 1)

Counsellors may bring special training, experience and expertise to the counselling relationship, to enable people to further their own growth and enhance their personal functioning. In this way, counsellors are enablers and facilitators, helping a client with a specific problem and focusing on evolutionary change.

Counselling is largely a general field, but it can also be quite specific, for example, redundancy counselling, marital or sexual counselling, debt counselling, HIV, retirement and health counselling, bereavement counselling etc.

BAC has a Code of Ethics and Practice for Counsellors, the aim of which is 'to establish and maintain standards for counsellors and to inform and protect members of the public seeking their services'. Also under this code, 'counsellors subscribe to principles in the areas of:

1. The nature of counselling.
2. Issues of responsibility.
3. Issues of competence' (British Association for Counselling, 1984, p. 1).

Counsellors may be eligible for accreditation through BAC, which has a Counselling at Work division as well as Personal, Family, Sexual and Marital divisions, a division for Pastoral Counselling, Counselling in Education and one for Counselling in Medical Settings.

Training in counselling usually lasts 1–3 years, although some people who become counsellors have no other qualifications than experience and expertise. Counsellors often argue, sometimes with good reason, that they do psychotherapy, as there is much overlap between the two areas. A well-trained counsellor may do work of equal value to that of people in other fields. Their focus, however, is *likely* to remain with more short-term work, with the less seriously disturbed members of the population, and with areas of life adjustment such as bereavement or career counselling or crisis support, guidance and problem solving, rather than in-depth work on a person's childhood. The task of counselling is to give the client an opportunity to explore, discover and clarify ways of living more satisfyingly and resourcefully. Counselling is thus not a destructuring and restructuring of personality, but aims to create the conditions through the counselling relationship wherein a person can connect with their basic drive towards health, and be enabled to adjust to changes of role situations and developmental states in life. Counsellors usually do not have psychology degrees and thus do not consciously use psychology as an academic discipline as a basis for their practice. Pastoral counselling centres (for example, the Westminster Pastoral Foundation) more usually train counsellors in psychodynamic theory and practice. The work of Rogers (1986) and Egan (1982) belongs in this field.

Clients can be sent to counsellors, or be self-referred, through their general practitioners or via friends or contacts. BAC publishes a directory of counsellors throughout the UK.

It seems at this stage to serve the two areas, counselling and psychotherapy, best by concentrating on where they are most different; that is, highlighting the polar opposites, rather than getting stuck in a quagmire of overlap. Counselling can be seen to focus on evolutionary change, whereas psychotherapy focuses on revolutionary change. B. Proctor (personal communication, 1989) talks about person-centred problem-solving in the here-and-now. Difficulties in distinguishing between counselling and psychotherapy do not absolve us from the responsibility of looking at the poles. Issues become clearer when we look at the two poles and just because the task is difficult does not mean it should not be done. Doing this, we can establish whether an issue is closer to one 'end' or the other. This is easier than making a boundary, because clearly there is considerable overlap.

Counsellors help to oil the wheels of someone's experience so that they manage to function better. It is for those whose script position is comfortable enough so that they could get through life very well without a metanoia or turnabout. Counselling seems most suited to a model of human growth in human beings, and indeed many counselling courses are predicated on the work of Carl Rogers, who emphasised that, through the creation of the necessary conditions of respect, empathy and genuineness, the human being will naturally learn:

> to *be* more of his experience – to be the feelings of which he has been frightened as well as the feelings he has regarded as more acceptable. He becomes a more fluid, changing, learning person...the motivation for learning and change springs from the self-actualizing tendency of life...to flow into all the differentiated channels of potential development, insofar as these are experienced as enhancing.
>
> (Rogers, 1961, p. 285)

Another characteristic of revolutionary change is that the starting conditions and basic components of the system have to be changed, and may even appear out of the regions of probable predictions.

Evolutionary change, in contrast, suggests that the same starting conditions and basic components can conceivably lead to the accomplished outcomes; that is, one could predict the range of probable outcomes. The juxtaposition of evolutionary and revolutionary change emphasises different sets of skills and different goals and methodologies. An individual's defensive structures can be left intact or strengthened in counselling, by using existing personality resources and the individual's potential for growth and self-healing.

Psychotherapy, on the other hand, focuses on discontinuous, revolutionary change. The justification for psychotherapy needs to be that such an expensive and time-consuming intervention is necessitated because, unless discontinuous change is implemented, serious tragedy may result. In this case, the medical model may be appropriate in terms of diagnosis (or at least assessment) leading to treatment implementing or seeking for a cure. It is appropriate when there is damage to the organism which has to be reversed before the organism can start reconnecting with its own innate healing process. Psychotherapy, in these authors' opinions, whether psychodynamic, behavioural, or humanistic/existential, concerns the destructuring and restructuring of the personality, whether it is conceived of as belief-and-behaviour systems, ego states, or super ego and self structures.

Sometimes counsellors lack the training and the facilities in screening, assessing and monitoring risks of suicide, homicide or psychosis which may only become apparent in the later stages of a helping relationship. Of course, this is not to suggest that all screening or assessment procedures, even when done by extremely experienced psychotherapists or psychiatrists, are always either effective or helpful. On the other hand there are also many reports of well-functioning individuals who set out to find someone to help them with a circumscribed problem such as a lack of interest in sex with a marital partner, and then end up several years later, having entered, for example, analysis three times weekly, with a sense of having been misled or misinformed. The point is not to suggest that there are absolute dividing lines between the work of the different professions, but to engage others (in and outside these professions) to continue to question and articulate what differences there may be; not so much in the areas of overlap, but in those areas that are more distinctly differentiated.

J. Loughly, during a conference on training in counselling and psychotherapy in 1985, put it in this way:

> Counselling and psychotherapy are not the same process, although I know there are some of you who would disagree with that statement. For me the difference between them is one of history. Counselling focuses on that which belongs to the now–here. It can be achieved through care and cognition, it is possible to think about it. Psychotherapy on the other hand, is to take the now as a living history: that the things learnt then are happening now but in a different context.

The psychotherapist thus helps the client to avoid allowing 'the things learnt then' to happen now in a context that is inappropriate.

Psychodynamic models of counselling, however, are about making information that brings the inner Child into an awareness that here-and-now is not there-and-then.

Gestalt counselling focuses on the existential aspect rather than the regressive, which would bring the client more into contact with the inner Child and is therefore psychotherapy.

The transactional analysis behavioural model fits into a counselling framework enabling a person to develop options on transacting differently, and moving the client from archaic Child to an Adult/Adult transaction position.

The Rogerian model is also existential, in that it also focuses on the here-and-now. Of course, all of these are approaches to counselling which may be used by counsellors at a counselling level or by psychotherapists at a psychotherapy level, depending on their level of training, their settings and their experience.

Undervaluing of counselling

It is important that the proper weight and value of counselling be acknowledged and appreciated. It is more, much more, than a chat over the garden fence or a cup of tea with a sympathetic listener or befriender. Many psychotherapists do not necessarily make good counsellors, and there is a danger in seeing pathology and making diagnosis where none exists. Iatrogenic disorders may occur – that is, problems may be created by the very treatment supposed to cure the problem, so that clients end up with problems which they did not have when they first came for help.

Counselling therefore can be seen as enabling and facilitating, whereas psychotherapy is concerned with intervention, treatment and reconstruction. Given that, in evolutionary change, the organism is striving, naturally and probably successfully, towards its fulfilment, the helper needs to be supportive, enabling and facilitating of this self-generated and self-directed process. In revolutionary change the focus is on interpretation, confrontation, destructuring and reconstruction. The risk of systemic disintegration is naturally greater in evolutionary change than in revolutionary change, and therefore the skills and experience involved in the latter are of a different order; but not necessarily better or worse than the skills of enabling or facilitation. Goal-setting and the educational task will therefore be more important in counselling training, and diagnosis of pathology more important in the training of psychotherapists.

It is less differentiating but, practically, still the case that counselling assists people in finding the solution to a particular problem, or dealing with a particular crisis, whereas psychotherapy helps people to develop new ways of solving problems which can become generalised to new situations. There is also sometimes a differentiation drawn between counselling as dealing with a current situation, contrasted with psychotherapy as dealing with a past situation. Sometimes it is suggested that the difference lies between counselling dealing with conscious phenomena, and psychotherapy dealing with unconsciousness phenomena. This is frequently an untenable position.

Psychotherapist

'Legislators and courts of law have found it almost impossible to define "psychotherapy" in such a way as to include, by universal agreement among therapists, that which *is* psychotherapy and to exclude that which *is not* psychotherapy.' (Watkins in Wolman, 1965, p. 142). The professional body for psychotherapists is the UK Council for Psychotherapy (UKCP).

The following definitions of psychotherapy have been published:

> Psychotherapy is defined as a form of treatment for mental illness and behavioural disturbances in which a trained person establishes a professional contact with the patient and through definite therapeutic communication, both verbal and non-verbal, attempts to alleviate the emotional disturbance, reverse or change maladaptive patterns of behaviour, and encourage personality growth and development. Psychotherapy is distinguished from such other forms of psychiatric treatment as the use of drugs, surgery, electric shock treatment and insulin coma treatment.
>
> (Freedman, Kaplan and Sadock, 1985, p. 2601)

> Psychotherapy is the treatment by psychological means of problems of an emotional nature in which a trained person deliberately establishes a professional relationship with a patient with the object of 1) removing, modifying or retarding existing symptoms, 2) mediating disturbed patterns of behaviour, 3) promoting positive personal growth and development.
>
> (Wolman, 1965, p. 118)

In some discussions at the UKCP the following definitions of psychotherapy have been used: 'the systematic use of a *relationship* between therapist and patient – as opposed to pharmacological or social methods – to produce changes in cognition, feelings and behaviour' (Holmes and Lindley, 1989, p. 3).

'Psychotherapy is aimed at helping the client to help himself with his own problems. After receiving psychotherapy the client should be able to manage the daily tasks of living without getting tied up in destructive or mundane patterns of behaviour or negative feelings' (Brady and Considine, 1988, p. 3).

The authors see the psychotherapeutic relationship as active in destructuring and restructuring the personality. It aims at revolutionary, rather than evolutionary, change. The relationship is used to remedy or improve an individual's difficulties in terms of feelings, behaviour and cognition.

The definition of psychotherapist is sometimes not very different from that of counsellor, as there is overlap between the two areas.

Previously, anybody could set up as a psychotherapist: that is, before the formation of the UKCP, whose aim is to create a profession and a register so that the public can identify appropriately trained practitioners who are subject to an enforceable Code of Ethics. The UKCP was founded in 1989 and now has 71 member organisations grouped into 8 sections. Each section contains a distinct kind of psychotherapy. It is expected that the voluntary Register due to appear early in 1993 will form the foundation of a Statutory Register of psychotherapists. A national audit of psychotherapy is in preparation and a variety of initiatives under way, including cooperation with the development of National Vocational Qualifications at the higher levels, and research into and management of the overlap between psychotherapy, counselling and counselling psychology. Following 2 years of an active steering committee, UKCP was present at the founding of the European Association for Psychotherapy (EAP) in Brussels on 3 July 1992. The Chair of UKCP was elected Vice-President of the EAP. In the professional literature, some 250 different schools or approaches to counselling and psychotherapy have been identified (Corsini, 1986). Karasu (1986) has talked of polling 450 models of counselling/psychotherapy nationwide in the USA. Dryden's book, *Individual Therapy in Britain* (1984) can be extremely useful to help understand the differences between the approaches.

There is now usually a minimum of 3 years' training – often 4, sometimes 7 years. Most psychotherapy training institutions involved in the UKSCP require most of their trainees to be in extended personal psychotherapy so that professionals who graduate from these training programmes have personal experience of the process and uses of psychotherapy themselves. Thus, personal psychotherapy is considered to be a vital part of most training. The personal psychotherapy of trainees usually is of a similar duration, type and frequency as that which they would be offering their clients.

Psychotherapists would expect to deal with more serious problems, for example, clinical aspects. Clients are seen frequently, in regular sessions at least once a week, perhaps more frequently. Clients may want to go far back into their past; repetitive patterns of behaviour are identified, worked on and cleared if they are having a negative effect upon the client's present life. Psychotherapists will usually have a wider range and greater flexibility in their working methods than psychoanalysts. People can be self-referred, or come via their general practitioners, friends or contacts.

In the UKCP, the psychotherapy training organisations are currently divided into the following sections.

1. *Analytic psychotherapy* Psychotherapists in this section usually see people for less than three hours per week. Their theoretical basis may be Freudian, Jungian or Kleinian or some combination of these with other psychoanalysts. The Institute of Group Analysis belongs in this section.
2. *Humanistic and integrative psychotherapy* Humanistic psychotherapists base their work on Maslow, Rogers, Frankl, Perls, Berne and Moreno, amongst others. Many integrate other approaches into their own.

   Integrative psychotherapists usually integrate the best of different psychotherapies. The intention is to look at common truths across the psychotherapies. Integrative approaches may or may not be primarily humanistic in orientation. However, at the time of writing, these approaches both belong to this section.

   In the USA, most psychotherapists say they are integrative; and it is likely in the next few years to become more established in the UK. Integrative psychotherapists look at commonalities, meta-models and 'different therapeutics' which means that different treatments may be suitable for different conditions. Another distinguishable grouping within this section is the transpersonal psychotherapies, who emphasise the transpersonal elements in human experience and psychotherapy.
3. *Family, marital, and sexual* The psychotherapy training organisations (their graduates and trainees) are specialists in marital or family therapy. (Therapists from other orientations may or may not have trained additionally in family or marital work.)
4. *Experiential constructivist therapy* These approaches are based on personal construct theory (Kelly, 1955) and neurolinguistic programming (Bandler and Grinder, 1975).
5. *Behavioural psychotherapy* This is the section for therapists who primarily use a behavioural or cognitive–behavioural approach, and contains a very large number of clinical psychologists.
6. *Hypnotherapy* These training organisations primarily use hypnosis or some form thereof for treating clients.
7. *Psychoanalytically based psychotherapy with children* This title is self-explanatory. These are psychotherapists trained with organisations belonging to other organisations who may also work with children from a different theoretical approach. These courses are based on Jung, Freud or Klein.
8. *Analytical psychology* This is the section for those whose theoretical basis is primarily Jungian.

Psychoanalyst

Freud gave several definitions of psychoanalysis. One of the most explicit is to be found at the beginning of an encyclopaedia article written in 1922:

> Psycho-analysis is the name (i) of a procedure for the investigation of mental processes which are almost inaccessible in any other way, (ii) of a method (based on that investigation) for the treatment of neurotic disorders and (iii) of a collection of psychological information obtained along those lines, which is gradually being accumulated into a new scientific discipline.
>
> (Laplanche and Pontalis, 1988, p. 367)

The word 'psychoanalysis' refers to a theoretical viewpoint concerning personality structure and function, in the application of this theory to other branches of knowledge and also to a specific psychotherapeutic technique. Although much developed since his time, this body of knowledge is based upon the discoveries of Sigmund Freud (British Psycho-Analytical Society, 1990, p.37).

Psychoanalysts usually follow Freud, Jung and Klein.

Psychiatrist

The *Shorter Oxford English Dictionary* defines psychiatry as 'healing, medical treatment.... The medical treatment of diseases of the mind' (Onions, 1968, p. 1700). Their professional body is the Royal College of Psychiatrists.

Psychiatrists have a medical degree, then undergo further specialist training in psychiatry. Many psychiatrists are not trained in psychotherapy. They can prescribe drugs and are specialists in the treatment and management of serious disturbances such as psychosis, schizophrenia, manic-depressive disorders and so on. They tend to work in hospital or psychiatric settings, unless they work in private practice settings. There is a clear difference between child and adult psychiatry.

Psychologists and Applied Psychologists

Psychologists are professionals with at least one degree in psychology. Many move on to further postgraduate studies in applied psychology, one of which is counselling psychology.

The dictionary definition of psychology as 'the science of the nature, functions and phenomena of the human soul or mind' (Onions, 1968, p. 1700) is somewhat restrictive in its view. Psychology is not only the 'science of the mind' but also the science of human behaviour in all its aspects. Psychology interprets the person (Carroll and Pickard, 1993) and results in a number of theories of personality and research methods for understanding the person. Its questions are person-related: why do people behave the way they do? What motivates the individual? How do people grow and begin to think and use language? Can we isolate stages of life as individuals progress towards old age? From its academic base, psychology is divided into a number of subsections, such as development psychology, cognitive, personality theory, biological basis of behaviour, abnormal psychology, psychological assessment. From this academic basis, psychologists move to apply their subject to the world.

The British Psychological Society is an amalgamation of the various applied psychologies. There are approximately 13 divisions, sections and special interest groups within the Society ranging through developmental psychology, educational, occupational, clinical, counselling, clinical neuropsychology etc. It can be difficult at times differentiating between the three: the occupational psychologist, the clinical psychologist, and the counselling psychologist.

Occupational psychologist

An occupational psychologist will have knowledge in relation to the following areas:

> Human–machine interaction, design of environments and of work, personnel selection and assessment, performance appraisal and career development, training (including identification of needs and evaluation), employee relations and motivation and organisation development.
>
> (BPS description provided by Gary Fitzgibbon)

Not many occupational psychologists train to do psychotherapy. Occupational psychology is better paid than clinical psychology, as they usually work in industry (as opposed to the National Health Service) and they may, for example, work on computers to make software programs.

Clinical psychologist

All clinical psychologists must belong to their professional body, the British Psychological Society, and they will then be on the Register of Chartered Psychologists. This document is available from the BPS, and it contains the names, qualifications and contact addresses of all the chartered psychologists in the UK. The BPS distinguishes between members who are prohibited from using MBPsS on publicity (British Psychological Society, 1991, pp. 26–27), and chartered psychologists who have done additional training in psychology in addition to holding a psychology degree.

A clinical psychologist will have studied psychology for a long time (usually a Bachelor's and often a Master's degree in psychology), and will have trained in clinical settings such as hospitals with clinical focus, for example, made special study of mental retardation, or management of phobias or behaviour disorders. Not all chartered clinical psychologists are trained in psychotherapy; many have not been in psychotherapy themselves. They do not prescribe drugs.

They are usually trained to do psychodiagnostics, for example, the use on clients of tests such as the Rorschach, Myer-Briggs, Minnesota Multiphasic Personality Inventory (MMPI) or Wechsler. 'The key tasks of clinical psychologists are: assessment, treatment, training/teaching and research (both patient and service related) as well as management' (British Psychological Society, 1988b, p. 4).

> The range of treatment techniques has grown considerably during the last twenty years, from the previously limited range of essentially educational or psychodynamic techniques.... Examples are the treatment of elimination disorders in children, phobic conditions in adults and the remediation of cognitive difficulties following different types of brain injury. Some of these treatments now offer positive alternatives to drug treatments (such as anxiety management procedures), and supplement medical treatments in people with long-term disabling conditions.
>
> (British Psychological Society, 1988a, p. 5)

Behavioural methods (such as desensitisation), methods based on social learning principles (such as social skills training) and cognitive methods, used especially for altered mood states, are now widely used. In addition, a wider range of psychotherapeutic approaches has been developed, based on theories that are not essentially psychodynamic (such as personal construct theory). It has become apparent that there are a number of non-specific factors which are relevant to many apparently different techniques. A number of these approaches are used by counsellors and other non-psychologists to help people with less serious conditions.

> [T]he boundaries between clinical psychology as a discipline and other academic and health-care disciplines, are not fixed.
>
> (British Psychological Society, 1988a, p. 1)

Counselling psychologist

This is highly likely soon to be an avenue to chartered psychologist status and an independent division of the BPS. At the time of writing it is a Special Group of the BPS, as Carroll (1991) makes clear:

> counselling psychology moved from being a 'Section' in 1982 to becoming a 'Special Group' in 1988 with increasing aspirations to becoming a Division

> within BPS. Its membership...is still probably the fastest-growing section of the BPS. ...Becoming a Division with BPS would bring with it major implications for training, training courses, career structure and pay levels, status, and supervision. A proposed new Diploma in Counselling has been outlined as the next step on the journey to Division status.
>
> (p. 74)

Within the near future, counselling psychologists will probably become ever more present in industry.

One important difference between counsellors and counselling psychologists, if not the most important, is the conscious use of academic psychology alongside practical counselling skills. Counselling psychologists have a basic degree in psychology, and then further training in counselling psychology (MSc). Counselling psychology is here conceptualised as the overlapping area between counselling and psychotherapy in the Venn diagram (see Figure 1.1) representing the three primary arenas of counselling, psychology and psychotherapy.

Counselling psychology is considered not to be identical with counselling (even when it is carried out by psychology graduates). In counselling psychology, there is an emphasis on the systemic application of distinctively psychological understanding, based on empirical research of the client and the counselling process, to the practice of counselling. The relevant psychological knowledge is partly concerned with the problems of presenting clients, and partly with the procedures and processes involved in counselling. It should be remembered that counselling psychology involves work in an organisational context as well as with individual clients, and synthesises elements of better developed areas of professional work such as clinical and occupational psychology. Life-span developmental psychologies, and the social psychology of interpersonal processes are among the areas that supply the academic foundations of counselling psychology. Of central scientific relevance, of course, are empirical investigations of the processes and outcomes of counselling and of related methods of psychotherapy.

> The psychological understanding of counselling derives not only from formal psychological enquiry but also from the interpersonal relationships between practitioners and their clients. The essence of such relationships is one of personal exploration and clarification in which psychological knowledge is used and shared in ways that enable clients to deal more effectively with their inter- and intrapersonal concerns. The capacity to establish and maintain such relationships ultimately rests upon the personal qualities and maturity of the individual counselling psychologist. Personal qualities such as non-defensiveness and a capacity to experience and communicate emphatic resonance, constitute essential resources which the counselling psychologist draws upon. Although these characteristics may be enhanced by skills training, they derive primarily from a foundation of personal experience and integrative maturity.
>
> (British Psychological Society, 1989, p. 1)

Emerging Issues

From the above, a number of interesting areas emerge as crucial to the ongoing dialogue.

First, the concept of change and what it means. There are different kinds of change possible within therapeutic settings: problem solving, environmental change, adjustment, re-negotiation (as in a relationship), developmental change (evolutionary) and revolutionary change (personality restructuring). Is it possible to look at the professional approaches above to see if certain approaches are more appropriate for certain kinds of change within the person and his or her environment?

A second area of interest is the area of relationship within therapeutic settings. Chapter 2 of this book, and Gelso and Carter (1985) outline different kinds of relationships appropriate to different therapeutic approaches or more applicable to different client groups. It may well be that such relationships are also in keeping with the professions above.

The third area is that of training. Carroll (1992) has outlined ways of connecting training and education in counselling, psychotherapy and counselling psychology which connects rather than diversifies them. He suggests a three-stage model depicting pathways in which counselling is:

1. Integrated in an already existing profession, for example, nursing or social work.
2. Seen as the primary work of the practitioner.
3. A specialisation in a given area or field, for example, employee counselling, student counselling, working with eating disorders, marital counselling (psychotherapy training and practice would enter here).

Further theory, practice and research that connects counselling and psychotherapy with psychology (or indeed another profession: counselling could be connected to sociology or education or politics) would add postgraduate qualifications to the above leading to Advanced Diplomas, MA or MSc degrees. Carroll (1992) has also pointed out the problems emerging if the three main organisations to whom counsellors, psychotherapists, and counselling psychologists are affiliated (the BAC, UKCP and BPS) become too isolated and ally themselves to rigid training which refuses to recognise other expertise.

Fourth, the arena of client groups emerges. Are there clients who could be designated as more appropriately the domain of one approach rather than another? This could be done in terms of the 'change' envisaged (or the degree of disturbance); it could be seen in terms of the training of the helper; it could be viewed from the assessed problem of the client. Or indeed, it might well be a combination of all three.

Conclusion

Research (Norcross, 1986) shows that theoretical differences between 'schools or approaches' are far less important in terms of successful outcome of counselling or psychotherapy, than the quality of the *relationship* between counsellor and client and certain client characteristics, including motivation for change and the willingness to take responsibility for their part in the process. The trend is nowadays towards integrative psychotherapy or integrative approaches to counselling which draw on many traditions and do not adhere to only one 'truth'. In the USA, most psychologists say they are integrative; and it is likely to become more established in the UK in the next few years (Dryden, 1984). As counselling psychology takes its place as a fully articulated profession, it is hoped that there will be a rich representation of both specialist and integrative approaches to the field.

References

BANDLER, R. and GRINDER, J. (1975). *The Structure of Magic: A Book About Language and Therapy,* Vol. 1. Pao Alto, CA: Science and Behaviour Books, Inc.

BRADY, K. and CONSIDINE, M. (1988). *The London Guide to Mind, Body and Spirit.* p.3. London: Brainwave.

BRITISH ASSOCIATION FOR COUNSELLING. (1984). *Code of Ethics and Practice for Counsellors* (Form no. 20, Sept. 1984). Rugby: British Association for Counselling.

BRITISH ASSOCIATION FOR COUNSELLING. (1989). *Invitation to membership* (Form no. 1, Oct. 1989). Rugby: British Association for Counselling.

BRITISH PSYCHO-ANALYTICAL SOCIETY. (1990). In *UKCP Member Organisations' General Information and Training Courses.* (Sept. 1990). London: United Kingdom Council for Psychotherapy.

BRITISH PSYCHOLOGICAL SOCIETY, DIVISION OF CLINICAL PSYCHOLOGY. (1988a). *MPAG Project on Clinical Psychology Services, Manpower and Training Issues: Key Tasks of Clinical Psychology Services.* Leicester: British Psychological Society.

BRITISH PSYCHOLOGICAL SOCIETY, DIVISION OF CLINICAL PSYCHOLOGY. (1988b). *The Representation of Clinical Psychologists: Interim Briefing Paper.* Leicester: British Psychological Society.

BRITISH PSYCHOLOGICAL SOCIETY, MEMBERSHIP AND QUALIFICATIONS BOARD (1989). *Report of the Working Party on the Diploma in Counselling Psychology,* November. Leicester: British Psychological Society.

BRITISH PSYCHOLOGICAL SOCIETY. (1991). *Code of Conduct, Ethical Principles and Guidelines* (March 1991). Leicester: British Psychological Society.

CARROLL, M. (1992). Counsellor training or counsellor education? A response. *Counselling,* **2** (3), 104–105.

CARROLL, M. and PICKARD, E. (1993) Psychology and Counselling. In: Dryden, W. and Thorne, B. (Eds), *Counselling: Interdisciplinary Perspectives.* Buckingham: Open University Press.

CORSINI, R. (Ed.) (1986). *Current Psychotherapies.* Illinois: F.E. Peacock.

DUFFY, M. (1990). Counselling psychology USA: Patterns of continuity and change. *Counselling Psychology Review,* **5** (3), 9–18.

DRYDEN, W. (Ed.) (1984). *Individual Therapy in Britain.* London: Harper and Row.

EGAN, G. (1982). *The Skilled Helper: Model, Skills and Method for Effective Helping.* Monterey, CA: Brooks/Cole.

FREEDMAN, A.M., KAPLAN, H.I. and SADOCK, B.J. (1985). *Comprehensive Textbook of Psychiatry* (vol. 2), p. 2601. Baltimore: Williams and Wilkins.

GELSO, C.J. and CARTER, J.A. (1985). The relationship in counselling and psychotherapy: Components, consequences, and theoretical antecedents. *The Counselling Psychologist,* **13** (2), 155–243.

HOLMES, J. and LINDLEY, R. (1989). *The Values of Psychotherapy* p. 3. Oxford: Oxford University Press.

KARASU, T.B. (1986). The psychotherapies: benefits and limitations. *American Journal of Psychotherapy*, **40** (3), 324–343.

KELLY, G. (1955). *The Psychology of Personal Constructs* (vols 1 and 2). New York: Norton.

LAPLANCHE, J. and PONTALIS, J.B. (1988). *The Language of Psychoanalysis.* London: Karnak Books. (Originally published 1973.)

NORCROSS, J. (Ed.) (1986). *Handbook of Eclectic Psychotherapy.* New York: Brunner/Mazel.

ONIONS, C.T. (Ed.) (1968). *The Shorter Oxford English Dictionary.* Oxford: Clarendon Press.

ROGERS, C. (1961). *On Becoming a Person: A Therapist's View of Psychotherapy.* London: Constable. (Originally published 1961.)

ROGERS, C. (1986). *Client-centred Therapy.* London: Constable

WATKINS, J.G. (1965). Psychotherapeutic methods. In: B.B. Wolman (Ed.),. *Handbook of Clinical Psychology,* pp. 1143–1167. New York: McGraw Hill.

Part II
Cornerstones of Psychotherapy: The Relationship, Change, Commonality and Difference

Part I

Chapter 2
A Multiplicity of Psychotherapeutic Relationships

Introduction

In this chapter, I intend to make explicit what is often implicit in psychotherapy literature regarding the variety and nature of psychotherapeutic relationships. It may remind experienced clinicians of what they might have forgotten, and novice psychotherapists of what they might still need to learn. Hopefully this may begin to clarify confusion in the literature, and contribute towards precision and purpose in practice.

Relationship can be defined as 'the state of being related; a condition or character based upon this; kinship' (Onions, 1973, p. 1786). Relationship is the first condition of being human. It circumscribes two or more individuals and creates a bond in the space between them which is more than the sum of the parts. It is so obvious that it is frequently taken for granted, and so mysterious that many of the world's greatest psychologists, novelists and philosophers have made it a lifetime's preoccupying passion. According to the received wisdom of the late twentieth century, of all the forces of nature, it is our familial relationships that often serve to cause the most damage. Statistically you are more likely to be killed by a relation than by a stranger.

According to the great existentialist psychotherapist Medard Boss, all illness and treatment develops out of the patient's disturbed human relationships: 'In focusing on the physician–patient relationship, Freud called attention to the true locus of all therapeutic efforts, whether they were surgical, internal, or psychotherapeutic' (Boss, 1979, p. 257).

This chapter reaches for an elucidation of relationship, the *betweenness* of people. It is common knowledge that ordinary human relationships can have therapeutic value. The old structures of religion, accepted moral order and extended family networks used to provide

From P. Clarkson (1990). A multiplicity of psychotherapeutic relationships. *British Journal of Psychotherapy*, 7 (2), 148–163, with permission.

supportive relationships and healing matrices for many people. These appear to have started to crumble in the twentieth century. Indeed it is possible that psychotherapy as an institutionalised profession became necessary as a consequence of such a decline in the society and quality of healing relationships which were available in previous centuries.

One way of conceptualising the healthy psychotherapeutic relationship is to conceive of it as the psychotherapist voluntarily entering into a kinship relationship with the patient. This, in some views, recapitulates the early familial maladaptions and in many perspectives it is construed as providing the arena for understanding, reparation or healing. Fundamentally, if a psychotherapist can establish a relationship with someone who has lost the capacity for relationship (such as a schizophrenic individual), he or she has been retrieved in their relatedness with others. Thus they can begin to rejoin the family of man.

Most forms of psychotherapy use this state of voluntary kinship or relationship more or less consciously and more or less in awareness. The Jungian Samuels states that: 'the psychology of the soul turns out to be about people in relationship' (Samuels, 1985, p. 21). Indeed there is growing recognition that patient characteristics and the helping relationship are the most significant components of successful treatment. Research results consistently show that the choice of a particular psychotherapeutic method appears to have little discernible influence. That is, success in therapy can best be predicted by the properties of the patient, therapist and their particular relationship (Norcross, 1986).

If indeed the therapeutic relationship is one of the most, if not the most, important factor in successful therapy, one would expect that much of the training in psychotherapy would be training in the *intentional* use of relationship. Some psychotherapies claim that psychotherapy requires the use of only one kind of relationship, or at most two. Some specifically exclude the use of certain kinds of relationship. For example, Goulding and Goulding (1979), transactional analysts, minimise the use of transference, whereas Moiso (1985) also in transactional analysis, sees it as a central focal point of classical Berneian psychotherapy. Gestaltists Polster and Polster (1973) and the existentialist May (1969) focus on the existential nature of the therapeutic relationship. Some psychotherapeutic approaches pay hardly any theoretical attention to the nature of the relationship and they may attempt to be entirely free of content (for example in some approaches to hypnotherapy or neurolinguistic programming, therapeutic changes are claimed to be made by the patient without the practitioner necessarily knowing what these changes may be). In most approaches, of course, stated policy and actual practice often diverge. As we shall see later, even the actions of Freud (speaking perhaps louder than his words) often belied the assumed orthodoxy of psychoanalytic practice. But a more recent psychoanalyst comments:

> The most neglected feature of the psychoanalytic relationship still seems to me to be that it is a relationship: a very peculiar relationship, but a definite one. Patient and analyst need one another. The patient comes to the analyst because of internal conflicts that prevent him from enjoying life, and he begins to use the analyst not only to resolve them, but increasingly as a receptacle for his pent-up feelings. But the analyst also needs the patient in order to crystallise and communicate his own thoughts, including some of his inmost thoughts on intimate human problems which can only grow organically in the context of this relationship.
>
> (Klauber, 1986, pp. 200–201)

The psychotherapeutic relationship is characterised by the facts that:

1. It is paid for according to a contractual agreement.
2. One of the parties in the relationship has been specifically trained to take part in it.
3. The stated goal is usually the amelioration of psychological problems or the improvement of mental health of the paying partner in the task.
4. The psychotherapist is willing to commit him or herself to the welfare of another human being in this way.

Working Alliance

The working alliance is probably the most essential relationship modality operative in psychotherapy. Without such a working alliance psychotherapy is certainly limited in its goals and restricted in scope. This working alliance is represented by the client's or patient's willingness to engage in the psychotherapeutic relationship even when they at some archaic level may no longer wish to do so.

In transactional analysis, the working alliance is conceptualised as a contract or agreement between the Adult of the psychotherapist and Adult of the client. In psychoanalysis it is 'the relatively non-neurotic, rational, and realistic attitudes of the patient toward the analyst.... It is this part of the patient–analyst relationship that enables the patient to identify with the analyst's point of view and to work with the analyst despite the neurotic transference reactions' (Greenson, 1967, p. 29). The attitudes and character traits that further the development of the transference neurosis are basically antithetical to those that further the working alliance (Stone, 1961; Greenson 1965, 1967). So it is unlikely that both can be operative at the same moment. Which one is allowed to become figure, or focus, must depend on the nature of the psychotherapeutic task at a particular time with each unique patient. Other modes of therapeutic relationship may also be present, but may be more in the background at a particular time.

For many psychotherapists, the working alliance is the crucial and necessary relationship for effective therapy (Dryden, 1984). It certainly is the necessary co-operation which even the general practitioner requires in order to work effectively with patients, be it simply at the level that the patient takes the medication as prescribed. Anecdotal evidence and research has shown that this working alliance is frequently missing in general practice (Griffith, 1990). 'The therapeutic alliance is the powerful joining of forces which energises and supports the long, difficult, and frequently painful work of life-changing psychotherapy' (Bugental, 1987, p. 49). Bordin (1979) differentiated goals, bonds and tasks – three aspects of the working alliance which seem to be required for any form of therapy to be successful. Several studies emphasise the importance of further common factors.

> Among the common factors most frequently studied have been those identified by the client-centred school as 'necessary and sufficient conditions' for patient personality change: accurate empathy, positive regard, nonpossessive warmth, and congruence or genuineness. Virtually all schools of psychotherapy accept the notion that these or related therapist relationship variables are important for significant progress in psychotherapy and in fact, fundamental in the formation of a working alliance.
>
> (Lambert, 1986, pp. 444–445)

In response to the client asking 'How are you?' the psychotherapist in working alliance mode is likely to make any reply that will enhance optimum conditions to accomplish the stated therapeutic task. For example the therapist may say 'Fine and how have you been?' or 'As you can hear from my husky voice, I am having a bit of a cold, but I am quite well enough to work with you today'.

The following dream encapsulates symbolically the person's previous engagement with her mother contrasted with the working alliance, the current choice with the psychotherapist:

> I was with you and we were working – or engaged in something serious but having an enjoyable time. My mother was coming at three o'clock and I had an arrangement to meet her. You didn't know that and you said, "I am available at three o'clock – why don't we carry on then?" I thought, "Oh God, if I stay with you [the therapist] then I won't be there for my mother, if I go I may lose the connection with you". I might break this thing that felt so good. It wouldn't actually be disastrous, since we would continue working again the next day, but it would be like breaking the energy. It is so pleasurable, the work is so good, we're both getting something from it. My mother is more of a shadowy figure than you are. I then decided to do neither and went off for a walk on my own. In this way I wouldn't be choosing one person or the other. I would be choosing myself. You would agree with that. If I went with my mother you would say, "You needed to do that, but it would be less wise". But you would absolutely appreciate me for doing my own thing.

In kinship terms, the relationship of working together can be likened to that between cousins. According to Charles Kidd (personal communication, 1988) at Debrett's the word 'cousins' has loosely indicated uncle/aunt/niece/nephew relationships as well as cousin relationships. The notion is meant to convey a metaphoric distance from the family of origin (different parents) but kindred loyalties to each others' welfare so that it is possible to have a blend of subjective altruism and an objective capacity which may make that relationship constructive.

Transferential/Countertransferential Relationship

The mode of therapeutic relationship that has been written about most extensively in psychoanalysis is that of transference. It is important to remember that Freud did not intend psychoanalysis to be a cure but rather a search for understanding and frowned upon people who wished to 'change' instead of analyse. So the transference relationship is an essential part of the analytic procedure as the analysis consists of inviting the transference and gradually dissolving it by means of interpretation (Greenson, 1967).

Laplanche and Pontalis (1988) describe transference as follows:

> For psycho-analysis, a process of actualization of unconscious wishes. Transference uses specific objects and operates in the framework of a specific relationship established with these objects. Its context *par excellence* is the analytic situation.
>
> In the transference, infantile prototypes re-emerge and are experienced with a strong sensation of immediacy. As a rule what psychoanalysts mean by the unqualified use of the term 'transference' is ***transference during treatment***.
>
> Classically, the transference is acknowledged to be the terrain on which all the basic problems of a given analysis play themselves out: the establishment, modalities, interpretation and resolution of the transference are in fact what define the cure
>
> (Laplanche and Pontalis, 1988, p. 455)

Freud (1912b) went so far at one point as to suggest that the analyst model himself on the surgeon, put aside his human sympathy and adopt an attitude of emotional coldness. 'This means that the analyst must have the ability to restrain his therapeutic intentions, must control his urge for closeness and must "blanket" his usual personality' (Stone in Greenson, 1967, p. 389). Freud advocated that the analyst should refrain from intruding his personality into the treatment, and he introduced the simile of the analyst being a 'mirror' for the analysand (Freud, 1912b, p. 118). This may not in fact be an accurate picture of what Freud had in mind. Perhaps, he emphasised certain 'unnatural' aspects of psychoanalytic technique because they were so foreign and artificial to the usual doctor–patient relationship and the customary psychotherapy of his day.

For example, in a paper written in the same year as the one where he cites the recommendations for emotional coldness and the mirror-like attitude, Freud stated:

> Thus the solution of the puzzle is that transference to the doctor is suitable for resistance to the treatment only in so far as it is a negative transference or a positive transference of repressed erotic impulses. If we 'remove' the transference by making it conscious, we are detaching only these two components of the emotional act from the person of the doctor; the other component, which is admissible to consciousness and unobjectionable, persists and is the vehicle of success in psycho-analysis exactly as it is in other methods of treatment.
>
> (Freud, 1912a, p. 105)

Alexander and French (1946) expressed the psychoanalytic principle as follows:

> The old pattern was an attempt at adaptation on the part of the child to parental behavior...the analyst's objective and understanding attitudes allows the patient...to make a new settlement of the old problem.... While the patient continues to act according to outdated patterns, the analyst's reaction conforms strictly to the actual therapeutic situation.
>
> (pp. 66–67)

Berne (1961) wrote:

> Transactionally, this means that when the patient's Child attempts to provoke the therapist's Parent, it is confronted instead with the therapist's Adult. The therapeutic effect arises from the disconcertion caused by this crossed transaction.
>
> (p. 174)

The patient's question 'How are you?' may often be met with analytic silence. Alternatively the analyst may reply: 'I wonder what prompts your concern for me? It may be that you are anxious again, like you were with your mother, that I will not be able to withstand your envy towards me.'

This transferential psychotherapeutic relationship can be compared to that of step-parent or godparent. Negative transference connects with the former (the witch of many traditional fairy tales, for example Hansel and Gretel) and idealising positive transference resonates with the godparent or fairy godmother relationship in that a putative family connection exists but it lacks the immediacy of a real parent. Whether or not the psychotherapist identifies with such projections, and how he or she handles them, may destroy or facilitate the psychotherapy. Clearly, the nature and vicissitudes of the countertransference are inextricably interwoven with the management of the transference relationship and efficacy of the psychotherapy may well be determined by it.

A narcissistic, apparently generous, but dynamically retentive patient whose mother overfed him physically while never responding to his real feelings of isolation, abandonment or rage reports the following dream: 'I am at a sumptuous banquet which is presided over by you [the psychotherapist]. I take the food from the table, but I don't eat it. I put it in a plastic bag so that you won't see and I throw it in a wastepaper basket. I want to continue to be invited, but not to have to eat the food.'

Jung stated that:

> The great importance of the transference has often led to the mistaken idea that it is absolutely indispensable for a cure, that it must be demanded from the patient, so to speak. But a thing like that can no more be demanded than faith, which is only valuable when it is spontaneous. Enforced faith is nothing but spiritual cramp. Anyone who thinks that he must 'demand' a transference is forgetting that this is only one of the therapeutic factors...
>
> (Jung, 1966, p. 172)

Reparative/Developmentally Needed Relationship

The reparative/developmentally needed relationship is another relationship mode that can occasionally be differentiated from the others. This is the intentional provision by the psychotherapist of a corrective/reparative or replenishing parental relationship (or action) where the original parenting was deficient, abusive or over-protective. The following dream shows a client separating out a developmentally needed relationship (for the client's future) from the transferential relationship (based on the client's past).

He dreams about two psychotherapists, both called the same name as his psychotherapist. The one psychotherapist says to him in the dream: 'How could you make such mistakes, this is terrible, you ought to be punished'. In the dream the other psychotherapist says, 'Look, I myself have received a D in this subject. I was not very interested in it and you can see that you do not have to be perfect in all things'. The first psychotherapist responds with anger and accusations of unethical conduct saying, 'How could you say such things, you are just encouraging him to make mistakes and setting a very bad example!' The client himself then steps in to arbitrate and explains to the first psychotherapist: 'Actually she is right. You have to understand what she is saying *in the right spirit*'. This is what the client needed to hear.

Dreams often act as unconscious communication about the progress of the psychotherapy from the unconscious of the client. In this dream the client is clearly telling the psychotherapist what he needs developmentally – what was absent in the original relationship where he veered between being the saintly, clean, little boy who has to play without getting dirty and the disgusting child who causes embarrassment and shame to his family if he as much as gets his hands dirty. (In his adult life he veers between saintly self-sacrifice and secret addictions.) The client is also communicating a most significant fact – not only has he internalised the psychotherapist and distinguishes the two personifications of the person of the same name, but happily he is siding with the psychotherapist who has his best interests at heart and least resembles the transferential parent who would 'write him off' for the smallest misdemeanour, or shame him for not getting the best marks in every subject regardless of his true interests (even the D is still a passing mark!).

The developmentally needed relationship as indicated in the cited dream refers to those aspects of relationship that may have been absent or traumatic for the client at particular periods of his or her childhood and which are supplied or repaired by the psychotherapist, usually in a contracted form (on request by or with agreement from the patient) during the psychotherapy. Sandor Ferenczi (1980) (one of Freud's early followers) attempted this early in the history of psychoanalysis. He departed from neutrality and impassivity in favour of giving nursery care, friendly hugs or management of regression to very sick patients, including one whom he saw anytime, day or night, and took with him on his holidays. Ferenczi held that there needed to be a contrast between the original trauma in infancy and the analytic situation so that remembering can be facilitative instead of a renewed trauma for the patient.

The advocacy relationship proposed by Alice Miller (1983; 1985) can be seen to be the provision of the developmentally needed force in a child's life which should have been provided by a parent or other significant caretakers but which the psychotherapist ultimately has to provide. The holding environment of Winnicott (1958) is another example of such provision, as are the re-parenting techniques of the Schiffs (Schiff et al., 1975) in transactional analysis.

Freud prescribed a mirror-like impassivity on the part of the analyst, who should him or herself be analysed, who should not reciprocate the patient's confidences, and should not try to educate, morally influence, or 'improve' the patient, and who should be tolerant of the patient's weakness. In practice, however, Freud 'conducted therapy as no classical Freudian analyst would conduct it today' (Malcolm, 1981), shouting at the patient, praising him, arguing with him, accepting flowers from him on his birthday, lending him money, visiting him at home and even gossiping with him about other patients!

The psychoanalyst Sechehaye (1951) was able to break through the unreal wall that hemmed in her patient Renee and bring her into some contact with life. In order to do this, Sechehaye not only took her on holiday to the seashore, as Ferenczi had done with one of his patients, but also took Renee into her home for extended periods. She allowed her to regress to the point where she felt she was re-entering her mother's body, thus becoming one of the first of those psychotherapists who have literally undertaken to 're-parent' schizophrenic clients. She allowed her to lean on her bosom and pretended to give milk from her breasts to the doll with whom Renee identified.

> That Sechehaye was far more involved personally than even the most humanistic of therapists usually are we can infer from the accounts of how she gave instructions for her meals, saw to her baths, and in general played for Renee the nourishing mother that she had been denied as an infant. That this took an emotional toll far beyond the ordinary is evident from Renee's own account that 'Mama was extremely upset' or that she regained consciousness and found Mama weeping over her.
>
> (Friedman, 1985, p. 188)

The psychotherapist's reply to a client who asks: 'How are you?' in this kind of relationship will be determined by the specific needs that were not appropriately responded to by their caretakers in childhood. In response to the adult who as a child was never allowed to show her care or love for the parent the therapist may reply: 'I'm fine thank you and I appreciate your caring'. Alternatively in response to the adult who as a child was burdened with parental intimacies, a therapist may reply 'It is not necessary for you to worry about me, right now I am here to take care of you and I am ready to do that.'

In the developmentally needed relationship, the metaphoric kinship relationship being established is clearly closer to a real parent and child relationship than any of the other forms of bonding in psychotherapy. In the words of J. Schiff (1977):

> I am as much part of the symbiosis and as vulnerable as any parent. While my attachments don't occur at the same kind of depth with each youngster, they have not been selective in favor of those kids who were successful, and several times I have experienced tremendous loss and grief.
>
> (p.63)

In view of the regressive nature of this kind of work and the likely length of time involved, the professional and ethical responsibilities of the psychotherapists are also concomitantly greater and perhaps so awesome that many psychotherapists try to avoid it. It is certainly true that this depth of long-standing psychotherapeutic relationship as the primary therapeutic relationship modality is more frequently reported between psychotherapists and more severely damaged patients.

I–You Relationship

The therapeutic relationship modality that shows most continuity with the healing relationships of ordinary life is that which Buber (1970) called the I–You relationship to differentiate it from the I–It relationship. The I–You relationship is referred to elsewhere in psychotherapeutic literature as the real relationship or the core relationship (Barr, 1987). It is very likely that those ordinary relationships that human beings have experienced as particularly healing over the ages have been characterised by the qualities of the I–You relationship (Buber, 1970).

With Freud's discovery of the importance of the transference relationship came deep suspicion of the real relationship – the therapeutic relationship most similar to ordinary human relationships. Certainly for some decades psychoanalysts' emotional reactions to their patients were usually understood to be a manifestation of the analysts' unresolved conflicts. It is only comparatively recently that analyst feelings or countertransference reactions have been seen as valid and important sources of information to be used effectively in the psychotherapy (Heimann, 1950).

Object relations theorists have offered psychotherapy profoundly useful concepts and theoretical understandings, but the I–You therapeutic relationship is the opposite of an object relationship. For Buber, the other is a person, not an object.

> Whoever says You does not have something for his object. For wherever there is something there is also another something; every It borders on other Its; It is only by virtue of bordering on others. But where You is said, there is no something. You has no borders. Whoever says you does not have something; he has nothing. But he stands in relation.
>
> (Buber, 1970, p. 55)

The emotional involvement in this relationship between psychotherapist and patient is that between *person and person* in the existential dilemma where both stand in a kind of mutuality to each other. Indeed, as Friedman (1985) points out, it is a kind of mutuality because the psychotherapist is also in role. However in the immediacy of the existential encounter, the mutuality is almost complete and the self of the therapist becomes the instrument through which the healing evolves.

An intuitive, introverted type of patient sadly remembers difficulty with right or left, physical discomfort in the real world and incomprehension when required to learn kinaesthetically. The psychotherapist bends down to show the scar on her leg which she used as a little girl to help her decide which side was left. The moment is unforgettable, the bonding person to person. Yet it is enacted by a professional person who, at that very moment, has taken responsibility for that self-disclosure in the psychotherapy, judging it appropriate and timely to trust or delight the patient with a sense of shared personhood. The two then become siblings in incomprehension, siblings in discovery, and siblings in the quest for wholeness.

Such self-disclosure needs, of course, to be done with extreme care and, in its worst abusive form, has been an excuse for unauthentic acting out of the psychotherapist's own need for display, hostility, or seductiveness. Genuine well-judged use of the I–You relationship is probably one of the most difficult forms of therapeutic relating. Doubtless this was the very good reason behind the early analysts regarding it with extreme suspicion. Also, of course, it is in the name of I–You relationship that many personal relationships have been destructive. It probably requires the most skill, the most self-knowledge and the greatest care because its potential for careless or destructive use is so great. Yet there are only a few trainings, for example in gestalt, which specifically address this experientially and theoretically. Sometimes lip-service is paid to the I–You person-to-person concept as if we know what it's about, or it is 'outlawed' in the analysis – as if this were possible.

'There can be no psychoanalysis without an existential bond between the analyst and the analysand', writes Boss (1963). 'This means that to imagine there can be analysis without countertransference, without involvement and response on the part of the analyst, is an illusion. The analyst can deny but cannot avoid having an emotional relationship with the analysand: even the objectifying attitude of indifference is a mode of emotional relating' (Friedman, 1985, pp. 79–80). The I–You relationship is characterised by the *here-and-now existential encounter* between the two people. It involves mutual participation in the process and the recognition that each is changed by the other. Its field is not object relations, but subject relations. The real person of the psychotherapist can never be totally excluded from an interactional matrix of therapy. Existential psychotherapy (Boss, 1963; Binswanger, 1968; May, 1969), specifically includes the I–You genuine encounter as a major therapeutic modality, but analysts are also addressing the issue.

> It is good for analyst and patient to have to admit some of the analyst's weaknesses as they are revealed in the interchange in the consulting room. The admission of deficiencies may help patient and analyst to let go of one another more easily when they have had enough. In other words, the somewhat freer admission of realities – but not too free – facilitates the process of mourning which enables an analysis to end satisfactorily. The end of analysis is in this way prepared from the beginning.
>
> (Klauber, 1986, p. 213)

To Fromm-Reichmann (1974), Sullivan's (1940) concept of the psychotherapist as 'participant observer' included spontaneous and genuine responses on the part of the psychotherapist and even, in some cases, reassuring touch and gestures of affection. This does *not* include transforming the professional relationship into a social one, nor seeking extraneous personal gratification from the dialogue with the patient. But it does include confirmation of patients as worthy of respect, and meeting them on the basis of mutual human equality.

Guntrip (1961) also rejected the traditional restriction of the functions of the psychotherapist to the dual one of a screen upon which the patient projects his fantasies and a colourless instrument of interpretative technique. Instead, he saw the real personal relationship between patient and analyst as the truly psychotherapeutic factor on which all others depend. For him, true psychotherapy only happens when the therapist and patient find the person behind each other's defences.

Deep insight, as Fairbairn (1952) points out, only develops inside a good therapeutic relationship. What is therapeutic, when it is achieved, is 'the moment of real meeting'. This experience is transforming for both psychotherapist and patient because it is not what happened before (that is transference) but what has never happened before, a genuine experience of relationship centred in the here-and-now.

What Freud calls 'transference' Boss (1979) describes as 'always a genuine relationship between the analysand and the analyst'. Despite the difference in their positions, the partners disclose themselves to each other as human beings. It seems that Freud and Boss are describing different therapeutic relationship modalities which are intrinsically different in intent, in execution, and in effect; not merely a semantic blurring.

Of course, the humanistically orientated psychotherapies (such as gestalt which emphasises here-and-now *contact* as a valid form of therapeutic relating) have greatly amplified the value and use of the person-to-person encounter in psychotherapy.

> The details of technique vary, but the strategy is always to keep a steady, gentle pressure toward the direct and responsible I–Thou orientation, keeping the focus of awareness on the difficulties the patients experience in doing this, and helping them find their own ways through these difficulties.
>
> (Fagan and Shepherd, 1971, p. 116)

For Rogers and Stevens (1967) too, the establishment of a relationship of genuineness, respect, and empathy became the cornerstone conditions for facilitating human growth and development.

In psychoanalysis, even Anna Freud called for the recognition that in analysis two real people of equal adult status stand in a real personal relationship to each other. 'There are differences in the ways in which we receive and send off patients, and in the degree to which we permit a real relationship to the patient to coexist with the transferred, fantasied one.' (A. Freud, 1968, p. 360)

It is the neglect of this side of the relationship, and not just 'transference' that may cause the hostile reactions analysts get from their patients according to Leo Stone (1961). He expressed concern lest the analyst's unrelentingly analytic behaviour subvert the process by shaking the patient's faith in the analyst's benignity. Stone declared that a failure to show reasonable human response at a critical juncture can invalidate years of patient, skilful work.

According to Malcolm (1981) honesty and spontaneity can correct the patient's transference misperceptions and make the psychotherapist's responses unpredictable and therefore less likely to be manipulated by the patient. The patient's distrust may be relieved when the psychotherapist provides the patient with a model of authentic being with which he can identify. Such authenticity on the psychotherapist's part may mean that the therapeutic relationship changes the therapist as much as the patient. Both Jourard (1971) and Jung (1966) held this as a central truth in all healing endeavour. Searles (1975) also believed that the patient has a powerful innate striving to heal the analyst (as he or she may have desired to heal the parents) which can and does contribute to greater individuation and growth for the psychotherapist as they are *both* transformed in the therapeutic dialogue.

'What is confirmed most of all is the personal 'realness' of the therapist that has arisen from and been brought into the therapeutic relationship.' (Archambeau, 1979, pp. 141–158). I also quote Greenson directly: 'A certain amount of compassion, friendliness, warmth, and respect for the patient's rights is indispensable. The analyst's office is a treatment room and not a research laboratory.' (1967, p. 391)

Greenacre (1959) and Stone (1961) are clear that analysts must be able to become emotionally involved with and committed to their patients. They must like them; prolonged dislike or disinterest as well as too strong a love will interfere with therapy. They must have a wish to help and cure them, and must be concerned with patients' welfare without losing sight of long-range goals.

The kinship quality of the person-to-person relationship is analogous to that of siblings – the shared empathetic understanding from a similar inherited frame of reference. Although they are different, they are of more or less equal standing and share the ambiguous and ambivalent legacy of existence.

In answer to the patient's question: 'How are you?' the psychotherapist may well reply: 'Physically I am fine, but lately I have been wondering about the helpless feeling I sometimes experience when you talk about the death of your baby. I guess it reminds me of losing my husband, and the fact that we are both grieving for loved ones in the same year'. Equally the reply may be much shorter, for example: 'Great – how about you?'

In all cases the person-to-person relationship will be honoured by truthfulness or authenticity – not at the expense of the client but in the spirit of mutuality. According to Buber, the genuine psychotherapist can only accomplish the true task of regenerating the stunted growth of a personal centre by entering as 'a partner into a person-to-person relationship, but never through the observation and investigation of an object' (1970, p. 179). Significantly though, this does not mean injudicious honesty. Buber further acknowledges the limited nature of the psychotherapeutic person-to-person relationship. 'Every I–You relationship in a situation defined by the attempt of one partner to act on the other one so as to accomplish some goal depends on a mutuality that is condemned never to become complete' (p. 179).

Transpersonal Relationship

This refers to the spiritual dimension of relationship in psychotherapy. 'If the analyst has been moved by his patient, then the patient is more aware of the analyst as a healing presence' (Samuels, 1985, p. 189). The transpersonal relationship in psychotherapy is characterised by its timelessness, and in Jungian thought is conceived of as the relationship between the unconscious of the analyst and the unconscious of the patient not mediated by consciousness (Guggenbuhl-Craig, 1971).

> The psychotherapist and the client find themselves in a relationship built on mutual unconsciousness. The psychotherapist is led to a direct confrontation of the unreconciled part of himself. The activated unconsciousness of both the client and the therapist causes both to become involved in a transformation of the 'third'. Hence, the relationship itself becomes transformed in the process.
>
> (Archambeau, 1979, p. 162)

There is surprisingly little documented about the transpersonal relationship in psychotherapy. Peck (1978) mentions the concept of 'grace', as has Buber before him, as the ultimate factor that operates in the person-to-person encounter and which may make the difference between whether a patient gets better or not. Berne, too, was aware of it when he quoted: '*Je le pensay, et Dieu le guarit* (we treat them, but it is God who cures them)' (L.R.C. Agnew in Berne, 1966, p. 63).

The nature of this transpersonal dimension is therefore quite difficult to describe, because it is both rare and not easily accessible to the kind of descriptions which can easily be used in discussing the other forms of therapeutic relationships. 'The *numinosum* is either a quality belonging to a visible object or the influence of an invisible presence that causes a peculiar alternation of consciousness' (Jung, 1969, p. 7). It is also possible that there may be a certain amount of embarrassment in psychotherapists who have to admit that after all the years of training and personal analysis and supervision, ultimately we still do not know precisely what it is that we are doing or whether it makes any difference at all. This is the kind of statement one can only be sure of being understood correctly by experienced psychotherapists who have been faced repeatedly with incomprehensible and unpredictable outcomes – the person of whom you despaired, suddenly and sometimes apparently inexplicably, gets well, thrives and actualises beyond all expectation.

At the other polarity, the client for whom the analyst had made an optimistic prognosis reaches plateaux from which in effect they never move, and the analysis is abandoned with a lingering sense of potential glimpsed but never to be reached.

The kinship relationship which is characterised by space and creation between the psychotherapeutic partners is analogous to that of the marital pair. Indeed in Jung's work the sexual relationship is used to represent the alchemical process of transformation (1966). Of course, the conjunction was to be symbolic, not consummated in an unethically incestuous way.

The transpersonal relationship is also characterised paradoxically by a kind of intimacy and by an 'emptying of the ego' at the same time. It is rather as if the ego of even the personal unconscious of the psychotherapist is 'emptied out' of the therapeutic space, leaving space for something numinous to be created in the 'between' of the relationship. This space can then become the 'temenos' or 'the *vas bene clausum* inside which the transmutation takes place' (Adler, 1979, p. 21). It implies a letting go of skills, of knowledge, of experience, of preconceptions, even of the desire to heal, to be present. It is essentially allowing 'passivity' and receptiveness for which preparation is always inadequate. But paradoxically you have to be full in order to be empty. It cannot be made to happen, it can only be encouraged in the same way that the inspirational muse of creativity cannot be forced, but needs to have the ground prepared or seized in the serendipitous moment of readiness. What can be prepared are the conditions conducive to the spontaneous or spiritual act.

A trainee reports: 'When I first started learning psychotherapy it was like trying to learn a new language, say French, but when I saw a very experienced therapist working it appeared to me that she was speaking an entirely different language such as Chinese. The more I have learnt the more I have come to realise that she does indeed speak French, she just speaks it very well. And sometimes she speaks Chinese.'

The context from which this comment arose is that of how he has perceived the supervisor at times intuitively to know facts, feelings or intentions of patients without there being any prior evidence to lead to the conclusions. It is these intuitive illuminations which seem to flourish the more the psychotherapist dissolves the individual ego from the therapeutic container, allowing wisdom and insight and transformation to occur as a self-manifesting process.

The transpersonal relationship refers to the metaphorical Chinese in the psychotherapy. In response to the client's question 'How are you?', the therapist's reply may be nothing or any of the above examples. The essence of the communication is in the heart of the shared silence of being-together in a dimension which is impossible to articulate exactly, too delicate to analyse and yet too pervasively present in psychotherapy to ignore.

Another trainee in supervision brought as an ethical problem the fact that he had seen a particular client for several years, who was seriously disturbed and showed no sign of improvement. He had utilised all the major interpretations and strategies for such cases to no avail. Indeed she refused to form any working alliance in the shape of an agreed goal for her psychotherapy. It was exceedingly uncertain what benefit there could be for her, yet she continued coming because (we speculated) this was the only single human relationship which was alive for her in a physically and emotionally impoverished life.

The psychotherapist responsibly questioned whether she should be referred to another treatment facility. Yet he feared that she would experience this as an abandonment. In our supervision we explored the possibility that he should let go of expectations that she should be different from the way she was. The psychotherapist was even willing and able to let go of the healer archetype, allowing himself to become an empty vessel, a container wherein healing could have space to manifest, or beingness could be validated without any expectation even of the acceptance. This needs to be truly done in good faith and not based on the trickery of paradoxical interventions where expectations are removed ***in order*** for the patient to change. The atmosphere is more a trance-like meditation, the quality of which is conveyed by the being-with of highly evolved psychotherapists with patients who are in acute psychosis such as Gendlin (1967) who affirm the spiritual dimension in psychotherapy.

(It is quite possible that psychotherapists may be deluding themselves in ways that may be dangerous for themselves and their clients if they mistakenly, prematurely or naively focus on the transpersonal and, for example, overlook or minimise transferential or personal phenomena.)

James and Savary (1977) contributed the notion of a third self created in such a dimension of betweenness when the inner core energies of the dialoguing partners merge. 'Third-self sharing, perhaps the most complete form of sharing, involves not only *self-awareness* (of the individual self) and *other-awareness* (of the relating self), but *together-awareness* (of the third self) ' (p. 325).

This resembles the archetype of the self which Jung refers to as the person's inherent and psychic disposition to experience centredness and meaning in life, sometimes conceived of as the God within ourselves. Buber was essentially concerned with the close association of the relation to God with the relation to one's fellow men, with the I–Thou which issues from the encounter with the ***other in relationship***. This dimension in the psychotherapeutic relationship cannot be proved and can hardly be described and Buber (1970) concludes: 'Nothing remains to me in the end but an appeal to the testimony of your own mysteries' (p. 174).

Conclusion

Five kinds of psychotherapeutic relationship available as potential avenues for constructive use have been described briefly. Some characteristics of each were indicated and hopefully an effort begun to clarify, specify and differentiate more acutely in theory and practice the nature and intentions of the multiplicity of psychotherapeutic relationships available in the consulting room. Different psychotherapies stress different relationships for different reasons.

It is perhaps time that psychotherapists acknowledged explicitly that these five forms of relationship are intentionally or unintentionally present in most approaches to psychotherapy. How explicitly and purposefully, which of these modes of psychotherapeutic relationships are used, may be one of the major ways in which some approaches resemble each other more and differ most from other approaches.

It may need to be recognised in most psychotherapy trainings that experience and supervision are required in distinguishing between such different forms of psychotherapeutic relationship and assessing and evaluating the usefulness of each at different stages of psychotherapy. Equally, different modes may be indicated for individuals with different characteristic ways of relating so that there is not a slipshod vacillation due to error or neurotic countertransference, nor a denial of the obvious.

Confusion and lack of clarity abound when types of psychotherapeutic relationship are confused with each other or the validity of one is used as necessarily substituting for the other. It is possible that human beings need all of these forms of relating, and that psychotherapists with flexibility and range can become skilful in the appropriate use of all of them, although not all are required in all psychotherapies or for all patients.

The far-ranging implications of this perspective for psychotherapy research, assessment and treatment need to be developed further. Integration of a multiplicity of therapeutic relationship modalities does not mean eclectic or unconscious use. Indeed if such is the declared field, the responsibility is awesome. Freedom does not mean that we forgo discipline. Courage in actively embracing the fullest range of potentials of the self, theory or the numinosum needs to be accompanied by the severest form of testing, and forged anew with each client from moment to moment, no matter what the prescriptions or proscriptions of theoretical orthodoxy.

References

ADLER, G. (1979). *Dynamics of the Self*. London: Coventure. (Originally published 1951.)

ALEXANDER, F. and FRENCH, T. (1946). *Psychoanalytic Therapy*. New York: Ronald Press.

ARCHAMBEAU, E. (1979). *Beyond Countertransference: The Psychotherapist's Experience of Healing in the Therapeutic Relationship*. Doctoral dissertation. San Diego, CA: California School of Professional Psychology.

BARR, J. (1987). Therapeutic relationship model. *Transactional Analysis Journal*, **17** (4), 141.

BERNE, E. (1961). *Transactional Analysis in Psychotherapy: A Systematic Individual and Social Psychiatry*. New York: Grove Press.

BERNE, E. (1966). *Principles of Group Treatment*. New York: Grove Press.

BINSWANGER, L. (1968). *Being-in-the-World*. New York: Harper Torchbooks.

BORDIN, E.S. (1979). The generalizability of the psychoanalytical concept of the working alliance. *Psychotherapy: Theory, Research and Practice*, **16** (3), 252-260.

BOSS, M. (1963). *Psychoanalysis and Daseinanalysis*, (L.B. Lefefre, trans.). New York: Basic Books.

BOSS, M. (1979). *Existential Foundations of Medicine and Psychology*. New York: Jason Aronson.

BUBER, M. (1970). *I and Thou*, (W. Kaufmann, trans.). Edinburgh: T. and T. Clark. (Originally published 1923.)

BUGENTAL, J.F.T. (1987). *The Art of the Psychotherapist*. New York: W.W. Norton.

DRYDEN, W. (Ed.) (1984). *Individual Therapy in Britain*. London: Harper and Row.

FAGAN, J. and SHEPHERD, I.L. (Eds) (1971). *Gestalt Therapy Now: Theory, Techniques, Applications*. New York: Harper and Row.

FAIRBAIRN, W.R.D. (1952). *Psychoanalytic Studies of the Personality*. London: Tavistock Publications.

FERENCZI, S. (1980). *Further Contributions to the Theory and Technique of Psychoanalysis*. London: Maresfield Reprints/Karnac Books. (Originally published 1926.)

FREUD, A. (1968). *Indications for Child Analysis and Other Papers 1945 to 1956, The Writings of Anna Freud*. Vol. 4. New York: International Universities Press.

FREUD, S. (1912a). The dynamics of transference. In: J. Strachey (Ed.), *The Standard Edition of the Complete Psychological Works of Sigmund Freud*, Vol. 12, pp.97–108. London: Hogarth Press.

FREUD, S. (1912b). Recommendations to physicians practising psycho-analysis. In: J. Strachey (Ed.), *The Standard Edition of the Complete Psychological Works of Sigmund Freud*, Vol. 12, pp. 109–120. London: Hogarth Press.

FRIEDMAN, M. (1985). *The Healing Dialogue in Psychotherapy*. New York: Jason Aronson.

FROMM-REICHMANN, F. (1974). *Principles of Intensive Psychotherapy*. Chicago: University of Chicago Press. (Originally published 1950.)

GENDLIN, E. (1967). Subverbal communication and therapist expressivity: trends in client-centred therapy with schizophrenics. In: C.R. Rogers and B. Stevens (Eds) *Person to Person – The Problem of Being a Human: A New Trend in Psychology*, pp. 119–149. Lafayette, CA: Real People Press.

GOULDING, M.M. and GOULDING, R.L. (1979). *Changing Lives Through Redecision Therapy*. New York: Grove Press.

GREENACRE, P. (1959). Certain technical problems in the transference relationship. *Journal of the American Psychoanalysis Association*, 7, 484–502.

GREENSON, R.R. (1965). The working alliance and the transference neurosis. *Psychoanalysis Quarterly*, 34, 155–181.

GREENSON, R.R. (1967). *The Technique and Practice of Psychoanalysis* (Vol. 1). New York: International Universities Press.

GRIFFITH, S. (1990). A review of the factors associated with patient compliance and the taking of prescribed medicines. *British Journal of General Practice*, **40**, 114–116.

GUGGENBUHL-CRAIG, A. (1971). *Power in the Helping Professions*. Dallas, TX: Spring Publications.

GUNTRIP, H. (1961). Personality structure and human interaction: the developing synthesis of psychodynamic theory. In: J.D. Sutherland (Ed.), *The International Psycho-analytical Library*, No.56. London: Hogarth Press and the Institute of Psycho-Analysis.

HEIMANN, P. (1950). On countertransference. *International Journal of Psycho-Analysis*, **31**, 81–84.

JAMES, M. and SAVARY, L. (1977). *A New Self: Self-therapy with Transactional Analysis*. Reading, MA: Addison-Wesley.

JOURARD, S.M. (1971). *The Transparent Self*. New York: Van Nostrand Reinhold.

JUNG, C.G. (1966). The psychology of the transference. In: *The Collected Works*, (R.F.C. Hull, trans.), Vol. 16, pp. 162–323. London: Routledge and Kegan Paul. (Originally published 1946.)

JUNG, C.G. (1969). Psychology and religion. In: *The Collected Works* (R.F.C. Hull, trans.), Vol. 11, pp. 3–105. London: Routledge and Kegan Paul. (Originally published 1938.)

KLAUBER, J. (1986). Elements of the psychoanalytic relationship and their therapeutic implications. In: G. Kohon (Ed.), *The British School of Psychoanalysis: The Independent Tradition*, pp. 200–213. London: Free Association Books.

LAMBERT, M.J. (1986). Implications of psychotherapy outcome research for eclectic psychotherapy. In: J.C. Norcross (Ed.), *Handbook of Eclectic Psychotherapy*, pp. 436–462. New York: Brunner/Mazel.

LAPLANCHE, J. and PONTALIS, J-B. (1988). *The Language of Psycho-analysis*. London: Karnac Books. (Originally published 1973.)

MALCOLM, J. (1981). *Psychoanalysis: The Impossible Profession*. New York: Knopf.

MAY, R. (1969). *Love and Will*. London: Collins.

MILLER, A. (1983). *The Drama of the Gifted Child and the Search for the True Self* (R. Ward, trans.). London: Faber and Faber. (Originally published 1979.)

MILLER, A. (1985). *Thou Shalt Not Be Aware: Society's Betrayal of the Child* (H. and H. Hannum, trans.). London: Pluto. (Originally published 1981.)

MOISO, C. (1985). Ego states and transference. *Transactional Analysis Journal*, **15** (3), 194–201.

NORCROSS, J.C. (1986). *Handbook of Eclectic Psychotherapy*. New York: Brunner/Mazel.

ONIONS, C.T. (1973). *The Shorter Oxford English Dictionary: On Historical Principles*, Vol. 2. Oxford: Clarendon Press.

PECK, S. (1978). *The Road Less Traveled: A New Psychology of Love, Traditional Values and Spiritual Growth.* New York: Simon and Schuster.

POLSTER, E. and POLSTER, M. (1973). *Gestalt Therapy Integrated.* New York: Random House.

ROGERS, C.R. and STEVENS, B. (1967). *Person to Person – The Problem of Being Human: A New Trend in Psychology.* Lafayette, CA: Real People Press.

SAMUELS, A. (1985). *Jung and the Post-Jungians.* London: Routledge and Kegan Paul.

SCHIFF, J.L. with SCHIFF, A.W., MELLOR, K., SCHIFF, E., SCHIFF, S., RICHMAN, D., FISHMAN, J., WOLZ, L., FISHMAN, C. and MOMB, D. (1975). *Transactional Analysis Treatment of Psychosis.* New York: Harper and Row.

SCHIFF, J.L. (1977). One hundred children generate a lot of TA. In: Barnes, G. (Ed.), *Transactional Analysis after Eric Berne*, pp. 54–57. New York: Harper's College Press.

SEARLES, H. (1975). The patient as therapist to his analyst. In: R. Langs (Ed.), *Classics in Psycho-analytic Technique*, pp. 95–151. New York: Jason Aronson.

SECHEHAYE, M. (1951). *Reality Lost and Regained: Autobiography of a Schizophrenic Girl.* (G. Urbin-Rabson, trans.). New York: Grune and Stratton.

STONE, L. (1961). *The Psychoanalytic Situation.* New York: International Universities Press.

SULLIVAN, H.S. (1940). *Conception of Modern Psychiatry.* New York: Norton.

WINNICOTT, D.W. (1958). *Collected Papers. Through Paediatrics to Psycho-analysis.* London: Tavistock Publications.

Chapter 3 Outcomes of Psychotherapy: A Diagnostic Pentagon

Introduction

One of the central tenets of transactional analysis is that people with psychiatric difficulties can be cured. 'This means not just the mildly neurotic, but the drug abuser, the severely depressed, the "schizophrenic", everyone with a functional psychiatric disorder.... The notion that psychiatrists could in fact "cure" the severe emotional disturbances of the people they work with was as radical and stunning a notion as has ever been introduced' (Steiner, 1974, p. 7).

Berne saw script analysis, (along with ego state analysis, transactional analysis and game analysis) as the primary avenue for curing people. According to him:

> Each person decides in early childhood how he will live and how he will die, and that plan, which he carries in his head wherever he goes, is called his script. His trivial behavior may be decided by reason, but his important decisions are already made: what kind of person he will marry, how many children he will have, what kind of bed he will die in, and who will be there when he does. It may not be what he wants, but it is what he wants it to be.
>
> (Berne, 1972, p. 31)

Newcomers to transactional analysis often find some difficulty with this apparent contradiction between the high predictability of script outcomes and our belief in and experience of major life and personality changes. 'For the transactional script analyst, as for the play analyst, this means that if you know the plot and the character, you know what his outcome will be, unless some changes can be made.' (Berne, 1972, p. 36)

Transactional analysis, as a fundamentally existential approach to

From P. Clarkson (1987). Outcomes of psychotherapy: a diagnostic pentagon. *Institute of Transactional Analysis News*, 17, 3–10, with permission. Also published in Dutch in *Strook Tijdschrift voor Transactionele Analyse*, 9 (4), 6–19 (1987).

human psychology, emphasises that our scripts were constructed by our own choice and can be reconstructed or abandoned by our own choosing. It is precisely because life scripts are so predictable that they can be brought into awareness and re-decided, which makes change truly possible.

However, knowing when or if a life script change or re-decision in therapy is indeed 'script cure' has intrigued and puzzled many authors, as witness a whole issue of the *Transactional Analysis Journal* (April, 1980) devoted to the subject.

In his last public address, Berne (1971) said that there was only one paper to write, which is called 'How to Cure Patients' (p. 12). He might have also been interested in this chapter, which hopes to differentiate 'cure' as he meant it, from other impostors, jokers, tricksters and clowns which masquerade as 'cure' on the psychotherapeutic stage.

Five types of change are discussed below.

Cure (OK Change)

Berne was interested in the kind of cure which meant that people could break out of their scripts entirely, putting their 'own show on the road with new characters, new roles, and a new plot and payoff. Such a script cure, which changes his character and his destiny, is also a clinical cure, since most of his symptoms will be relieved by his re-decision' (Berne, 1972, p. 362).

The metaphor he repeatedly used was to change princes and princesses (who had become 'frogs' through social and parental influences) back into princes and princesses so that they could continue their development into autonomous, intimate, spontaneous and aware individuals. Erskine (1980) describes script cure as observable from the cessation of behaviours syntonic with the individual's script. He emphasises that such a cure involves changes at behavioural and intrapsychic levels (affective and cognitive) as well as psychological levels. OK type change or script cure also has a number of phenomenological characteristics. Clients who have made such fundamental changes of character and destiny often report an 'ad lib' quality to their lives and relationships. They no longer 'know what to say' and their social networks frequently undergo considerable oscillation, for example, spouse considers personal psychotherapy or divorce, change of friends is almost always a consequence, and career or name changes are not unusual. If script decisions determine the most important aspects of a person's life, script re-decisions will affect them too.

Often people experience some 'nostalgia' for 'the person I used to be' and may need to do some mourning for a valued archaic self even though it is now defunct or dangerous as a survival adaptation. Script change can also be uncomfortable in another way. 'He is then faced with the existential problems of necessity, freedom of choice, and absurdity, all of which were previously evaded in some measure by living with the illusions of his script' (Berne, 1966, p. 311).

The person who has 'flipped in' has a frame of reference in which changing is experienced as satisfying and autonomous. Not only are changes imposed by the environment or natural cycles (ageing, for example) welcomed as learning opportunities, but such 'cured' individuals also *seek* change and growth in their continuing ways. They develop and nourish their own particular needs and levels for stimulation and excitement, complexity and diversity which Selye (1957) referred to as 'eustress'. The change process itself is experienced as energising and they are pro-active and creative. Such people *act* upon their world. They have overcome the subjective 'learned helplessness' (Miller and Seligman, 1975) which reinforces the powerlessness of script-bound individuals and collectives such as women, ethnic minorities, and the physically handicapped. Research (Kiev and Cohn, 1979) has shown that senior levels of management derive satisfaction from working under 'stresses' which middle managers may experience as 'distress'. It is hypothesised that this is due to the feeling that their decisions actually affect the outcomes they initiate. The corollary with experienced power over your life is clear.

Characteristically, change after termination of psychotherapy (permanently or temporarily) continues to be important for the individual, but it is essentially post-pathological; away from cure and towards growth. It has to do with responding adaptively and creatively to life's stresses (Holmes and Rahe, 1967) and progressing with increasing autonomy and assurance through adult development stages (Erikson, 1968; Levinson, 1978).

Real and lasting script cure is achieved when the new decision, for example, 'I will still not commit suicide' is stable under ordinary and extreme stresses. Some vicissitudes of life such as bereavement, loss of jobs, natural disasters, war and concentration camps can challenge the script-change profoundly. 'The last of the human freedoms' which Frankl (1969, p. 65) defines so poignantly as the freedom to choose one's attitude in any given set of circumstances, even in Auschwitz and Dachau.

> Every day, every hour, offered the opportunity to make a decision, a decision which determined whether you would or would not submit to those powers which threatened to rob you of your very self, your inner freedom; which determined whether or not you would... become molded into the form of the typical inmate.
>
> (pp.65–66)

If you are still following a 'script' based on other people's directives it is probably impossible continuously to live responsibly under such severe testing.

The archetypal image is that of Odysseus transforming himself and his life on the adult voyage/journey through life. Aristotle summarised it as follows: 'A certain man has been abroad for many years. Poseidon is lying in wait for him, and he is alone. Matters at home, too, have reached the point at which his property is being squandered and his son's death is plotted by suitors to his wife. He arrives there after terrible sufferings, reveals himself, and falls upon his enemies. The story concludes with his salvation and their destruction. This is all that is proper to the Odyssey; the rest is episode' (Aristotle, 1963, p. 31).

This seems a truly apt metaphor for a man who seems compelled by his destiny to end up lonely and dethroned, bereft of all that he holds precious while he fights other men's battles. Revealing himself, in his innate 'princeliness' under severe stress, his journey ends in triumph.

'Making Progress' (Non-change)

This outcome of psychotherapy (short or long term) is not a true change at all, but mere fluctuations that may be mistaken for real change. 'The patient fights being a winner because he is not in treatment for that purpose, but only to be made into a braver loser. This is natural enough, since...if he becomes a winner, he has to throw away all or most of his script and start over, which most people are reluctant to do' (Berne, 1972, p. 37).

This type of 'change' is a masquerade of living creatively within very narrow norms of maintaining what Steiner (1974) calls 'banal scripts'. By moving three steps forward, two back and two steps forward, three back, the client can give impressions that there is movement or progress, but a hard contractual check over any length of time, will prove that in fact no significant long-term stable change has been accomplished.

Repeatedly in his writing, Berne referred scathingly to this outcome of psychotherapy: 'something called getting better, or 'progress', which in effect is making more comfortable frogs' (1966, p. 290).

People who feel they have accomplished change but have in fact 'made progress' usually place great value on the maintenance of a single world view, and tend to find reinforcing experiences which support the future avoidance of both positively and negatively valued stresses. Even in fantasy, changing, or the stimulus to change, is perceived as negative, destabilising and therefore undesirable. Their goal is homeostasis or stability within very narrow but predictable limits. Psychotherapy may end up by widening the limits somewhat, but the basic restrictions on autonomy and creativity are stretched or redefined, not changed.

However, making progress *obviously* has some value and should be encouraged where the alternative may be a third-degree payoff or a prematurely forced change against resistance which results in the therapist being in effect 'the-rapist' and the client responding by disintegration or catastrophe.

Changing requires not only the willingness to take full responsibility for your life, but also courage. After many years of virtual imprisonment in her home, an agoraphobic patient has a job, a driving licence and hope. She needs/wants to leave her kind and gentle husband who supported her incapacitation in a collusive but well-meaning way. As she is poised for 'cure', he has a stroke that leaves him paralysed. Who will judge for another what price happiness?

People need to change at the pace and rhythm and depth they can manage and not according to their therapist's countertransferral need for stimulation or peacefulness (excitement or 'an easy life').

A characteristic response to such a change is that this system is in a continual state of stress, holding in bound energy, archaic experiences and the influence of introjected others, while at the same time avoiding true contact with the here-and-now experiences which could potentially destabilise a delicate balance. Essentially these people are chronically stressed, rigid in their attitudes and may frequently experience a chronic low level of fatigue and a minimum tolerance for deviance, uncertainty or ambiguity.

The response pattern of clients who are 'making progress' is recognisably reactive to the initiative of others, the environment or habit. These people are passive in response to stimuli from the environment and from others and do not actualise their own lives. These may be the people Berne (1972) describes as 'waiting for Rigor Mortis' (pp. 49–51). They often accumulate 'awareness' at the expense of real change or speak in terms of intellectual knowledge, not really 'feeling different in the gut' as a result of it.

The archetypal image is encapsulated in the story of Echo on whom Juno cast a spell so that ever afterwards she would only repeat the other person's last words. After Narcissus rejected her love, she grieved until all her flesh shrank away and only her voice was left. Echo was doomed by her script forever to repeat the introjected words of a significant other, never giving voice to her autonomous existence in the world (Graves, 1986a, p. 287).

Disillusionment – Impossible Change

This is the outcome of psychotherapy when the client says disappointedly: 'Is that all?', much to the mystification of therapists who thought that they were giving the client exactly what he wanted. (This is a paraphrasing of Berne, 1972, p. 153.)

Misguided Utopian hope is indeed one of the problems that humanistically oriented therapies, including transactional analysis, are particularly heir to, because of their own belief in achieving the seemingly impossible (for example, self-actualisation) and their emphasis on the possibilities (rather than the impossibilities) of changing lives. Much heartbreak can be avoided by recognising and then confronting in a wise and timely fashion the realism and achievability of contracts, goals and expectations which are so out of awareness that they may only become known towards the end or after the termination of the psychotherapy. This kind of disillusionment occurs where either overtly or covertly the outcome of therapy, or script cure is confused with the attainment of omnipotence, irresistability or practical immortality. The desired change is experienced as essentially inappropriate. 'This is the most painful task which the script analyst has to perform: to tell his patients finally that there is no Santa Claus' (Berne, 1972, p. 153).

Furthermore even after the huge investment of time, thought, emotion, money and sacrificed treasured life beliefs required in therapeutic change, there will still be people who are unjust or unkind to her, trains will still break down, death and disaster may still be visited upon him, she may never achieve fashionable thinness without injury to her health, he will never achieve the easy-going phlegmatic attitudinal responses of his colleague with a constitutionally different temperament (Thomas, Chess and Birch, 1977).

There is substantial independent research evidence (for example, Eysenck, 1968) that people are different in terms of their neuropsychological make-up. The introvert can probably never change the biochemical–electrical activity of his cortex to resemble that of his extrovert friend (or therapist?). The task for therapists as well as friends, partners, spouses and parents is rather to value and celebrate each other's different qualities than to do violence to them according to some standard of mass conformity quoting what some expert or statistical report defines as 'normal' or 'healthy'. Personality and character can be changed; temperament can but be allowed for, influenced and enjoyed.

Well-trained psychotherapists can avoid getting involved with a fruitless quest for this type of change by (amongst other procedures) clarifying contracts, checking third-party involvement, learning about the physiological bases of behaviour and forever being vigilant against the cardinal sin of amateur psychologist – extrapolating from your own psychology.

Script is not changing who we are, but how we are in the most important aspects of our lives. This may be the cause of the confusion between people who claim that script cure is impossible when what would be accurate to say is that temperament change is highly unlikely. 'Script' is not that which we do not like or do not understand about other people! According to Berne, whatever behaviour fits in with the formula: Early parental influence – Programme – Compliance – Payoff – is part of the script, and 'whatever behaviour does not fit in with it is not part of script. Every script will fit this formula and no other behaviour will fit it' (Berne, 1972, p. 419).

Characteristic of this misdiagnosis of achieved or non-achieved script change is that the system is simply not designed for the function required of it and so suffers despair and breakdown. Plastic surgery may make noses smaller and people shorter. Ordinary human beings can walk on fire (as I have done), but no amount of 're-deciding' can change the past or give a foolproof guarantee that other people will behave in honourable ways towards you. The world is the world and pigs don't fly.

This system cannot tolerate the attempts to change in an organismally impossible way, nor the stress of attempting to maintain the impossible change. Disillusionment may then mar or ruin a possible script while in vain seeking to change the impossible.

The archetypal myth is that of Icarus, who was given wings made by his father Daedalus to escape from Crete. Because he flew too close to the sun, the wax melted and he plummeted into the sea (Onions, 1973, p. 1012, definition of Icarian). Even in ancient myth, people might fly, but wax will still melt near the sun!

Disintegration (Not OK Change)

This outcome of therapeutic change is not just destabilising, but also disintegrating. Unlike Icarus' change, the desired change is possible, but it is under the influence of Mortido (Federn, 1977), the death instinct.

The motivating frame of reference is that the world does not correspond to the ideal or desired view of it. The stimulus to change is imagined as noxious, and the person may insist that unless homeostasis is maintained on her own terms, destruction will result. The response pattern is acting out, often at a third-degree level, resulting in accidents, imprisonment or hospitalisation. This is the outcome of psychotherapy (or encounter groups) referred to in the popular mind and in literature as a 'therapeutic casualty'.

Berne realised the real potential of this type of change in several places in his writings, for example: 'Well, the husband looks a little paranoid to me, and I'm afraid to cure paranoids because in my experience...they often get a very serious physical disorder like a perforated ulcer or diabetes or a coronary' (1971, p. 10).

Change that strips away a person's defences without the simultaneous provision of protection, skills, knowledge and resources can result in such destructive disintegration. Closing (at appropriate times in the therapy process) the escape hatches, for example, 'no suicide', 'no homicide', 'no going crazy outside of the therapy room', is vitally important in avoiding the likelihood of such eventualities. Also important would be attending to the impact of the change on the person's psychosociological network, the re-learning or acquiring of developmentally impaired skills, maintenance procedures, and reinforcement practice for stability under stress.

On the other hand, no matter how conscientiously a therapist honours a client's contract, there is always still the possibility that the client (or workshop participant) may be more interested in forwarding the script than in creative change.

> The demon is the jester in human existence, and the joker in psychotherapy. No matter how well Jeder lays his plans, the demon can come in at the critical moment and upset them all, usually with a smile and a ha ha. And no matter how well the therapist plans his psychotherapy, the patient always has the upper hand. At the point where the therapist thinks he has four aces, Jeder plays his joker, and his demon wins the pot. Then he skips merrily off, leaving the doctor to leaf through the deck trying to figure out what happened.
>
> (Berne, 1972, p. 122)

A person may still choose to work out her script curse non-contractually despite impeccable ethical and therapeutic procedures on the part of the therapist or workshop leader. Just about any topic may 'bring up material' which a script-bound individual could use to potentiate a script payoff.

The archetypal image is that of Medea who, when her husband threatened to leave her, reacted to this impending change not by accepting it, nor by working through the difficulty with him, nor by finding another man who actually wanted to be with her, but by destroying her rival (Glauke) and being responsible for the deaths of her own two children (Graves, 1986b).

Illusion of Autonomy (Counterscript Change)

> Jeder...carries out his script because it is planted in his head at an early age by his parents, and stays there for the rest of his life, even after their vocal 'flesh' has gone forevermore. It acts like a computer tape or a player-piano roll, which brings out the responses in the planned order long after the person who punched the holes had departed the scene. Jeder meanwhile sits before the piano, moving his fingers along the keyboard under the illusion that it is he who brings the folksy ballad or the stately concerto to its foregone conclusion.
>
> (Berne, 1972, pp. 65–66)

The motivation is Hubris – the belief that you have changed fundamentally when it is actually a cosmetic change. Changes in the person's behaviour have an introjected quality – it seems as if they have adopted new behaviour and belief systems, even a new language (such as transactional analysis) in the service of the pathology. Instead of 'hurrying up' to kill themselves, they may be 'hurrying up' to be perfectly self-actualising, transactional analysis people who always ask straight for strokes and let out their 'free Child' at parties!

The fantasy is that of having achieved autonomy and having escaped the script payoff – what I describe as 'counterscript cure' or what Freudians mean by 'flight into health' (Greenson, 1967, p. 276). This person may have re-decided to 'be close' and 'be aware of their drivers' without a 'fundamental transformation' (metanoia) or a re-organisation in the archaic script-driven Child or compelling Parental ego states. The person is acting as if change at a deep structural level has occurred.

There is the story of the family who lived in a haunted house. After much deliberation they decided to move to another part of the city to get away from the ghost. On the day of the move, having packed the van with all their furniture and goods, one of the neighbours chanced by. 'What's happening?' he asked. A skeletal hand then lifted up a corner of the tarpaulin and said: 'We're moving!'

Counterscript change can be a valuable bridge to lasting script change, but it is not to be confused with the destination. Schiff (1975) has mentioned that over-adaptation has the benefit of good thinking supporting it and as such is a better choice of passive behaviour than incapacitation or escalation into violence. The danger of over-adaptation to the therapist *as an interim measure* is often greatly exaggerated. If a client stops sexually abusing his children as an adaptation to his therapist, he may start receiving positive reinforcement of his new behaviour which acts as a powerful motivation for constructive change and possible permanent script re-decision. As Berne (1972) said, we all know that you can talk a man into drinking or committing suicide, and therefore you can talk him out of it. As stageposts along the way to metanoia, counterscript change is not necessarily illegitimate and may be distinctly beneficial or even life-saving.

The problem with counterscript change (where the therapist's directives, permission, values and example are substituted for the original counterscript messages of one or both parents) is not that it *happens*, but that therapist and client may mistake it for the goal post. If people get stuck here and terminate psychotherapy without changing at a more fundamental 'script level', such contractual changes are unstable under stress and unreliable over time. Figure 3.1, the 'counterscript cure' diagram, shows how, according to the third rule of communication, the script outcome will still be determined by the original psychological level message.

For example, a client who has been cured of vertigo, when climbing a mountain thereafter may fall 'accidentally' over a cliff to her death. The underlying curse and the decision to comply might possibly have

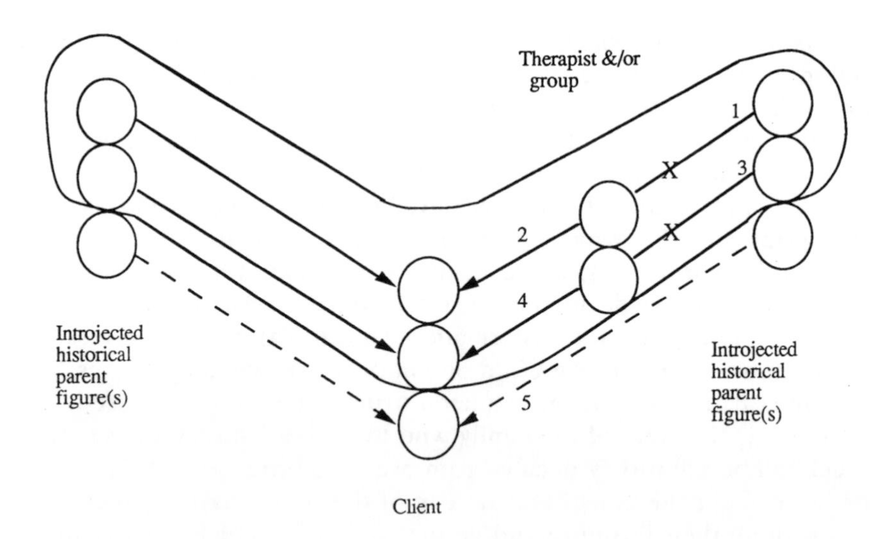

Figure 3.1. Counterscript cure diagram. 1. Original counterscript message. 2. Substitute counterscript message incorporated from therapist or psychological/ ideological system. 3. Old programme. 4. New examples/role models incorporated from therapist and other group members. 5. Unchanged script message manifesting payoff under stress (psychological message). 6. Area of counterscript/counterscript change.

not been revoked in a therapy which paid attention primarily to change at a behavioural level or allowed premature re-decisions not grounded in the total context of her life script, its supports and survival defences. Most experienced clinicians can adduce similar examples.

The compelling potency of 'script power' against 'will power' (original or new counterscript) is poignantly and chillingly illustrated in a recent newspaper report of a man who was warned by his doctor that cigarette smoking would kill him. He indeed succeeded in giving up cigarettes, but choked to death on a piece of nicotine-substitute chewing gum (*The Sun*, 1986).

The symbolic or mythological archetype chosen to illustrate this type of change is that of Oedipus who believed that he had foiled his destiny. He ended up by killing his father and marrying his mother, so fulfilling a 'prophecy' made early in childhood. Aristotle (1963) also rumbles the 'self-deception' of Oedipus: 'It seems unlikely that Oedipus, seeking to discover who had slain Laius, should have overlooked the clue provided by the murder which he himself had committed' (p.27). The functional 'blindness' of Oedipus leads to the loss of his father, his mother, his wife, his kingdom and his eyes. He preserved the illusion of his autonomy but at the price of his ultimately predictable script payoff.

Figure 3.2 facilitates the use and teaching of this material.

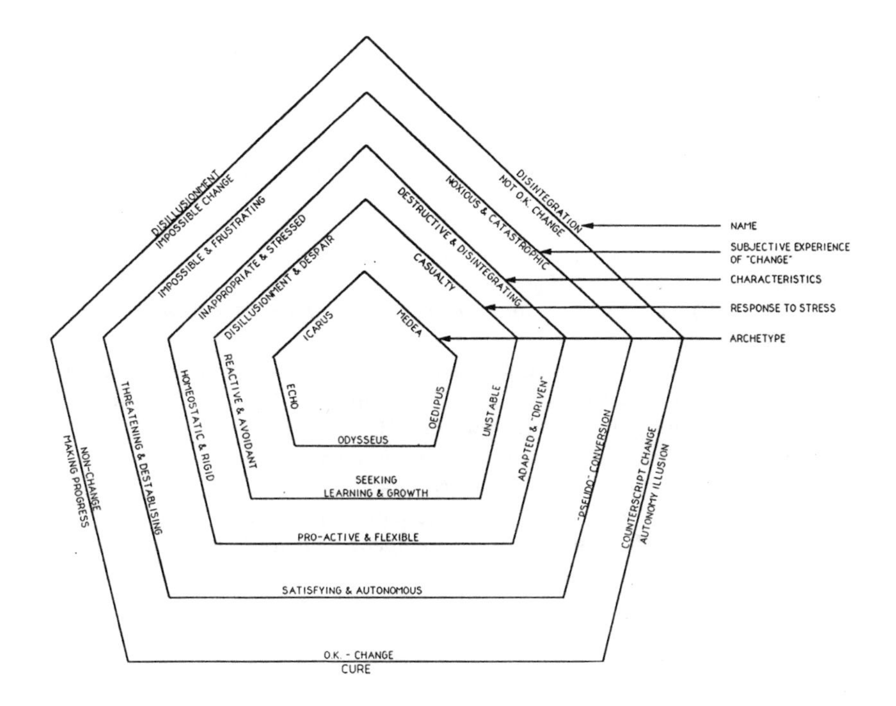

Figure 3.2. The change pentagon: a summary diagram.

I know of no better way to conclude this discussion of different types of change than to remind both client and psychotherapist of the prayer attributed to St Francis of Assisi:

> Lord, give me the courage to change the things I can;
> The serenity to accept the things I cannot change;
> And the wisdom to know the difference.

References

ARISTOTLE (1963). *Poetics.* (J. Warrington, trans.). London: Dent and Sons.

BERNE, E. (1966). *Principles of Group Treatment.* New York: Grove Press.

BERNE, E. (1971). Away from a theory of the impact of interpersonal interaction on non-verbal participation. *Transactional Analysis Journal,* **1** (1), 6–13.

BERNE, E. (1972). *What Do You Say After You Say Hello?* New York: Grove Press.

ERIKSON, E.H. (1968). *Identity, Youth and Crisis.* New York: W.W. Norton.

ERSKINE, R.G. (1980). Script cure: behavioral, intrapsychic and physiological. *Transactional Analysis Journal,* **10** (2), 102–106.

EYSENCK, H.J. (1968). *Handbook of Abnormal Psychology.* London: Pitman Medical Publishing.

FEDERN, P. (1977). *Ego Psychology and the Psychoses.* London: Maresfield Reprints. (Originally published 1953.)

FRANKL, V. (1969). *Man's Search for Meaning.* London: Hodder and Stoughton.

GRAVES, R. (1986a). *The Greek Myths: 1.* Harmondsworth: Penguin.

GRAVES, R. (1986b). *The Greek Myths: 2.* Harmondsworth: Penguin.

GREENSON, R.R. (1967). *The Technique and Practice of Psychoanalysis,* Vol. 1. New York: International Universities Press.

HOLMES, T.H. and RAHE, R.H. (1967). The social readjustment rating scale. *Journal of Psychosomatic Research,* **11**, 213–218.

KIEV, A. and COHN, V. (1979). *Executive Stress: An AMA Survey Report.* New York: Amacom.

LEVINSON, D.J. (1978). *The Seasons of a Man's Life.* New York: Ballantine Books.

MILLER, W.C. and SELIGMAN, M.P. (1975). Depression and learned helplessness in man. *Journal of Abnormal Psychology,* **84**, 228–238.

ONIONS, C.E. (Ed.) (1973). *The Shorter Oxford English Dictionary.* Oxford: Clarendon Press.

SCHIFF, J.L. with SCHIFF, A.W., MELLOR, K., SCHIFF, E., SCHIFF, S., RICHMAN, D., FISHMAN, J., WOLZ, L., FISHMAN, C. and MOMB, D. (1975). *Cathexis Reader: Transactional Analysis Treatment of Psychosis.* New York: Harper and Row.

SELYE, H. (1957). *The Stress of Life.* London: Low and Brydone.

STEINER, C.M. (1974). *Scripts People Live.* New York: Grove Press.

The Sun 29th October, 1986, p. 7. London: News International.

THOMAS, A., CHESS, S. and BIRCH, H. (1977). *Temperament and Development.* New York: Brunner/Mazel.

Chapter 4
Metanoia: A Process of Transformation

This chapter defines *metanoia* (a concept referring to the *turning point* in life and in psychotherapy), reviews the major circumstances under which it occurs, and indicates its commonly occurring features. The aim is to place psychotherapy in a wider context and perhaps broaden the consciousness of psychotherapists to adjacent fields of human enquiry and endeavour. Transactional analysis is one of many psychotherapies that have a particular interest in conditions which bring about change. Closer study of the elements of metanoia or turning points of different kinds can contribute to the learning, understanding and perhaps the clinical practice of transactional analysts. It is intended as an overall map of the territory and not as a detailed study of each of the individual circumstances and features.

In many psychotherapies, especially as represented in scientific publications such as the *Transactional Analysis Journal*, acknowledgement of transpersonal perspectives often seems conspicuous in its absence. Yet, even if the psychotherapist does not adhere to any spiritual vision at all, it is undeniable that he or she shares a similar field of endeavour with those who have such transpersonal perspectives, that is, healing changes. Religious experiences are included here, alongside experiences of love, crisis and education, as important factors in deepening our understanding of the change processes at work in psychotherapy.

The material is drawn from clinical casework, literature and film, as well as anecdotal sources. It is not my intention to be definitive about this vast topic, but rather to provide initial starting points and questions which could serve as springboards for further development and research in the field of psychotherapy.

From P. Clarkson (1989). Metanoia: a process of transformation. *Transactional Analysis Journal*, **19**, 224–234, with permission. A version was also published in *Institute of Transactional Analysis News* **23**, (4), 5–14 (1989). Also published in Dutch in *Strook Tijdschrift voor Transactionele Analyse*, **11**, 62–79 (1989) and in French in *Actualités en Analyse Transactionelle*, **16** (61), 3–9 (1989).

Definitions

Metanoia is derived from the Greek verb *metanoeo* which means:

1. To perceive afterwards or too late
2. To change one's mind or opinion
3. To turn around.

The classical Greek translation also suggests 'to change one's mind on reflection' (Liddell, 1963, p. 439). In the old religious language, metanoia involves confession and repentance. Jung refers to his personal 'mental transformation' as 'a metanoia' (Jung, 1956, p. *xxvi*).

Metanoia is elsewhere defined as 'a change of the inner man' and a 'turning about' (Burchfield, 1976, p. 911). It also means a fundamental change of mind, a fundamental transformation of mind or character. It was taken up in Christianity from the ancient Greek and in ecclesiastical context came to denote the idea of repentance in what the early Christians meant by 'seeing your way and changing'. It is to see the way you have come, and change the direction you are going in the future. It is emphatically not always a religious experience, since many people report such a *volte face* when talking about decisive changes in their lives. 'During this period I was full of indecision, it was a turning point in my life – I would have to decide one way or the other' (Boyle, 1977, p. 240).

Sam Keen (1985) – an existential psychotherapist – also indicates that we can talk about metanoia in many ways. He sees metanoia as the opposite of paranoia and akin to 'repentance, re-owning the shadow, turning around' away from the persona toward the self (p. 146).

The change that is referred to in a metanoia is, for all practical purposes, a permanently transformed state of being, whether it is a spiritual or psychological transformation: 'Something more active and fruitful, the setting up of an immense new inward movement for obtaining the rule of life' (Burchfield, 1976, p. 911).

To the transactional analyst, one of the most fascinating questions is how can we facilitate this turning, transformation or fundamental change?

> Our ordinary alterations of character, as we pass from one of our aims to another, are not commonly called transformations, because each of them is so rapidly succeeded by another in the reverse direction; but whenever one aim grows so stable as to expel definitely its previous rivals from the individual's life, we tend to speak of the phenomenon, and perhaps to wonder at it, as a 'transformation'.
>
> (James, 1985, p. 199)

William James writes about the 'the hot place in a man's consciousness, the group of ideas to which he devotes himself, and from which he works' (James, 1985, p. 200). When there is a long-lasting shift in this habitual centre of personal energy, there is a new centre of gravity in the person and a new frame of reference from which he or she lives.

These changes may appear to occur suddenly or over a period of time. Usually people will report some turning point in their experience, after which they no longer felt it possible to return to their previous way of being. These transformations often involve a paradigm shift or second-order change (Watzlawick, Weakland and Fisch, 1974) which can happen on any level. However, it usually involves physical, mental, emotional, social and sometimes spiritual re-organisation. Such turning points in life and in psychotherapy are often revolutionary, but may equally be the result of evolutionary processes. What appears to be a sudden and dramatic shift may be the result of long preparation and incubation. As a successful actor once put it, 'It took me 12 years of preparation to be an overnight success'. On the other hand, sometimes the change within the person is indeed suddenly precipitated and appears to be totally discontinuous with a person's past history.

In the context of this chapter, metanoia is used with its commonly accepted positive connotation, that is, a fundamental and long-lasting change for the better as defined by the person *and* significant others. In-depth considerations of who defines this 'better' must be left to another enquiry. For my purposes, the positive value of the turning point in a person's life does not depend on the process (the suddenness or gradualness of its achievement), but on its results.

Circumstances in Which Metanoia Occurs

Having summarised some definitions and connotations of metanoia, I attempted to find scientific studies which investigated circumstances in which such transformational changes occur in people's lives. By studying different circumstances which apparently lead to similar outcomes, clinicians learn ways of enhancing their task within the bounds of psychotherapy. They also discover those things they are doing which are similar in process and structure to what other change agents are doing in disparate but adjacent fields of endeavour. Unfortunately, little research has been done although, by activating these initial tentative propositions, it is hoped that either such research may be stimulated or extant studies may be brought to light.

In view of the dearth of scientific, psychological research into the conditions under which script change or fundamental life changes of any kind take place, it seems appropriate to follow Berne's advice:

> What script analysts have to do in practice is read biographies, keep track of their friends' successes and their enemies' failures, see large numbers of patients with various types of early programing, and project backward and forward in the lives of people they are clinically acquainted with for a reasonably long period.
>
> (Berne, 1972, p. 302)

Although fundamental changes appear in infinite variety, five major categories of contingencies can be distinguished. Occasionally they may overlap or aspects of one may shade into another. These categories are:

1. Psychotherapy
2. Religious/political conversion
3. Crisis
4. Falling in love
5. Education/re-education.

Psychotherapy

> Psychotherapy is defined as a form of treatment for mental illness and behavioural disturbances in which a trained person establishes a professional contract with the patient and, through definite therapeutic communication, both verbal and nonverbal, attempts to alleviate the emotional disturbance, reverse or change maladaptive patterns of behavior, and encourage personality growth and development. Psychotherapy is distinguished from such other forms of psychiatric treatment as the use of drugs, surgery, electric shock treatment, and insulin coma treatment.
>
> (Freedman, Kaplan and Sadock, 1975, p. 2601)

The task of the psychotherapist is to facilitate the desired change in the patient or client. There are many accounts of people's life changes as a result of psychotherapy. For example, *I Never Promised You a Rose Garden* by Hannah Green (1986) poignantly described the course of psychotherapy of a schizophrenic young woman. The character of her psychotherapist is based on that of Dr Frieda Fromm-Reichman and the book vividly evocates a tormented young woman in a mental ward making her way towards reality.

Another inspiring account of a fundamental transformation of a person's life, in this case as a result of group therapy, is contained in *A Sense of Freedom* by Jimmy Boyle (1977). From being considered Scotland's most violent criminal he became a sculptor, an author and a contributor to the improvement of prison conditions. When he was finally released from prison he set up a centre called Gateway to provide succour for young people in trouble.

Most psychotherapists can probably adduce from their personal and clinical experience many examples of contributing to, participating in and witnessing changes of a dramatic and totally transformative nature, whether these occur slowly and gradually or suddenly and intensely.

Religious conversion

> Conversion, however it may be described, involves a complete change from one life-style to another. It may require abandoning an aimless and unsatisfying perspective in exchange for a new and promising incentive to live a

> more meaningful life. Sometimes the fact and experience of conversion are related to the search for intellectual truth or the longing for moral purity and goodness. At other times, and these make up the more graphic accounts of dramatic conversions, deep emotional earthquakes erupt out of the past, shatter the present, and make way for a new tomorrow.
>
> (Kerr and Mulder, 1984, p. 9)

It is necessary to point out that conversion does not have to be religious or theological but may be purely ethical or even political, such as a previously selfish and materialistic person becoming committed to a socialist ideology.

The classic case of religious conversion is that of the apostle Paul (Acts 9:1–19, 22:1–21; 26:1–23, in the *New English Bible with the Apochrypha,* 1974). This experience changed Paul in a decisive and determinative way for the rest of his life. But there are also cases, such as that of Malcolm Muggeridge (Kerr and Mulder, 1984, pp. 303–305), whose conversion was not so much a dazzling and divine visitation, but more in the nature of intellectual self-persuasion.

In the classic *Varieties of Religious Experience* by William James (1985), there are many case histories of conversion experiences. He describes these from a purely psychological point of view without, however, detracting from the respect for the transpersonal or spiritual dimensions of the human experience.

Crisis

Crisis occurs

> [W]hen a person faces an obstacle to important life goals that is, for a time, insurmountable through the utilization of customary methods of problem solving. A period of disorganization ensues, a period of upset, during which many abortive attempts at solutions are made.
>
> (Caplan, 1951, p. 18)

Even though most people, lay or professional, can report anecdotes or personal experiences of how crisis, whether personal, environmental, intrapsychic or interpersonal, precipitated changes of a profound and lasting nature to their whole way of living and their view of life, there appears to be a dearth of scientific research into the positive transformative qualities of crisis.

> But a new perception, a sudden emotional shock, or an occasion which lays bare the organic alteration, will make the whole fabric fall together; and then the centre of gravity sinks into an attitude more stable, for the new ideas that reach the centre in the rearrangement seem now to be locked there, and the new structure remains permanent.
>
> (James, 1985, pp. 201–202)

> Near-death experiences are frequently reported as similar to the symbolic death of initiating rites in tribal cultures, after which a person returns with a different and deeper perspective on life, often with a spiritual consciousness which enhances their lives and the lives of those associated with them.
>
> (Lorimer, 1987)

In *Life Wish*, Jill Ireland (1987) describes her recovery from cancer – one of many autobiographical accounts which document how a crisis ranging from a diagnosis of a life-threatening disease to having a child trapped under a car can change people's lives. There are many films which illustrate the possibility of transformation following on the impact of crisis in the person's life.

> Emotional occasions, especially violent ones, are extremely potent in precipitating mental rearrangements. The sudden and explosive ways in which love, jealousy, guilt, fear, remorse, or anger can seize upon one are known to everybody. Hope, happiness, security, resolve, emotions characteristic of conversion, can be equally explosive. And emotions that come in this explosive way seldom leave things as they found them.
>
> (James, 1985, pp. 202–203)

In Tennessee Williams' play, *Cat on a Hot Tin Roof* (1959), Brick also demonstrates a metanoia of a kind. In the film starring Paul Newman and Elizabeth Taylor, Brick's movement from a defensive racket position through anger to sadness, to fear, to a genuine breakthrough is most poignantly dramatised. This may be another case where the novelists and the playwrights tread intrepidly on the terrain which the psychologists have hardly begun to identify.

Of course, crisis intervention theory (Parad, 1969) is based on the assumption that crisis conditions can be used advantageously as transformational vortices in individual lives and in family systems. Webster defines crisis as a 'decisive' or 'crucial' period, a 'turning point' (Webster, 1944, p. 240). 'Indeed the Chinese character for crisis combines those for opportunity and danger' (Clarkson, 1988). However, accounts of positive changes subsequent to crisis still tend to be reported in magazines and newspapers rather than attracting funding for serious psychological research. Perhaps this book may draw some attention to this unexplored, but profoundly exciting, aspect of human psychology, and readers are invited to write to me contributing case-studies, literary sources and personal experiences.

Love

The experience of love, or falling in love, can be a transformational force in the lives of many people. Lord Byron, for example, ended a life style of dissipation and sexual excess in 1819 when he fell in love with a countess who left her rich husband to live with him. As a result of this, Byron rapidly turned from an aimless, self-indulgent profligate into a serious and committed man in the service of the European liberation movement.

> If two people who have been strangers, as all of us are, suddenly let the wall between them break down, and feel close, feel one, this moment of oneness is one of the most exhilarating, most exciting experiences in life. It is all the more wonderful and miraculous for persons who have been shut off, isolated, without love.
>
> (Fromm, 1966, p. 11)

The experience of falling in love has often been compared to a kind of conversion. Again, most of us have experienced the total change in frame of reference and suspension of old ways of behaving. Many people have described being in love as a temporary state of blissful insanity and it is certainly a frequent clinical observation that people appear temporarily to suspend their script payoffs while in the state popularly referred to as 'being in love'. The stability of character transformation as a result of falling in love (or falling out of love) is highly questionable. However, there are again many autobiographical accounts of how a loving relationship has permanently transformed a person's life for the better. An interview with Alison Bryce who survived a rare and deadly form of cancer, was recently reported in the *News of the World*.

> Surgeons removed a cyst on her ovary which turned out to contain a massive tumour. And doctors found she had *more* cancerous cells in her body. But she has proved doctors wrong by giving birth to a bouncing, healthy baby. They warned her that intensive chemotherapy might have left her sterile. But this year she amazed everyone by becoming a mum – without any medical help. And cuddling five-month-old wonder-tot Lauren, blonde Alison revealed: 'I've such a lovely life with my husband Jamie that I know I'm no longer at risk. Jamie is all I ever dreamed of in a husband. I'm far too happy to be ill.'
>
> (Hall, 1986, p. 31)

One of the most famous stories testifying to the power of love as a transformative force is that of Elizabeth Barrett Browning. From the age of 16, Elizabeth, as the result of a spinal injury, was an invalid. She was confined, by her own frailty and her father's authoritarianism, to her sick room with her dog Flush as her constant companion (Mander, 1980). Elizabeth eventually fell in love with Robert Browning, the poet. She then recovered her health sufficiently to elope with Browning against her father's wishes, and to do extensive travelling in Italy including climbing the steps of the cathedral in Milan. She eventually gave birth to a healthy son. When the Brownings settled in Pisa the maid declared that Mrs Browning was 'transformed rather than improved', and when Wordsworth died she succeeded him as Poet Laureate of England (Stephen and Lee, 1917, pp. 78–82).

Education

Education has always been considered to be a powerful way of bringing about change, in either gradual or dramatically sudden ways. This can range from the old Jesuit saying, 'Give me a child until he is seven and he will be mine for life' to the extensive use of re-education or brainwashing used in some countries to indoctrinate innocents and opponents (Sargent, 1959).

A recent film, *The Last Emperor* (Bertolucci,1988), captures vividly the transformation through so-called 'educational processes' of a person brought up to become the Emperor of China to becoming a humble gardener spending his days in poverty and obscurity with apparently genuine acceptance of his condition.

The educational aspects of psychotherapy have been conceptualised by Frank (1973; 1982) as a provision by the therapist of a new perspective for the client, 'the process by which the therapist provides the client with a new assumptive world' (1973, p. 181).

> Therapists provide novel information about clients themselves, about their situations, or about how to view the world; this may be presented directly to clients as interpretations, advice, or information giving, or it may be communicated more subtly through modelling or selective reinforcement.
>
> (Stiles, Shapiro and Elliott, 1986, p. 172)

Masterson (1985), although a psychoanalyst, also stresses the educative tasks of psychotherapy, particularly for borderline and narcissistic patients:

> The therapist deals with this immaturity by providing a learning experience.... Therefore, as it begins to emerge in treatment, all of these relatively obvious and almost commonsense notions about the reality of life and interactions between people have to be not relearned, but learned for the first time.
>
> (pp. 58, 89)

Commonly Occurring Features of Metanoia

In an attempt to learn more about the nature of change, five different circumstances under which metanoia is reported to occur have been compared along with some characteristic features common to several different circumstances.

In this ongoing survey of biographical accounts, clinical cases and anecdotal material, several features of metanoia emerged with regularity. These features seem to be common to two or more of the aforementioned categories. The following features have been identified and abstracted:

1. Intensity
2. Despair
3. Surrender
4. Void (Bridges, 1980)
5. Importance of relationship
6. Community validation
7. Sense of mission
8. Appearance of archetypal images of transformation in dreams and in art.

Each of these are defined and discussed with examples. While these overlap and influence each other, they are here separated for purposes of discussion and further development.

Intensity

Intensity of emotional experience frequently correlates positively with life-changing events or experiences of metanoia. 'A high level of arousal of any emotion increases susceptibility to changes in consciousness' (Conway and Clarkson, 1987, p. 18). The heightened states of emotional intensity developed at some religious events, such as Sufi whirling or fundamentalist evangelical meetings, is a well-observed phenomenon. The atmosphere at Lourdes is said to intensify the positive expectations of thousands of pilgrims, some of whom are permanently healed.

Psychotherapy (and its variants) also makes deliberate and intentional use of increases of emotional and/or physical intensity by heightening the transference through frequent sessions per week (psychoanalysis), breathing techniques that bring people in touch with their primal pain (rebirthing or bioenergetics), use of the techniques to bring the past vividly alive in the here-and-now (Polster and Polster, 1974), and heightening procedures (McNeel, 1976).

Boyle (1977) described the impact of his experiences preceding his life change as follows:

> I have simply been on a journey and experienced terrible pain of a physical, spiritual and emotional nature and I want to stop those of my ilk from doing the same.... It was all of these thoughts that were racing through my mind and I hasten to add they were not all of an altruistic nature, but the complexity and intensity of them were giving me a hard time. For the first time in my life I was having to think very deeply about violence and other methods of gaining status.
>
> (pp. 239–240)

Frequently in psychotherapy, as in homeopathy, patients appear to get worse before they get better. However, such emotionally intense experiences may often herald a profound and long-lasting change for the better. At times it takes the visionary in the therapist to believe in its possibilities.

> 'Not sicker.' Doctor Frieda said at the meeting of the D-ward staff. 'Not sicker at all'. The ward personnel listened politely and attentively, but it seemed unbelievable to them that the bursting stream of gibberish and the uncontrolled and useless violence was not a great change for the worse.
>
> (Green, 1986, p. 183)

Despair

Despair is a frequent feature that precedes a metanoia. Eldridge Cleaver converted to Christianity at the most profound point of discouragement and despair in his life.

> I returned to the Mediterranean coast and began thinking of putting an end to it all by committing suicide. I really began to think about that. I was sitting up on my balcony, one night, on the thirteenth floor – just sitting there.
>
> (Kerr and Mulder, 1984, p. 308)

Another example is cited by James (1985):

> In Tolstoy's case the sense that life had any meaning whatever was for a time wholly withdrawn. The result was a transformation in the whole expression of reality. When we come to study the phenomenon of conversion or religious regeneration, we shall see that a not infrequent consequence of the change operated in the subject is a transfiguration of the face of nature in his eyes.
>
> (James, 1985, p. 158)

Like many alcoholics who become members of Alcoholics Anonymous, Jimmy Boyle had to hit his own kind of rock-bottom before he changed. 'I knew that the screws in the Special Unit had this fear in their minds that Larry and I would react violently to the sentences if they were very long. They didn't realise that once you have reached a certain depth you can go no lower' (Boyle, 1977, p. 235).

Surrender of previous frame of reference

The individual's frame of reference provides him or her with 'an overall perceptual, conceptual, affective end action set, which is used to define the self, other people, and the world, both structurally and dynamically' (Schiff et al., 1975, p. 51). A change in the individual's frame of reference seems to accompany most major life changes. For example, James (1985) wrote, 'Self surrender' and 'new determination,' though seeming at first sight to be such different experiences, are 'really the same thing. Self-surrender sees the change in terms of the old self; determination sees it in terms of the new' (p. 217).

And in her book, Jill Ireland (1987) offered, 'I thought to myself, "It looks as if I have to die so that I can live." It was clear to me now that certain lifelong behaviour and convictions had to die so I could survive' (p. 152).

The experience of the void

In gestalt therapy the void is between the satisfaction and completion of an old need and the emergence of a new need – it is the emptiness through which we pass as we let go of one set of experiences in order fully to engage with a new set of experiences. The outcome determines whether 'the void' has been 'futile' or 'fertile' (Van Dusen, 1975, pp. 89–95). In transition theory, Bridges (1980) refers to this as the neutral zone – the empty space after ending and before a new beginning. In the rights of passage of ancient or primitive tribes, people were educated and instructed in techniques (fasting, dehydration in the sweat lodge) and mental states (dreaming and psychotrophically induced hallucinations) which heightened their availability to new and transformative experiences. The education of Carlos Castaneda by Don Juan in the Yaqui teachings provides many examples of how this neutral zone is cultivated as a source for renewal and change (Castaneda, 1968, p. 110).

> In taking the initiate out into the wilderness and enervating him or her with fasting and fatigue, in suppressing the initiate's old consciousness with chanting and rhythmical movements, in enlivening the imagination with mythical tales and symbolical procedures of various sorts...
>
> (Bridges, 1980, p. 117)

According to clients and clinicians, tolerating, encountering and exploring the awesome emptiness of the void is often the turning point for therapeutic change.

The following Zen story also points to the importance of emptiness as a prelude to enlightenment.

> Nan-in, a Japanese tea master during the Meiji era, received a university professor who came to inquire about Zen. Nan-in served tea. He poured the visitor's cup full, and then kept on pouring. The professor watched the overflow until he could restrain himself no longer: 'It is overfull, no more will go in.' 'Like this cup', Nan-in responded, 'you are full of your own opinions and speculations. How can I show you Zen unless you first empty your cup?'
>
> (Reps, 1971, p. 17)

Relationship

There is substantial and extensive evidence that successful psychotherapy is predicated on the nature of the relationship between client and psychotherapist and that this aspect is more crucial for successful therapeutic change than choice of technique or theoretical approach (Frank, 1979; Hynan, 1981; Norcross, 1986).

> General Booth, the founder of the Salvation Army, considers that the first vital step in saving outcasts consists in making them feel that some decent human being cares enough for them to take an interest in the question whether they are to rise or sink.
>
> (James, 1985, p. 207)

Frequently someone stands by to help and encourage in conversion experiences. In Colson's case, it was his friend Tom Phillips, President of the Raytheon Company, who gave him a copy of C.S. Lewis's *Mere Christianity* (Kerr and Mulder, 1984, p. 310).

The following dialogue between therapist and patient illustrates more experientially the importance and vitality of the healing relationship.

> 'Well, what?' Deborah said, good and loud.
> 'Well, did I ever say it would be easy? I cannot make you well and I do not want to make you well against your own wishes. If you fight with all the strength and patience you have, we will make it together.'
> 'And what if I don't?'
> 'Well, there are lots of mental hospitals, and they build more every day.'
> 'And if I fight, then for what?'
> 'For nothing easy or sweet, and I told you that last year and the year before that. For your own challenge, for your own mistakes and the punishment for them, for your own definition of love and of sanity – a good strong self with which to begin to live.'
>
> (Green, 1986, pp. 182–183)

Community validation

In many experiences of change, the wider community also assumes an important role. For Jimmy Boyle in prison, the acceptance and validation by his new community becomes the bridge to the new man.

> If it was the opposite and someone needed support due to some problem, then everyone would reach out and touch him, and by that I mean help him over the bad patch. Either way the group meeting was a very powerful force.
>
> (Boyle, 1977, p. 245).

> The key to the whole thing lies in the relationships of the people within the group, and the understanding that no one person is bigger than the Community, that the commitment is to the Community and not the individual.
>
> (p. 252)

In initiation rites, it is the community's task to welcome back the initiate and accept him into the community in his new role. In many of the important rituals of our modern Western World (marriage and graduation, for example), the participation of the community deepens the experience of the event and gives the change in status, or metanoia, added profundity and meaning.

Sense of mission/sharing

A frequent consequence of deep and profound experiences of personal change is that people want to share their experience with others. Evangelism commonly occurs subsequent to conversion (Kerr and Mulder, 1984). Clients who make major life changes in psychotherapy often suggest a similar route to their friends or acquaintances. Boyle (1977) also reports this epi-phenomenon of metanoia.

> I was concerned with helping myself and building for my own future but there was the wider issue in that I was now committed to helping the general situation on the penal and social fields. It was now that I was tasting a short spell on the outside that I realised just how committed I was to proving that people in hopeless situations like myself, who are serving very long sentences, can act responsibly and through their own experience, give something back into society.
>
> (Boyle, 1977, p. 257)

Archetypal images of transformation

There are several psychological moments in the turning-about-point (as discussed before). There are also correspondingly different images which point to them as collective representations through fairy tales or myths and biblical stories. Jung refers to these as archetypes:

> And the essential thing, psychologically, is that in dreams, fantasies, and other exceptional states of mind the most far-fetched mythological motifs and symbols can appear autochthonously at any time, often, apparently, as the result of particular influences, traditions, and excitations working on the individual, but more often without any sign of them. These 'primordial images,' or 'archetypes,' as I have called them, belong to the basic stock of the unconscious psyche and cannot be explained as personal acquisitions. Together they make up that psychic stratum which I have called the collective unconscious.
>
> (Jung, 1969, p. 112)

There are naturally a variety of such archetypal transformational images such as the phoenix – a well-known symbol of death and rebirth by fire (Jung, 1964). Certain archetypes occur with great frequency in the clinical experience of psychotherapists from many theoretical persuasions.

The image of death and rebirth is frequently diagnostic of script change in many circumstances.

In a spiritual context, the image of Christ being buried in the tomb for three days is often an image for the void, the lostness, the place beyond human help. It is like dying and going beyond death into the place where one cannot be reached, and there is no hope, there is no light, and there is no succour; and then from the depths emerges a new person.

By way of illustration, Jung (1956) recounts Frobenius' rendition of the following legend of transformation which contains many of the 'moments of metanoia' so far discussed:

> A hero is devoured by a water-monster in the West.... The animal travels with him to the East (*sea journey*). Meanwhile, the hero lights a fire in the belly of the monster... and feeling hungry, cuts himself a piece of the heart.... Soon afterwards, he notices that the fish has glided on to dry land...; he immediately begins to cut open the animal from within (*opening*); then he slips out.... It was so hot in the fish's belly that all his hair has fallen out.... The hero may at the same time free all those who were previously devoured by the monster.
>
> (p. 210)

And in another example, Boyle (1977) wrote from prison 'I personally felt that the best way for me to adjust to this new way was to look on it as a rebirth; it is true to say that I was experiencing lots of things for the first time in my life' (p. 247).

A psychotherapy client describes her experience as 'Daring to be new. Being able to be where the light is inside myself.' And New England Puritan Joseph Alleine wrote 'Conversion is not the putting in a patch of holiness; but with the true convert holiness is woven into all his powers, principles, and practice. The sincere Christian is quite a new fabric, from the foundation to the topstone. He is a new man, a new creature' (James, 1985, p. 230).

The following is a verbatim transcript of a dream reported to the author during the termination phase of a client's psychotherapy treatment.

> I was in the presence of two older women. One of them seemed to be my 'difficult' grandmother. But she faded into the background immediately. Both women were engaged in religious and spiritual pursuits. But the stranger definitely was more level-headed. She suggested I should do an 'exercise'. I was puzzled. She called it shedding of the skin. As she was explaining it to me a young woman was in fact performing the exercise. She put her head onto her chest. And it disappeared into her body. That's all I saw. Although I was slightly scared and apprehensive I told the woman I wanted to do the exercise. So I put my head onto my chest...[I]t entered my body. And from then on I had to completely trust the woman. I felt her hands curling my skin across my bones. I was completely soft. Even my

bones. She proceeded to peel me, turn me inside out. I felt like a sausage, with an unsavoury skin. I felt this as I was 'peeled.' I remember thinking, 'How nice to get rid of that skin.' But at the same time I still didn't know if I'd ever get out of this very awkward position! I could get completely stuck half-way through.... Those fearful thoughts crept through my mind as I felt my skin being pushed on my outside. I was still inside. It was awfully dark.... And then I felt hands quite hard pushing at my head. And I saw light. I saw it from the inside of my own vagina. And I realised I was actually born from myself. I saw the shedded skin and even the umbilical cord, which had been cut off. I can't remember how I got 'out' – but when I was OUT I had a new skin and felt VERY fresh all over. And glowing....

Aspiration

Finally, I want to draw attention to a frequently neglected concept in transactional analysis – the autonomous *aspirations* of the individual's own choice. 'In this regard, Berne's script diagram which includes the aspiration arrow, represents one of the most powerful images in transactional analysis literature of the potential of human beings to liberate themselves from the deterministic constraints of their scripts' (Clarkson, 1988, p. 12).

Aspiration may, after all, be the most determinative element in personal change. Berne represented Aspiration (Figure 4.1) as an arrow

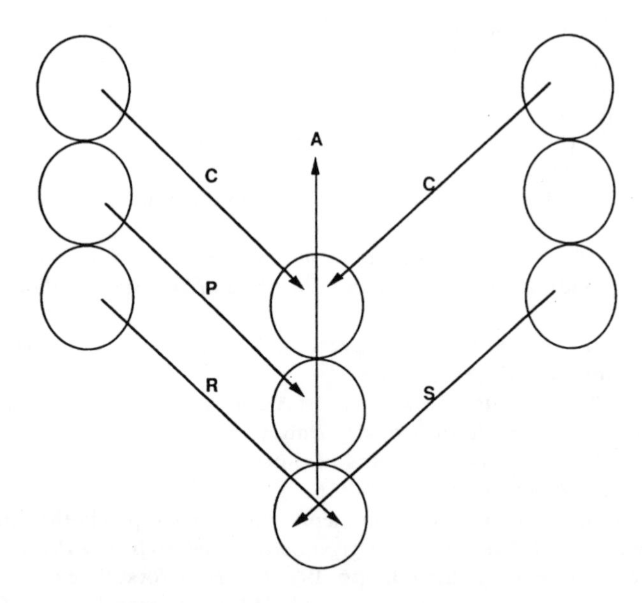

Figure 4.1. Script matrix showing aspiration arrow. S = script; C = counterscript; R = release; A = aspiration; P = pattern. (Adapted from Berne, 1972, p. 128.)

rising from the ground of the Child ego states, moving through the Adult and through the Parent and emerging well above the script matrix with the head of the arrow pointing ever upward (Berne, 1972, p. 128).

> The object of script analysis is to free Jeder and Zoe so that they can open the garden of their aspirations to the world. It does that by cutting through the Babel in their heads until the Child can say: 'But this is what I want to do, and I would rather do it my own way.'
>
> (Berne, 1972, p. 131)

Conclusion

It has been my aim to begin a participatory dialogue with other transactional analysts about the subject of fundamental and long-lasting life change by considering it in the light of definitions, circumstances and characteristics of metanoia. It is hoped that further research will be encouraged and shared. It is a small beginning to a vast undertaking which is, after all, the essence of the psychotherapeutic task – the therapy of the psyche, the soul. However, for both client and therapist it may be well to remember that: 'The practice of metanoia requires the rarest type of courage – the courage to be wrong, to repent, and to begin again' (Keen, 1985, p. 148).

References

BERNE, E. (1972). *What Do You Say After You Say Hello?* New York: Grove Press.

BERTOLUCCI, B. (director) (1988). *The Last Emperor*. London: Columbia.

BOYLE, J. (1977). *A Sense of Freedom*. London: Pan Books.

BRIDGES, W. (1980). *Transitions*. Reading, MA: Addison-Wesley.

BURCHFIELD, R.W. (Ed.). (1976). *A Supplement to the Oxford English Dictionary*, Vols 1–4. Oxford: Oxford University Press.

CAPLAN, G. (1951). A public health approach to child psychiatry, *Mental Health*, **35**, 18.

CASTANEDA, C. (1968). *The Teachings of Don Juan*. New York: Ballantine.

CLARKSON, P. (1988). Crisis and aspiration. *Institute of Transactional Analysis News*, **21**, 12.

CONWAY, A. and CLARKSON P. (1987). Everyday hypnotic inductions. *Transactional Analysis Journal*, **17** (2), 17–23.

FRANK, J.D. (1973). *Persuasion and Healing: A Comparative Study of Psychotherapy* (rev. ed.). Baltimore: Johns Hopkins University Press.

FRANK, J.D. (1979). The present status of outcome studies. *Journal of Consulting and Clinical Psychology*, 47, 310–316.

FRANK, J.D. (1982). Therapeutic components shared by all psychotherapies. In: J.H. Harvey and M.M. Parks (Eds), *Psychotherapy Research and Behavior Change: An Empirical Analysis*, 2nd edn, pp. 191–232. New York: Wiley.

FREEDMAN, A.M., KAPLAN, H.I. and SADOCK, B.J. (1975). *Comprehensive Textbook of Psychiatry – II*, Vol. 2, 2nd edn. Baltimore: Williams and Wilkins.

FROMM, E. (1966). *The Art of Loving*. London: Unwin Books. (Originally published 1962.)

GREEN, H. (1986). *I Never Promised You a Rose Garden* (rev. Pavanne edn). London: Pan. (Originally published 1964.)

HALL, U. (1986). Miracle of the anti-cancer marriage. *News of the World,* 30th November, p. 31. London: News International.

HYNAN, M.T. (1981). On the advantages of assuming that the techniques of psychotherapy are ineffective. *Psychotherapy: Theory, Research and Practice,* **18,** 11–13.

IRELAND, J. (1987). *Life Wish.* London: Century Hutchinson.

JAMES, W. (1985). *Varieties of Religious Experience.* Glasgow: Fount Paperbacks, William Collins and Sons. (Originally published 1977.)

JUNG, C.G. (1956). Symbols of transformation: an analysis of the prelude to a case of schizophrenia. In: *The Collected Works,* Vol.5. (R.F.C. Hull, trans.). London: Routledge and Kegan Paul.

JUNG, C G. (1964). *Man and his Symbols.* London: Aldus Books.

JUNG, C.G. (1969). Constitution and heredity in psychology. In: *The Collected Works,* Vol.8, 2nd edn, pp. 107–113 (R.F.C. Hull, trans.). London: Routledge and Kegan Paul. (Originally published 1929.)

KEEN, S. (1985). *The Passionate Life.* London: Gateway Books.

KERR, H.T. and MULDER, J.M. (1984). *Conversions: The Christian Experience.* London: Hodder and Stoughton.

LIDDELL, H.G. (1963). *A Lexicon Abridged from Liddell and Scott's Greek-English Lexicon.* Oxford: Oxford University Press.

LORIMER, D. (1987). The near-death experience and spiritual health. *Holistic Medicine,* **2,** 179–184.

MANDER, R. (1980). *Mrs. Browning.* London: Weidenfeld and Nicolson.

MASTERSON, J.F. (1985). *The Real Self.* New York: Brunner/Mazel.

MCNEEL, J.R. (1976). The parent interview. *Transactional Analysis Journal,* 6 (1), 61–68.

New English Bible with the Apocrypha. (1974). Harmondsworth: Penguin.

NORCROSS, J.C. (Ed.). (1986). *Handbook of Eclectic Psychotherapy.* New York: Brunner/Mazel.

PARAD, H.J. (Ed.) (1969). *Crisis Intervention: Selected Readings.* New York: Family Services Association of America. (Originally published 1965.)

POLSTER, E. and POLSTER, M. (1974). *Gestalt Therapy Integrated: Contours of Theory and Practice.* New York: Vintage. (Originally published, 1973.)

REPS, P. (1971). *Zen Flesh, Zen Bones.* Harmondsworth: Penguin.

SARGENT, W. (1959). *Battle for the Mind.* London: Pan.

SCHIFF, J.L. with SCHIFF, A.W., MELLOR, K., SCHIFF, E., SCHIFF, S., RICHMAN, D., FISHMAN, J., WOLZ, L., FISHMAN, C. and MOMB, D. (1975). *Cathexis Reader: Transactional Analysis and Treatment of Psychosis.* New York: Harper and Row.

STEPHEN, L. and LEE, S. (Eds). (1917). *The Dictionary of National Biography,* Vol. 3. Oxford: Oxford University Press.

STILES, B., SHAPIRO, D. A. and ELLIOTT, R. (1986). Are all psychotherapies equivalent?, *American Psychologist,* **41** (2), 165–180.

VAN DUSEN, W. (1975). Wu wei, no-mind and the fertile void. In: J.O. Stevens (Ed.), *Gestalt Is,* pp. 87–93. Moab, UT: Real People Press.

WATZLAWICK, P., WEAKLAND, J.H. and FISCH, R. (1974). *Change.* New York: W.W. Norton.

WEBSTER, N. (Ed.) (1944). *Webster's Collegiate Dictionary,* 2nd edn. Springfield, MA: Miriam Webster.

WILLIAMS, T. (1959). *Cat on a Hot Tin Roof.* Harmondsworth: Penguin.

Chapter 5
Dilemmas of Difference

Introduction

The ideas cited here are designed to evoke questioning of what the therapist can and cannot hope to facilitate, and what the couple realistically can or cannot hope to achieve, in couples counselling or therapy. Exploring the feasibility or likelihood of effective therapeutic action towards different therapeutic goals can sometimes prevent disillusionment and despair. Clarifying the kind of goals and achievability or morality of certain desired changes in couplehood seems to me vitally important, and sometimes a neglected aspect of couples work. Disagreement about the categories of difference I put forward here is to be welcomed and explored between the partners and the therapist. Such disagreement can be used to enrich the viability and usefulness of this contribution to the resources of the couples therapist.

It has been my experience in doing couples work, including training and supervising, that by sorting such desired changes into different categories, all parties can focus on more realistically achievable goals. Thus they can potentially reach greater satisfaction. It is therefore an attempt to put into couples work the spirit of the famous prayer usually attributed to St Francis of Assisi:

> God, grant me the serenity to accept the things I cannot change;
> The courage to change the things I can;
> And the wisdom to know the difference.

In order to deepen my understanding of my work with couples, my personal journey and my experiences of organisations, I have found it useful to study macrosystems such as nations in the processes of change. Often the large systems reflect similar processes to the smaller ones and the microsystems reflect learning about the macrosystems.

From P. Clarkson (1992). Dilemmas of Difference. *Journal of Couples Therapy*, 3 (4), with permisson.

Nations are the large-scale experiments in humans living together where good outcomes lead to peace, harmony and creativity. As with couples, however, misunderstandings about differences between peoples can also explode into war.

Three Categories of Difference

I wish to draw out some patterns currently apparent to me which apply both to couples and nations. This is done in the knowledge that I cannot, and am not attempting to, do justice to the full complexity of a matter that has preoccupied the human race since the dawn of time, and will continue to do so *ad infinitum*. For the moment I am separating out three categories of problem. These categories of difference can be termed *unacceptable behaviour, negotiable issues*, and *unchangeable aspects of self*. I think that they apply usefully in doing work with couples and may also apply usefully in mediation with groups, organisations and larger systems such as nations.

Unacceptable behaviour

The first category of difference between partners concerns areas of unacceptable behaviour. In other words: 'This is what I won't accept from you'. It is the behaviour of the other person or other party which is essentially non-negotiable and in an ultimate moral sense should not be up for negotiation. This concerns the basic human needs for security, economic well being, a sense of belonging, recognition, and control over one's own life (Fisher and Ury, 1983, p. 50). Whenever any of these needs are threatened, absent or denied, effective reconciliation or mediation work is substantially impeded, if not impossible, because one cannot meaningfully negotiate between a torturer and a victim until the victim is at least on an equal footing with the torturer. Any such *negotiation* is an attempt to escape victimhood, not to exchange value. Such cases are not genuine transactions between equal human beings, both of whom deserve respect.

A woman's economic well being is totally at the mercy of a vengeful and vindictive husband when he deprives her of either information or influence about how even her own earned income is spent. In couples therapy they cannot be said to be in a negotiating position on an equal basis. Where basic human needs are not honoured, war or war-like actions follow almost inevitably.

> Negotiations are not likely to make much progress as long as one side believes that the fulfilment of their basic human needs is being threatened by the other. In negotiations between the United States and Mexico, the US

> wanted a low price for Mexican natural gas. Assuming that this was a negotiation over money, the US Secretary of Energy refused to approve a price increase negotiated with the Mexicans by a US oil consortium. Since the Mexicans had no other potential buyer at the time, he assumed that they would then lower their asking price. But the Mexicans had a strong interest, not only in getting a good price for their gas, but also in being treated with respect and a sense of equality. The US action seemed like one more attempt to bully Mexico; it produced enormous anger. Rather than sell their gas, the Mexican government began to burn it off, and any chance of agreement on a lower price became politically impossible.
>
> (Fisher and Ury, 1983, p. 50–51)

Domination (for example, when a wife is over-ruled through superior financial or physical strength of her partner), violence, a threat to the person or to their property, disenfranchisement (for example, when blacks are deprived of their right to vote in South Africa), all mean that the possibility for effective therapy or resolution is drastically reduced, if not made impossible.

I had an initial consultation with a couple where the man was quite a high-ranking member of the professional community. The wife pleaded with him to come to couples therapy with me because he frequently threatened her and on more than one occasion had pushed her around or even hit her. She was frightened by his behaviour and yet unwilling or unable to call for help. Because of his standing in the community and his public reputation for being kind and generous she hoped that this could be resolved in couples therapy. He was, however, completely unwilling to accept personal responsibility for his threats of violence, for the terrorising nature of driving fast and recklessly with her as a passenger when he was angry with her, for throwing large objects in her direction when he felt aggravated with her, or for engaging in acts of self-mutilation such as head banging, or breaking objects.

Naturally, this was very frightening to her and, although she loved him, she could find no way to control him in such explosive rages. During these times he believed that she was accusing him of being mad or bad. The only way that she could escape from the verbal and threatened abuse was to leave the scene. Yet her love and concern for him seemed to rivet her to the interaction. She was trying to relieve his distress and of course deal with her own terror. He merely experienced it as further provocation and an incitement to more and more psychotic behaviour.

At their initial consultation I asked him if he was willing to agree not to be violent or to threaten violence with her again. His statement was 'Of course I can do that – unless she provokes me'. What constitutes provocation in situations where one person is at the mercy of another physically or financially, is open to a great deal of interpretation. Victims are often kept in this position by the abuser telling them that they are paranoid, oversensitive, or lying (Dorfman, 1992). The secrecy that surrounds marital or physical and sexual child abuse makes it notoriously hard for the child or the injured spouse to be believed. Yet we now know that this is one of the most potent acts of healing to begin a journey back to personal empowerment (Miller, 1985; 1987). Blaming victims for their abuse at the hands of others is a collectively well-documented phenomenon, in the same way that children can be blamed or blame themselves for the fact that they were party to abusive situations (Caplan, 1985). A prisoner who refuses half rations of food, or objects to inhuman conditions, is often considered a troublemaker and a provocateur, only to be punished more violently if he or she complains of such treatment (Makhoere, 1988).

I asked the woman whether she was willing to call in the police next time he terrorised her. She was unwilling to do this knowing that he had a psychiatric history. Confronted with his unwillingness to offer his wife a basic sense of security, I refused to work with them as a couple. This was not only because it was an emotional victim/persecutor situation, but because she was actually in danger if he was so unwilling or unable to accept responsibility for his own violence. Her justifiable distress was exacerbated because of her loving concern not to expose his secret brutality at the expense of his professional reputation.

So any form of fascism where one person of a couple is enforcing through physical, financial or emotional violence or threats of violence, the compliance of the other person, constitutes for me an area of unacceptable, non-negotiable behaviour. I do not think that couples work is appropriate at this level in many cases. What is more appropriate is to separate out the abused spouse/partner until he or she has reclaimed his or her basic human rights and can feel emotionally and financially like an equal human being. This is often impossible while they are still in a mutually self-reinforcing abusive system. Only when their basic human rights have been protected can threatened or abused individuals genuinely go into the arena of reclaiming their emotional and psychological equality.

Extreme cases, such as the ones mentioned above, are quite easy to recognise. Couples work where one gets habitually drunk and aggressive, whether it be on alcohol or jealousy, is notoriously difficult unless the co-dependency of the partner and their covert consent to their partner's brutality is withdrawn. Often separate work with each of the partners is indicated (Dryden, 1985). There are less extreme examples of unacceptable behaviours which, I believe, must be articulated between couples, usually in the beginning stages of their relationship, if they are not to lead to explosive or embittered breakdowns later. Ideally, these pre-requirements would be discussed early on in the relationship so that each partner understood as clearly as possible what the other partner considered to be absolutely non-negotiable ground for breakdown, and unforgivable.

People differ surprisingly as to what they consider to be unacceptable. For one person it may be lying (by commission or omission); for another it may be infidelity; and for another it may be financial betrayal. This area is different for different people, and is often not the same for both partners in a couple. One may find casual sex forgivable but not a genuine, loving relationship with another person outside the couple (whether platonic or otherwise). One person may find it easy to live with somebody who is unreliable and unpredictable about time or keeping their promises. For another person, violations of such contracts would constitute grounds for irreparable breakdown. Having unprotected sex with another person has now entered the unacceptable area for most couples, whereas invasion of privacy, such as reading your partner's diary, or going through their private papers, might not be considered so unforgivable by some.

It is important to note that sometimes one spouse in a couple may accept the violation of their bodies, dignity or autonomy early on in the relationship. They may even welcome or collude with abusive behaviour, particularly if it is secret and confined to the privacy of the bedroom. However, when the abused spouse, for example, goes into psychotherapy and begins to experience and assert his or her basic human rights to freedom from physical threat and financial influence over their own lives, the other partner may experience this as extremely disturbing. The partner who is threatened with loss of control over the other may escalate threatening or abusive behaviour. It may seem to them as if the original psychological level contract between them is failing. Their request to 'Be the person that I married' – that is, stop changing and becoming autonomous, is often based on fear of the threat of change, and a desperate wish to defend the rightness of precedent – however unfair it was.

The kind of couples therapy required in this category of difference is obviously radically different from less third-degree issues (potentially harmful to life or property) such as miscommunication, sexual adjustment, and differences about parenting. In extreme situations what is most important and most required may be education about basic human freedoms, prisoners' rights, legal or police protection, refuges, and so on.

Sometimes what is unacceptable to one partner is not concerned with a basic human right but is particular to their history, or their individual sensibilities. Veronica was sexually abused while being almost strangled as a child. When her breathing is restricted during lovemaking she gets very anxious. I believe that this kind of difference should not be labelled pathological because she finds it unacceptable. Whether or not the person has been traumatised in a particular fashion, an equal and respectful relationship must be based on concern and consideration for each other's psychological lesions (Berne, 1980), belt lines (Bach and Goldberg, 1983), and fears, whether or not they seem understandable or 'reasonable' to the partner.

If something falls into the category of unacceptable behaviour, we are discussing the pre-requirements for establishing a relationship, or the ground conditions for continuing a relationship; for example, 'I will not stay with you if you continue drinking'. It is, therefore, more figural and emphasised towards the beginning or ending of relationships. If these issues are not resolved further, couples work may even cause damage. For example, continuing to work in couples therapy on communication styles when a woman's life or economic freedom is endangered does not constitute good psychology. People are not free to take emotional risks, or to grow and develop in partnership, when their basic rights are threatened or denied. We are thus talking here about the essential pre-conditions for effective couples counselling; or to put it another way, if these issues are not resolved then the therapist may be colluding with cruelty or injustice at some level, because to remain neutral is to favour the aggressor in many such cases. Continuing without an agreed foundation, or with a wrongly assumed foundation to the relationship may also cause damage; and this is to be found both in the microcosm of couples relationships and also in the macrocosm of inter-racial and international issues, such as the current situation in South Africa.

I have been a voluntary exile from South Africa since 1976 when black schoolchildren were being killed in increasing numbers for protesting against the injustices of the South African Bantu education system. Many black people rebelled against the infamous apartheid laws which attempted conformity by forcing them to be educated in a language not their own. They also rightfully resisted the attempt to make cultural and skin colour differences the basis for their oppression and disenfranchisement. After the release of Mandela and the lifting of the state of emergency in 1990, I returned to work and learn for a short while in the country of my birth. The heritage of injustice, cruelty and abuse over generations remains appalling. Recent changes are only somewhat ameliorating and do not reach to the heart of the abuses perpetrated over centuries. Notwithstanding appearances, people are still being tortured, still disenfranchised, still discriminated against. Yet I found that the hope of change for the better is still possible as long as we can retain our empathy for others as human beings.

> Unbelievably...there is an astonishing level of compassion, love and tolerance still left. They call it *ubuntu* – which means fellow human feeling – and it is because of this that she still feels tremendous hope that the horrendous problems that are South Africa can progress towards peace.
>
> (Clarkson, 1990, p. 11)

It is important to separate non-negotiable from negotiable areas of work in couples therapy. It should not be negotiable to be treated with respect as a human being – to experience ***ubuntu*** or fellow-feeling. Even criminals or prisoners of war are protected by law from cruel and unjust treatment, and no matter what provocative thing a spouse may *say*, nothing within our legal or moral system should justify acts of violence and cruelty in response. When these non-negotiable areas are no longer in dispute, the abusing spouse can be relied upon both to cease his or her abusive behaviour, and the abused spouse can be relied upon to protect him- or herself. Mutual respect becomes the foundation for dealing with issues which can be negotiated between two equal human beings.

Negotiable issues

The next category concerns those issues that are essentially negotiable between a couple. This is the area where most couples work of an understanding, improving, reconciling and transformative nature can take place. Once a couple are clear about what is and what is not acceptable as pre-requirements, or what would constitute grounds for an irretrievable breakdown, then they can begin to deal with the differences in attitudes and behaviours which they can, and may be willing to change. It is helpful if these are concerned with those aspects of attitude and behaviour which are genuinely changeable. It concerns the area of: 'This is what I do or don't want you to do, and this is what you do or don't want me to do'.

This is the area where the relationship can be worked – where it becomes a yoga for individual development and interpersonal bonding. We have *chosen* specific people to be our partners, and in that sense they can bring us some of the most significant developmental opportunities that can ever come our way. It is in this most intimate relationship with another person that we can get to know ourselves most truly, and risk knowing another most profoundly. It is in this space between two people that new life and new meaning can arise. From such an alchemical marriage a philosopher's stone of great wisdom, compassion and transformative potential can be formed. I have often called life the great co-therapist because it brings so many opportunities to my clients and myself, often at exactly the most critically sensitive periods, to develop, change, transform or abandon aspects of my self, defences, potential or my capacity for intimacy. In this way our partners bring us, I think perhaps even in a karmic sense, specific existential opportunities for healing and creative evolution (Clarkson, 1991).

Most literature on couples therapy concerns issues in this category of negotiable changes (Satir, 1978; Gellert, 1983). For the purposes of this chapter I would like to draw attention to selected specific issues. It is frequently said that marriage is a case of give and take. It may be a fallacy, though, that both people need to give or take the same kind of things. If one person in the couple likes sitting in the front row at the theatre and the other in the second row, it can be a simple matter in an equal relationship to take turns, one time both sitting in the front row, the next time both sitting in the second row. Preferences for sexual activities, providing they are not in the unacceptable area for either, can be swapped, exchanged, or even traded in similar way: 'Tonight I'll scratch your back for you because you really like it, and tomorrow night you'll brush my hair for me because I really like that'.

One of the most frequently occurring misunderstandings which I encounter in the area of changeable attitudes and behaviours in couples work is the erroneous belief that my partner likes or should like what I like, or dislike what I dislike. One of the commonest and most prevalent sources for misunderstanding is the human inclination to give others what *we* want rather than to give them what they want. In the simplest terms, Mary likes to be hugged and cuddled and taken to bed when she is upset, and Jim likes to be distracted and taken out for a meal or a movie. When Jim finds Mary upset, he takes her out to distract her and finds it difficult to understand why she is not delighted with his attempts to amuse and entertain her. On the other hand, when Jim is upset, Mary feels puzzled and alienated when he does not respond to her nurturing and caretaking offers to put him to bed and bring him dinner there. The variations of misunderstandings on this theme are too numerous to contemplate. 'I like surprise parties therefore I'll give you one', not thinking (or believing) that you can be so different from me that you hate them (even though you've told me this before!).

> Consider...the two sisters quarrelling over an orange. Each sister wanted the orange, so they split it, failing to realise that one wanted only the fruit to eat and the other only the peel for baking. In this case as in many others, a satisfactory agreement is made possible because each side wants *different* things. This is genuinely startling if you think about it. People generally assume that differences between two parties create the problem. Yet differences can also lead to a solution.
>
> (Fisher and Ury, 1983, p. 76)

This may also apply to helping each other solve problems. Mary does not want Jim to give her solutions until she has had time to explore her feelings, and cry and rage if she wants to. It is helpful to her if Jim shows her empathy and unconditional acceptance while she explores her own feelings and options, but she enjoys coming to her own solutions. Jim has a different style of problem-solving. He likes being given advice or quick-fire solutions as soon as he has stated his problem, and finds talking about it and exploring his emotions frequently a waste of time. When Mary comes home with a problem, he bombards her with solutions, and when Jim comes home with a problem, Mary withholds all suggestions and fruitlessly encourages him to find solutions.

The biggest confusion seems to be a common distortion of love between how *I* want to be loved and how *you* want to be loved. According to Fromm (1966), 'Love is the active concern for the life and the growth of that which we love' (p. 25). He writes that certain basic elements – care, responsibility, respect, and knowledge – are common to all forms of love. Some of the most tragic misalignments of loving can occur when self-knowledge is assumed to be knowledge about the other.

As one woman said to me:

> He keeps telling me he loves me, he tells everybody else he loves me and, as he loves me in his way, I feel like a *pâté de foie gras* goose that is being stuffed with food I hate. My eyes are burning, my throat is sore, I yearn for different food, the kind I've asked for. But as I'm being lovingly force-fed on someone else's definition of love, I am torn between guilt that I somehow cannot experience this as love, and deep resentment that my individual unique desires for the kind of love I would appreciate are so totally ignored while the indulgent display continues. Sometimes he blames me and says that I am never satisfied. Indeed, this is true – I can never be satisfied when I am blamed for not liking that for which I never expressed a preference, and ultimately have come to loathe. The alternative is a desensitisation of my own desires, my unique needs, and a fundamental alienation from my organismic self.'

It seems a simple matter if you love someone, to love them in the way they want to be loved. However, this has rarely been any child's experience. Too often we were loved in a way that suited our parents. Jamel had to put on a sweater when his mother was cold, Lila said that her mother wore her like an expensive brooch as public testimony to what a good mother she was. Indeed, loving someone in the way that he or she wants to be loved calls for considerable consciousness and a commitment to the relationship, instead of just using your partner as a vicarious receptacle for your own unmet needs. If she takes a longer time and needs soft music and sweet words to become sexually aroused, it seems a matter of both selfish and loving interest to do this. Perhaps he likes to be jumped on the stairs or groped in the restaurant in order to feel turned on, so perhaps what is needed is that she does that for him. Any couple or couples therapist can probably adduce many more examples of similar negotiable or changeable behaviours, communication patterns, or present-giving styles.

Contracts for change behaviour are often quite easy to implement providing there is rational goodwill between the couple and they are willing to acknowledge each other as different (not worse). This can, of course, only happen when there is care, responsibility, and respect for the other person. One of the most important things to realise is that it course, only happen when there is care, responsibility, and respect for the other person. One of the most important things to realise is that it is not the objective reality of, for example, whether or not there is a draught, that settles disputes between couples and avoids war, but an understanding of each other's subjective experiences – each one's inner phenomenological world. Changes to one's holistic perception can be experienced as extremely threatening.

Because I have always been interested in the bringing down of walls and the building of bridges of understanding, I booked the first possible flight to Berlin on 11th November 1989 on hearing that the Wall was being demolished. One of the most enlightening insights gained from this experience was the incredible psychological threat which people experienced in very suddenly changing their frame of reference. Festinger (1957) referred to this as *cognitive dissonance*. Whereas many people welcomed and celebrated the change, for some border guards the challenge was too much. 'No precise figures are yet available but when the Berlin Wall fell, several East German soldiers chose to commit suicide. Rather than attempt to make the painful transition to a new reality where those who yesterday were the "enemy" today become the "friend", some guards preferred the strange safety of death' (Clarkson in George, 1990, p. 14).

Of course the problems of peace in Germany have by no means solved the excruciating problems still facing the country in the future. A decision to stay in the marriage or to try again, does not necessarily means that the work is ended – sometimes the hardest work has still to follow the reconciliation.

Somewhere I have learned the phrase that 'feelings are facts'. In working with couples and organisations this is certainly true. Another saying is 'A man convinced against his will, is of the same opinion still'. The husband experiences his wife as shouting at him when she raises her voice. She doesn't define it as shouting but his feeling constitutes a *fact* in the couple's domain, whether or not it can be shown to be consistent with objective decibel measurements. If she genuinely wants to solve the problem she could find a way of assessing, or responding to a signal from him, when her voice grows so loud that he can no longer pay attention to the content of what she is trying to say to him.

> Morocco and Algeria quarrel over a section of the western Sahara.... The detailed history and geography of the western Sahara, no matter how carefully studied and documented, is not the stuff with which one puts to rest that kind of territorial dispute. As useful as looking for objective reality can be, it is ultimately the reality as each side sees it that constitutes the problem in a negotiation and opens the way to a solution.
>
> (Fisher and Ury, 1983, pp. 22–23)

Unchangeable aspects

This is the category which concerns those aspects of the self which are essentially unchangeable, or very hard to change without injury to one's integrity in some important way. In this case the issues are not about attitudes or behaviour; they have to do with selfhood. It concerns those deepest characteristics of what we feel as our integrity, authenticity, or those values which are not open to change. This category includes the kinds of values, beliefs or convictions for which people may choose to be martyred rather than change. It is very important to note that these are not demands on the other person to be different (as in the unacceptable category), but are essential qualities or convictions of the self. 'This is who I am. This is who you are'.

The reasons that couples or nations give for making war, coming together or seceding are varied and complex. The act of seceding is here defined (MacDonald, 1972) as: 'to withdraw, esp. from a party, religious body, federation, or the like' (p. 1329). I use this phrase because it covers national choices to declare independence, as well as implying separation or divorce on the smaller scale of the human couple. Rarely are the reasons that are stated in the official communiques the same as those experienced by the ordinary soldiers or the people of a country. The separating effect when difference exceeds the interest in keeping connected is exemplified in the process of states seceding from the Soviet Union.

On a recent visit to Russia to teach gestalt (which coincided with the second Russian revolution), we met Russians of all political, national and religious persuasions. As we talked with people it became clear that sometimes the urge for individuality becomes stronger than the desire for commonality or bonding. This also happens in couples relationships, sometimes as a result of one or both partners changing as a result of therapy, personal counselling or another impetus to personal growth and change.

Heraclitus said (Guerriere, 1980) that war is 'the father of all things' (p. 91). From a gestalt perspective, healthy aggression is the root of all good human contact and the ground for intimacy. It is our need for others and for intimate intercourse which is one of the most fundamental of human needs (Fairbairn, 1952). The root of the word aggression is 'to reach out' (Clarkson, 1989, p. 10). I believe that because we, as human beings, have not yet learnt how to be comfortable with and constructively channel our aggressiveness, we still have such enormous potential for imminent destruction. Although the threat of nuclear war seems to be receding, there is still the possibility that we may die engorged with the detritus of our unthinking, uncaringly aggressive exploitation of our planet. Whether it is the war between the Serbs and the Croats in the former Yugoslavia, or *The War of the Roses* on our cinema screens, the eternal tension between Eros and Thanatos, between love and war, continues to preoccupy the individual human soul in the dark and lonely night hours, and spills the blood of children in the streets of Beirut.

I am not saying that these characteristics, beliefs or preferences cannot be influenced, modified or shaped in important ways. I am emphasising a category of problem which, in some crucial sense, constitutes concerns about the essence of the personality of one or both of the partners. Such unchangeable areas do not necessarily always remain unchangeable. For example, people may change their religious convictions over time or due to circumstance. However, at the time that the couple comes for help it is often very helpful to separate out the issues which fall into this category. They do not threaten the viability of couples work in the same way as those concerns in the unacceptable behaviour category. However, getting caught up in turning a basically shy, introverted person into an extroverted, life-of-the-party soul in order to please a wife who has grown more socially confident over time, may demand a fruitless quest from the couples therapist. A highly sexed husband with a wife who is naturally not very interested in sex may make some adjustments to each other, but sometimes their temperamental preferences for frequency of lovemaking may never truly be compatible. Each may have to compromise their own natural preferences. Tragically sometimes, even though they love each other, a couple may choose to separate rather than live for all their lives with a partner whose fundamental life rhythms are completely 'out of synch'.

For the purposes of this chapter I will highlight such minimally unchangeable areas: temperament, personality, personal convictions and sexual arousal or preferences.

Temperament

Temperament, or what I call one's *first nature*, is one such practically unchangeable area. Sometimes people may even try to change their basic temperamental type, but they cannot do it. More importantly, I think they should not because, if they did, they would be violating some important aspect of their organismic integrity which no human being can do for long without damage to themselves and perhaps others. I have referred to this as 'first nature' to distinguish it from *second nature*. I have been concerned over many years as a psychotherapist with the potential oppressiveness for mental or emotional health, of externally imposed criteria, rather than due respect for the intrinsic temperament of each unique human being.

Studies (for example, Thomas et al., 1977) have shown that babies have identifiably different temperaments (which are genetically transmitted), even at birth. In later life these temperamental traits may remain unchanged or may be somewhat modified by environmental circumstances. Damage may be done to children whose temperamental styles are very different from that of their parents, and the parents may be unwilling to see, respect and value such temperamental difference (Rowe, 1988). Rowe has also drawn attention to the importance of valuing temperamental differences.

Personality

Personality typologies, for example, that of Jung (1944) which was further developed by Myers and Briggs Myers (1976), have also been very useful in helping to differentiate between very different personality types but removing any implication that some are better or healthier than others.

Eysenck (1968) compiled substantial independent research which indicated that people are different in terms of their neuropsychological make-up, their learning styles, and their personality types. The introvert can probably never change the biochemical–electrical activity of his cortex to resemble that of his extrovert friend. The task for therapists, as well as friends, partners, spouses and parents, is to value and celebrate each other's different qualities, rather than to do violence to them according to some standard of mass conformity, quoting what some expert or statistical report defines as *normal* or *healthy*. Temperament is defined as an 'inborn, constitutional predisposition to react in a specific way to stimuli' (Freedman et al., 1975, p. 2607). Personality and character can be changed; temperament can but be allowed for, influenced and enjoyed.

> Psychotherapists can avoid getting involved with a fruitless quest for this type of change by (amongst other procedures) clarifying contracts, checking third-party involvement, learning about the physiological bases of behaviour and forever being vigilant against the cardinal sin of the amateur psychologist – extrapolating from your own psychology. Script is not changing *who* we are, but *how* we are in the most important aspects of our lives.
>
> (Clarkson, 1988, pp. 32–22)

Personal convictions

Another type of unchangeable area is that of one's deepest convictions, such as religious beliefs or political views. A woman who is an Orthodox Jewess is deeply in love with a man who returns her love. He is not Jewish and does not want to convert. He will not and cannot consider in his integrity that, should they marry, their children would be brought up in the Jewish faith. One's heart goes out to such potential couples, thwarted by differences of religion, politics, divisions of war, opposing families, such as played out in the tragedies of Romeo and Juliet or Heloise and Abelard. Perhaps in our more modern world such loves do not have to end in suicide or convents. However, the unfulfilled yearning for a soulmate which has been found, yet cannot be celebrated, must constitute one of the deepest and most abiding injustices of human destiny.

Sexual arousal or preferences

Of almost similar poignancy are differences that concern the most fundamental biologically based responses, for example, sexual arousal. In a couple where the man needs to cross-dress in order to become sexually aroused and his wife responds to this with physiological feelings of disgust or revulsion, the couples therapist may be faced with a long-standing and difficult issue which may indeed end in war, if not secession. If she can overcome her physiological responses enough to trade some of her fantasies with some of his, there may be a very satisfactory conclusion. However, wherever this is not possible, the love which brought them together may ultimately be shot through with the bitter ashes of resentful self-sacrifice or the incessant gnawing of guilt, knowing that we are asking someone else to do something which they, at a physiological level, find deeply offensive. I often refer to the *animal* in each of us – the layer of chemical attraction or repulsion that may have to do with the rhinencephalon – one of the oldest structures in the brain associated with smell and therefore with pheromones. How our partners smell to us is an ineradicable element of sexual arousal.

These are the differences that lead to war – when Islam is pitted against Christianity, or northern and southern Irish kill each other in terrorist attacks. Difference of personality, conviction or physiology, is probably the source of its greatest tragedy of human existence as well as the fount of the greatest joy. Because it is in these differences between individuals, partners, nations, that diversity can flourish and variety can come to flower. When there is an erosion of such differences there is a drift towards conformity, an imposition of the norm of mediocrity, and an attenuation of sexual desire in the couple.

Perhaps we can change our attitudes towards such differences, and the couples therapist can help the couple towards working on accepting and celebrating such differences. Of course, frequently the qualities that first attracted us to a partner can become the source of later irritation.

An ambitious high-powered woman executive who marries a gentle, sensitive residential social worker who has no ambition except to become more perfectly attuned with nature, needs to decide before she marries him that this is who he is and make a commitment that she will not embark on a change programme to turn him into somebody different later in the relationship. The same may apply to him. If she needs to be active, energetic, and goal-achieving, and this is healthy and good for her, it is very necessary that he is willing to support her in her self-actualisation, however different it may be from his. If they can do this, this mutual appreciation of each other's different qualities, can become and remain the core of a continuing spring of wonderment, pleasure and creative tension, mutually enhancing each other's lives from different sources. All of us have the drawbacks of our virtues and for the long-term loving couple it is essential to separate out changes in attitudes and behaviour, which may be necessary or desirable, from changes in the essential quality of the person which, in effect, would make them very different from the person you love.

Conclusion

I have briefly surveyed three major categories of conflict and negotiation between couples and I have also briefly juxtaposed these with similar issues between nations at war, at peace and in the process of secession. I hope that I have shown the importance of separating issues to do with human rights from issues between equal negotiating partners, and that I have made the beginnings of the case for the importance of celebrating difference, modifying the drawbacks of our virtues, but cherishing the qualities in our partners which, by their very otherness, become the fulcrum for greatest attraction and most significant mutual transformation. Although I cannot in any ultimately significant way influence the fates of nations, I hope that this perspective on how to affect the fate of loving, warring, or separating couples may prove useful to others who are also engaged in the endeavour to be a better, loving partner and in the struggle to make this a better world.

References

BACH, G. BACH, G. and GOLDBERG, H. (1983). *Creative Aggression: The Art of Assertive Living.* London: Anchor Books. (Originally published 1974.)

BERNE, E. (1980). *Transactional Analysis in Psychotherapy.* London: Souvenir Press. (Originally published 1961.)

CAPLAN, P. J. (1985). *The Myth of Women's Masochism.* New York: E. P. Dutton.

CLARKSON, P. (1988). Script cure? – a diagnostic pentagon of types of therapeutic change, *Transactional Analysis Journal,* **18** (30), 211–219.

CLARKSON, P. (1989). *Gestalt Counselling in Action.* London: Sage.

CLARKSON, P. (1990). Despair before change. *Counselling News,* **1**, 11.

CLARKSON, P. (1991). Facets of the dance. *Journal of Couples Therapy,* **2** (3), 71–82.

DORFMAN, A. (1992). *Death and the Maiden.* London: Nick Hern Books. (Originally published 1991.)

DRYDEN, W. (Ed.) (1985). *Marital Therapy in Britain*, Vols 1 and 2. London: Harper and Row.

EYSENCK, H. J. (1968). *Handbook of Abnormal Psychology*. London: Pitman Medical.

FAIRBAIRN, W. R. D. (1952). *Psycho-analytic Studies of the Personality*. London: Tavistock.

FESTINGER, L. (1957). *A Theory of Cognitive Dissonance*. Stanford: Stanford University Press.

FISHER, R. and URY, W. (1983). *Getting to Yes*. London: Hutchinson.

FREEDMAN, A. M., KAPLAN, H. I. and SADOCK, B. J. (1975). *Comprehensive Textbook of Psychiatry – II*. Baltimore: Williams and Wilkins .

FROMM, E. (1966). *The Art of Loving*. London: Unwin Books. (Originally published 1957.)

GELLERT, S. D. (1983). *Nuts Come in Pairs*. Huntington Station, NY: Cite Press Inc.

GEORGE, E. (1990). Shortwave: heard in the global village (interview with P. Clarkson). *Wave*, (Autumn), 14.

GUERRIERE, D. (1980). Physis, sophia, psyche. In: J. Sallis and K. Maly (Eds), *Heraclitean Fragments: A Companion Volume to the Heidegger/Fink Seminar on Heraclitus*, pp. 87–134. Tuscaloosa; AL: University of Alabama Press.

JUNG, C. G. (1944). *Psychological Types or the Psychology of Individuation*. (H. G. Baynes, trans.) London: Kegan Paul, Trench, Trubner.

MACDONALD, A. M. (1972). *Chambers Twentieth Century Dictionary*. Edinburgh: T. and A. Constable. (Originally published 1901.)

MAKHOERE, C, K. (1988). *No Child's Play*. London: The Women's Press.

MILLER, A. (1985). *Thou Shalt Not be Aware: Society's Betrayal of the Child*. (H. and H. Hannum, trans.) London: Pluto Books. (Originally published 1981.)

MILLER, A. (1987). *The Drama of Being a Child*. (R. Ward, trans.) London: Virago. (Originally published 1979.)

MYERS, K. C. and BRIGGS MYERS, I. (1976). *Myers-Briggs Type Indicator*. Palo Alto, California: Consulting Psychologists Press.

ROWE, D. (1988). *The Successful Self*. London: Fontana/Collins.

SATIR, V. (1978). *Conjoint Family Therapy*. London: Souvenir Press. (Originally published 1967.)

THOMAS, A. L., CHESS, S. and BIRCH, H. (1977). *Temperament and Development*. New York: Brunner/Mazel.

Chapter 6
Individuality and Commonality in Gestalt

Introduction

This chapter concerns itself with several major interrelated gestalt themes – individuality, change, commonality and growth. It finds traces of a natural gestalt legacy which has existed since the dawn of time, and reaches out for the findings of physics and chaos theory today. It is painted in broad brushstrokes. Like gestalt itself, it is a whole in which many other wholes are imbedded and which changes even as it temporarily loses its dynamic movement on paper. It concerns the person, psychotherapy and gestalt as an approach to psychotherapy. Whenever any one of these become figure, the others implicitly inhabit the field. It is difficult, if not impossible, to separate them out from one another. These themes themselves have fractal qualities (Gleick, 1988) – elements of the whole are recurringly repeated in every fragment and they spiral off each other towards creative evolution.

The whole is thus represented in any fragment of itself. It is in the nature of holons or wholes that we experience different facets differently at different times. This does not negate the intrinsic wholeness of the phenomenon. But neither does it exclude its containment of opposites. Whatever is said fully and completely, the opposite also begins to be true. In 500 BC this quality of a whole was referred to as a *'coincidentia oppositorum* – a coincidence of opposites' (Guerriere, 1980, p. 102). This is in the nature of the notion of polarities, turning into each other at their apotheosis. Both Jung (1968) and Perls refer to this by the name of 'enantodromia'. In chaos theory this phenomenon is known as the 'flipover' effect and in gestalt we are familiar with it in terms of the paradoxical theory of change.

In the training of gestalt psychotherapists, intentionality, reactivity and flexibility, range and spontaneity, as well as intelligence and under-

From P. Clarkson (1991). Individuality and commonality in gestalt. *British Gestalt Journal,* 1 (1), 28–37, with permission.

standing can be valued. Gestalt cannot be studied or served in intellectual or practical isolation from its surrounding field whether that be the psychotherapy scene of the 1990s in Europe or the intellectual fields from which Perls, Hefferline and Goodman (1951) drew their inspiration and their knowledge. These fields were: science, particularly so-called modern physics, gestalt psychology and philosophy. ***Science*** concerns the world, ***gestalt psychology*** concerns the person and perceptual processes of the person, and ***philosophy***, of course, concerns the large questions, such as being (ontology), knowledge (epistemology), goodness (ethics), and meaning (metaphysics).

It is my intention to briefly bring the complexity, diversity, richness and vastness of our discipline momentarily into figure or awareness. It is not my goal to oppose a more singular view of gestalt, but to complement and complete it. The material here contains left-hemispheric as well as right-hemispheric evocations. Much of what follows may be familiar to you, albeit in different guises. There is of course no way I can do it justice. You may be able to recognise how much you already have assimilated from your own study, training and psychotherapeutic experience in terms of the breadth and depth of gestalt. Fortunately, the idea that gestalt has to be a totally 'headless' approach, only concerned with experimentation and inspiration of bodies and feelings, is well dead by now. It is well recognised that gestalt is intrinsically an holistic approach. Therefore, it must encompass passion as well as compassion, emotions as well as intelligence, and minds as well as hearts.

Individuality in Gestalt

> I do my thing and you do your thing.
> I am not in this world to live up to your expectations
> And you are not in this world to live up to mine,
> You are you and I am I,
> If by chance we find each other, it's beautiful.
> If not, it can't be helped.
>
> (Perls, 1969b, p. 4)

Known as the 'gestalt prayer', the spirit of these few lines has on occasion in the past been used to justify a rampant polarity of individualism at the expense of consideration for the other person. It is no doubt partly attributable to the 'Perls-ism' (Dublin, 1977). He refers to it as that kind of gestalt which is *not* gestalt therapy *nor* existential gestalt therapy, but the particular articulation of Fritz Perls's personal hedonism which found its manifestation in the sexual exploitation of clients and trainees, neglect of commitment to other people, and a rejection of many attempts at commonly agreed ethics, values or standards. At the extreme of one polarity this culminated, particularly in parts of

America and Europe, in gestalt teaching which included 'insemination', humiliation and exploitation.

This spirit of individualism, anarchy and iconoclasm served the purses, the purposes and the egos of people who may not otherwise have been acceptable to the professional bodies of their time or their countries. Furthermore, this spirit sharpened a figure or focus of individualism which had not until then, in the field of psychology, been voiced by such exuberantly rebellious and exhilarating charismatic teachers. It liberated many fine minds and free spirits from the constraining strictures of the psychology and the ethos of that time. Perls and his colleagues attacked the establishment with such vigour that their movement drew to it many who, for good or ill reasons, wished to emphasise de-structuring at the expense of structuring. This breaking down of the morality, psychological assumptions and cliched forms of relationship was a significant and intrinsic part of the *Zeitgeist* of the 1960s. All this was very necessary at the time when Fritz and Laura began to develop gestalt therapy in South Africa.

As Fritz Perls himself would insist, any unipolar articulation of experience cannot truly be gestalt as gestalt always implies figure-in-background, organism in environment, content in context. Times have changed. To quote Perls, 'Everything is in a state of flux – even the density of the same substances with differences of pressure, gravitation and temperature.' (Perls, 1969a, p. 22). The same applies to gestalt itself.

The national and international context or background of psychotherapy has changed in profound and far-reaching ways. Whereas once gestalt was listed as the sixth most prevalent form of psychotherapeutic orientation, the excesses of some of the practitioners of the 1960s, perhaps necessary as they were, have resulted in a widespread and pervasive distrust of gestalt therapy in public as well as professional domains. This is only gradually and recently beginning to shift.

The more belligerent, hostile and destructive people were in some places, the more authentic and 'pure' gestalt they were considered to be. This was a reaction against the conformity, repression and formalism particularly of psychoanalysis of the 1950s. That was a long time ago. But there are still gestaltists who cling to this outdated ethos, so that it can become ossified into a new tyranny. As Perls himself said 'But how can you have sameness in this rapid-changing world? So of course anybody who wants to hold onto the status quo will get more and more panicky and afraid' (Perls, 1969b, p. 30).

Historically, Perls considered gestalt as one of three types of existential therapy along with Frankl's logotherapy and the daseins therapy of Binswanger. He goes on to say that gestalt therapy is the first existential philosophy that stands on its own feet:

> Existentialism wants to do away with concepts, and to work on the awareness principle, on phenomenology. The setback with the present

> existentialist philosophies is that they need their support from somewhere else. If you look at the existentialists, they say that they are non-conceptual but if you look at the people, they all borrow concepts from other sources. Buber from Judaism, Tillich from Protestantism, Sartre from Socialism, Heidegger from language, Binswanger from psychoanalysis, and so on. A rich heritage, indeed. Gestalt therapy is a philosophy which tries to be in harmony, in alignment with everything else, with medicine, with science, with the universe, with what is. Gestalt therapy has its support in its own formation because the gestalt formation, the emergence of the needs, is a primary biological phenomenon.
>
> (Perls, 1969b, pp. 15–16)

There is still, even nowadays, a little game in the gestalt world which is called 'My gestalt is purer than your gestalt'. So, sometimes this little game of 'mine is purer than yours', is played in the following way – as long as it can be found in *Gestalt Therapy* by Perls et al., the gestalt can be claimed to be extremely pure. In some ways of course this is very silly, because Perls himself was no purist. He was a synthesiser of other people's ideas *par excellence*; an intellectual and philosophical magpie, collecting concepts, theory and technique from a most diverse range of sources. With or without acknowledgement he drew from Jung, Freud, Friedlaender, Koffka, Wertheimer, Kohler, Reich, Rank, Horney, Frankl, Neitzsche, Sartre, Moreno, the New Physics of his time including Heisenberg, biology, Deustche, Federn, Zen, Einstein, Abraham, Landauer, Fromm, Gandhi, Goldstein, Anna Freud, Kant, Korzybski, D'Alembert, Mach, Avenarius, Mauthner, the physicist Joule, Lewin, Sullivan, Whyte, Yoga, Rolf, Maslow, Dewey, Adler, Aurelius, Descartes, Schachtel. He was an original synthesiser, yes – a free-standing original, no. So, a pure gestalt therapist would study all of these, adding the few books incorporating the words 'gestalt therapy' and 'gestalt psychology' in their titles.

When Perls said 'Lose your mind and come to your senses', he was probably sloganeering to undermine intellectualism for its own sake. Erv Polster said he often did this kind of thing (personal communication, 1989). He was not seeking to undermine intelligence. Clearly he was an intelligent man. In any field perspective, the passions of the heart and body cannot be divorced from the mind and still lay any claim to wholism. In view of the above, it is my contention that Perls would have been in favour of the creative adjustment of gestalt therapy to the changed and changing environment of Europe in the 1990s. Clinging to the shibboleths of the 1960s would accord with neither the tone nor the spirit of a man for whom change was his very life's blood. (He had many lovers, lived in several countries and made massive changes of technique or emphasis during his career.)

Gestalt therapy itself needs to go through the cycle of experience – sensing, becoming aware, mobilising, acting, achieving final contact, allowing satisfaction and withdrawal from favourite concepts or techniques – as the background to gestalt therapy and the environment of psychotherapy itself changes. To paraphrase what Perls was saying about an individual, it is not organismic for gestalt therapy as a system to interrupt itself by egotism whereby its adherents become 'ideal products'. When this happens to a person or a system of psychotherapy, the experience has not been integrated or assimilated. This will prevent the person or the system from truly giving or receiving at the moment of contact with the environment. This way lies not de-structuring, but annihilation.

Perls, Hefferline and Goodman had this to say:

> But any one who sympathetically surveys the various schools and methods of psychotherapy, as we have been doing...also thinks a new thought: the basic human nature is in part given...but in part...it creates itself; and this creative adjustment in favourable circumstances is itself an essential of the basic human nature. It is the same essential power that is *prima facie* evident in *any* worthwhile human experience. The problem of psychotherapy is to enlist the patient's power of creative adjustment without forcing it into the stereotype of the therapist's scientific conception.
>
> (Perls, Hefferline and Goodman, 1951, p. 281)

And this must apply to gestalt therapy itself.

Change in Gestalt

Of course I doubt very much whether Fritz, if he were alive, would still be practising or rebelling in the way that he used to – but, I believe, he would still be making changes. Unfortunately, according to Resnick (1984) and others, many gestalt psychotherapists became fixed for the rest of their professional lives on an introjection of Fritz Perls at a particular time and in a particular place of his development. In contrast, the man himself kept moving on and changing. Of course, Perls was originally a psychoanalyst. Freudian psychoanalysis too, largely influenced by Descartes and Newton and, in turn, so responsible for the way so many ordinary people see themselves, has no conceptual framework for interpersonal relationships. Indeed it does not even consider such relationships its proper business. As the author of *A Critical Dictionary of Psychoanalysis* puts it: 'This is because psychoanalysis is a psychology of the individual and therefore discusses objects and relationships only from the point of view of a single subject' (Rycroft, 1972, p. 101). In some ways gestalt therapy can be seen as the embodiment of Perls' rebellion against analysis, but he carried this emphasis on the individual unquestioningly to an extreme for many years. Eventually he even changed this. He, towards the end of his life, apparently responded to a confrontation from Erv Polster about his relationships with other people (personal communication, 1989). Perls attempted to create a *community* at Lake Cowichan.

The structure of the actual situation, the here-and-now of the 1990s is different from the here-and-now of the 1960s, and in order to continue growing, gestalt will need to continue changing. Of course the idea of ever-returning changes between the emergence of the gestalt and its disappearance, the sense that the situation is in eternal cyclic flux, was not originated by Perls.

The idea has actually been around since 500 BC when Heraclitus (perhaps the first gestaltist) was busy with a similar notion in his time.

> The Divine Flux of Heraclitus [implies] that all things, conscious and material, derive ultimately from one common source. 'God is day and night, winter and summer, war and peace, surfeit and hunger; but he takes various shapes, just as fire, when it is mingled with spices, is named according to the savour of each.... Men do not know how what is at variance agrees with itself.'
>
> (Zohar, 1990, p. 38)

Preceding Perls's existentialist concerns with being by two and a half thousand years, Heraclitus was working with a concept of being in a uniquely transitional configuration. I quote directly: 'The cycle is the compact experiential reconciliation of permanence and degeneration. Mythic man exists [*sic*] the cycle or the whole' (Guerriere, 1980, p. 88).

Two thousand five hundred years later, I have written a book based on this very topic – so the cycle continues! (Clarkson, 1989). The familiar cycle paradigm I used was developed from Zinker (1987) and the original outline in Perls et al. (1951). They put it thus: 'The present is a passage out of the past toward the future, and these are the stages of an act of self as it contacts the actuality' (p. 374). The cycle of gestalt formation and destruction seems to be one of the most eloquent and economical models for conceptualising changes in nature, in the individual person and in society.

Since writing the book, I think I have recognised the prototype for the gestalt cycle (which bears fruitful comparison) in *Holism and Evolution* by Smuts (1987). Smuts was a great South African general who catalysed the formation of the League of Nations and the Pan-African Congress. Perls was greatly influenced by Smuts, visited him at his home in Pretoria and incorporated the concept of holism into the infancy of gestalt therapy while he was in South Africa. ('An holistic approach to the person embraces and affirms complexity, inclusion and diversity, and resists reductionism' (Clarkson, 1989, p. 8).

This is what Smuts had to say:

> Elements both of the actual past and of anticipated future experience are fused with the present experience into one individual act, which as a conscious object of the mind dominates the entire situation with the

> purview of the purpose or plan. It involves not only *sensations* and *perceptions*, but also concepts of a complex character, *feelings and desires* in respect of the end desired, and volitions in respect of the act intended; and all these elements are fused and blended into one unique purpose; which is then put into *action* or *execution* [all italics added].
>
> (Smuts, 1987, p. 258)

Change is a matter very dear to my heart, because on personal and collective levels, I have desired to change many things. And the changing of certainties (whether convictions about my own limitations – such as fear of walking on fire, or the barriers between nations, such as the Berlin Wall) has been a *leitmotiv* of my life's work. 'If a man will begin with certainties, he shall end in doubts; but if he will be content to begin with doubts, he shall end in certainties' (Francis Bacon in Goold, 1964, p. 3). Yet these very certainties will again in time certainly transform into new doubts. Even what I am writing today, I can well believe will change in future, perhaps it will have changed even by the time this book is published. This is an effect of the ever-changing Heraclitean flux which appears to be the nature of human existence. Such is the interplay between figure and ground, faces and vase, permanence and transience, individuality and commonality. The cycle describes the nature of change on both microscopic and macroscopic scales – on the one hand, the inhalation and exhalation of breath, and on the other, the rise and fall of nations.

Commonality in Gestalt

This beat, or pulse, seems essential to the lives of individual organisms in order to preserve their individual and separate existences. Yet, scientific studies have found that cells have a natural cooperativeness, they seek to work together (Fox, 1983). Living cells, separated from each other and pulsing to different beats, will eventually become synchronised in their pulsing. This phenomenon has also been observed in shops where they sell clocks – the clocks tend to synchronise their ticking. Even in women's dormitories or wards, women's menstrual cycles tend to coincide (Leonard, 1978). The emphasis here is on the modern scientific evidence for the interconnectedness of all life on earth. In the true nature of cycles, this one has been around several times, beginning with the following statement recorded three hundred years before Christ:

> All the world is working together. It is all one living whole, with one soul through it. And, as a matter of fact, no single part of it can either rejoice or suffer without all the rest being affected. The man who does not see that the good of every living creature is his good, the hurt of every living creature is his hurt, is one who wilfully makes himself a kind of outlaw or exile: he is blind, or a fool.
>
> (Murray, 1915, p. 37)

Nowadays, Lovelock (1979) calls this the Gaia hypothesis.

Up until now I have emphasised the individualism of Perls. However, imbedded in his book, *Gestalt Therapy Verbatim*, is the following, rather neglected quotation which shows that Perls et al. (1951), at least at some level, took the *sociality* of human beings perhaps almost for granted. It was ground for them whereas individuality was the figure to emphasise at the time. The following quotation points to the close affinity between Perls and Merleau-Ponty.

> For consider it a moment in the following way: the common 'human nature' (whatever the conception is) is a sharing of not only animal but cultural factors; and the cultural factors, especially in our society, are very divergent – the *co-existence of divergences is perhaps the defining property of our culture* [italics added]. Besides, there are undoubtedly original eccentric dispositions of individuals and families. And more important still, the self-creation, the creative adjustment in various circumstances, has been going on from the beginning, not completely as an extrinsic 'conditioning' that can be 'de-conditioned', but also mainly as true growth.
>
> (Perls et al., 1951, pp. 281–282)

Apparently, if a plant has been injured in the presence of another plant, the surviving plant resonates with the distress of its injured neighbour and even appears to recognise the aggressor subsequently (Watson, 1974). In human beings this phenomenon can be referred to as visceral empathy, which means that we feel with the pain of others in our bodies and our souls. Providing we have not become desensitised, as experiments show human beings can become, this visceral experience of pain in the presence of another's pain is an organismic healthy response. Most of us have experienced this empathic visceral resonance with others in group psychotherapy situations.

> Dillard explains that all the entire green world of plants consists of chloroplasts. If we analyze a molecule of chlorophyll we see 136 atoms of hydrogen, carbon, oxygen, and nitrogen arranged 'in an exact and complex relationship around a central ring'. At the center of the ring is a single atom of magnesium. Amazingly, human blood is *identical* to this cholorophyll, *except* that at its center is a single atom of iron. Thus, our red power is a kissing cousin to the greening power all around us. These stories emerging from contemporary science are awe-some; they are both mystical and scientific. They are part of our learning to live once again *in the cosmos*.
>
> (Fox, 1983, p. 2 of 'Afterword')

The distinction between plants and human beings is thus not as great as one might think. Rinzler (1984) emphasises that only people who have become desensitised to their own organismal nature, their own biological roots, could cause the damage that they do to our planet.

Estrangement from the embodied, sensing self results in an alienation from the other.

Such is the state of affairs, for example, in South Africa, which was where I came to gestalt in the late 1960s. My teachers were first of all South African members of the clergy – spiritual people (who were serving the Good through the I and Thou encounter). They had gone to Esalen – the high mecca of gestalt at that time – to learn gestalt in order to help them in the struggle of transforming a country where the battles between individuality and commonality are fought – fought in prison, in torture chambers and in the starving bellies of the disenfranchised. As gestalt was about human liberation it was deeply relevant to our situation. During this time I was part of an encounter group in the ecumenical community of Wilgespruit where these trainers brought together black and white people who were questing for individual and collective freedom. The first awareness experiment many of us remember was in touching the face and hair of the first black person consciously encountered as an embodied equal. This may be a terrible thing to be true, but it was.

I became convinced that change was the most exciting, interesting process in the whole world. To study, participate in and master the principles of personal and collective change became my life's work. That is why I have called our institute metanoia – a turning around, a transformation, in short, change.

At the core of metanoia's philosophy is the concept of individual responsibility for individual behaviour (whether conscious or unconscious), *as well as* responsibility towards others. So, while we seek excellence of individual development, we attempt to encourage this within a framework of respect for the person and our shared common humanity. In the training of counsellors, psychotherapists and organisational consultants, we have acted on the belief that the person needs to be suitable and their performance needs to meet certain standards. I have had to struggle since the beginnings of becoming conscious with the separation between being and doing, between valuing and respecting people no matter how different they are from me because they are human beings and share their humanity with me and, on the other hand, taking and inviting responsibility for our actions – for the work we do in the world. I noticed if everybody only looked after themselves we could never complete the work that needed to be done. I noticed even as a little girl that everybody had to look after themselves *and* after others. I understood that we were all fettered, not only the imprisoned helpless ones, but also the keepers, the torturers, the people who made laws out of fear were trapped.

It is our 'first nature' to be connected, to be in organismic empathy. This 'un-connectedness', unawareness, being 'out of empathy' is 'second-nature'. It is not first nature, developed as a defence against our biological and social truth. Second nature usually means that which is automatic or 'a deeply-ingrained habit' (Macdonald, 1972, p. 1223). I conceive of first nature as that which is our truest, most real and most biologically rooted temperamental authentic self. We may have become inured to the plight of our fellow inhabitants of the planet, desensitised to the assaults on the planet herself, conditioned by philosophies and economies which glamourise individualism against social responsibility. But this is not truly organismic. This is not the situation of the living organisms in a healthy field.

Perls et al. affirm this in the following words:

> We have been at pains to show that in the organism before it can be called a personality at all, and in the formation of personality, the social factors are essential.... The underlying social nature of the organism and the forming personality – fostering and dependency, communication, imitation and learning, love-choices and companionship, passions of sympathy and antipathy, mutual aid and certain rivalries – all this is extremely conservative, repressible but ineradicable. And it is meaningless to think of an organism possessing drives which are 'anti-social' in this sense, opposed to his social nature, for this would be a conserved inner contradiction; it would not be conserved. But there are, rather, difficulties of individual development, of growing-up, of realizing all of one's nature.
>
> (1951, p. 333)

Here Perls is similar to the gestalt phenomenologist Merleau-Ponty, as well as the existentialist Marcel (1952). The latter has been sadly neglected in gestalt in favour of Sartre, the existentialist who stressed the nausea and entrapment given for our relations with others. Marcel, against this background developed the equally *existentialist gestalt themes* of embodiment, I and Thou, the nature of Being, and our simultaneous need for connectedness and individuation.

Compare his following words with Perls above:

> I find myself engaged along with others in a world which makes demands on me: I respond to others and undertake responsibilities to and for them. [This is so different from the old gestalt prayer.] So far from my being myself the ground of my certainty in knowing and the motive of my constancy in willing, it is the existence of another that gives me my primary notion of existence and it is in so far as I believe in the existence of others and act on that belief that I affirm my own existence.

> Life is achieved by resolving the tension in responsive feeling and creative activity, in which having is not eliminated but is assimilated to being, in which one and another become I and thou; in which science is integrated with metaphysics; in which autonomy (managing my own affairs) is transcended in liberty, which is participation; in which my body and the world with which it is consubstantial and which enlarges and multiplies its powers is the place in which I bear witness to Being; in which I work out my fidelity

> and my hope and keep myself open, fluid and ready to spend.
>
> (Marcel, 1952, p. 66)

'Spend' has Victorian connotations with 'coming' or a sexual climax. This is close to Hildegarde of Bingen's conception of the human soul whose work Matthew Fox is reviving. She saw spirituality as firstly biological. According to her, our souls need to be moist and green and juicy. Fox derives inspiration from her to plead for human relationships with our planet on the basis of erotic justice (Fox, 1983, p. 295). When we dry up, we can't have intercourse, it hurts. When we desensitise ourselves we destroy what is organismically valuable whether this be natural resources or an intellectual heritage. This the field perspective of gestalt.

G.M. Yontef's definition (unpublished) of gestalt as 'applied phenomenology' focuses us on the subjective experience, giving primacy and priority to people's actual feelings and seeing that as the true source of knowledge. This is uniquely characteristic of gestalt. I have become more and more convinced that psychology should get beyond object-relations to subject-relations – people in relationship to people. Gestalt is an approach that does do this. It can bring back the moistness, the human experience and the vivid, pulsating life of the subject in relation to others and in relation to the world. Merleau-Ponty has talked of a social universe where we participate and co-create each other. Our relationship to the social is, like our relationship to the world, deeper than any expressed perception or any judgement. It is as false to place ourselves in society as an object among other objects, as it is to place society within ourselves as an object of thought. In both cases the mistake lies in treating the social as an object. We must return to the social with which we are in contact by the mere fact of existing, and which we carry about inseparably with us before any objectification.

This section closes with a quotation from Merleau-Ponty on the nature of subject-to-subject dialogue.

> In the experience of dialogue, there is constituted between the other person and myself a common ground; my thought and his are interwoven into a single fabric, my words and those of my interlocutor are called forth by the stage of the discussion, and they are inserted into a shared operation of which neither of us is the creator. We have here a dual being, where the other is for me no longer a mere bit of behaviour in my transcendental field, nor I in his; we are collaborators for each other in consummate reciprocity. Our perspectives merge into each other, and we co-exist through a common world. In the present dialogue, I am freed from myself, for the other person's thoughts are certainly his; they are not of my making, though I do grasp them the moment they come into being, or even anticipate them. And, indeed, the objection which my interlocutor raises to what I say draws

> from me thought which I had no idea I possessed, so that at the same time that I lend him thoughts, he reciprocates by making me think too.
>
> (Merleau-Ponty, 1962, p. 354)

Of course with an increase in commonality, another kind of shadow comes into being – the envy and spite towards individuals who threaten the norm by being too different whether for worse or for better. Again the ancient Greeks also had experience of this problem:

> The Ephesians would do well to hang themselves, every grown man,
> and leave the polis to the beardless boys,
> for they have banished Hermodorus, the ablest man among them, saying:
> 'No one shall be the ablest of us;
> or, if there be such, let him be it elsewhere and among others.'
>
> (Guerriere, 1980, p. 123)

These are old stories, not new.

We have seen that in any biological or sociopsychological investigation, the concrete subject-matter is always an organism/environment field. Field theory, particularly as developed by Lewin (1952) is one of the theoretical cornerstones of gestalt. There is no function of any animal that is definable except as a function of such a field. Organic physiology, thoughts and emotions, objects and persons, are abstractions that are meaningful only when referred back to interactions of the field.

The field as a whole tends to complete itself, to reach the simplest equilibrium possible for that level of field. But as the conditions are always changing, the partial equilibrium achieved is always novel; it must be grown to. An organism preserves itself only by growing. Self-preserving and growing are polar, for it is only what preserves itself that can grow by assimilation, and it is only what continually assimilates novelty that can preserve itself and not degenerate. So the materials and energy of growth are: the conservative attempt of the organism to remain as it has been, the novel environment, the destruction of previous partial equilibria, and the assimilation of something new.

'Homoeostatic' self-regulation is only one polarity. We can get carried away with homoeostasis in gestalt. As Perls et al. (1951) stated, gestalt is not concerned with seeking 'equilibrium in general' (p. 350).

Creative Growth in Gestalt

Perls, Hefferline and Goodman were among the most vociferous proponents for change and they posited an organismic drive towards increasing wholeness and increasing perfection or goodness. 'Repeating an action to the point of mastery is the essence of development. A mechanical repetition without perfection as its aim is contrary to organic life, contrary to "creative holism" (Smuts)' (Perls, 1969a, p. 102). That gives enormous substance to striving, to aspiration, to excellence, to becoming well.

> No natural animal and no plant exists that will prevent its own growing. So the question is, how do we prevent ourselves from maturing? What prevents us from ripening? The word 'neurosis' is very bad. I use it, too, but actually it should be called *growth disorder*.
>
> (Perls, 1969b, p. 28)

In Prigogene's physics within open systems, unlike those driven by entropy, order always increases (Prigogene and Stengers, 1984). A healthy open system could not maintain its drive towards increased order in a static or homogeneous universe, a universe at equilibrium (creativity happens at far from equilibrium conditions). Homeostasis is, in fact, contrary to continuing, evolving life. To have a steady homoeostatic rhythm may be nonproductive and maybe even dangerous. This has been discovered in chaos theory as well (Gleick, 1988). Apparently an absolutely regular heart beat is the herald of impending death. It is the nature of growing things to be in *and* out of alignment. In Tai Chi, for example, in order to be in the best position for effective action, one needs to be in continual movement, moving in *and* out of balance.

Zohar describes the process in modern physics thus:

> Quantum field theory takes us even further beyond Newton's dead and silent universe, giving us a vivid picture of the dynamic flux which lies at the heart of an indeterminate being. Here, even those particles which do manifest themselves as individual beings do so only briefly.... [It gives a] graphic picture of the emergence and return, or the beginning and ceasing, of individual subatomic particles at the quantum level of reality [which] holds out deep implications of our way of looking at the nature and function of individual personalities or the survival of the individual self.
>
> (1990, p. 13)

So in modern physics as well, gestalt principles remain true and are enriched.

> Given the novelty and indefinite variety of the environment, no adjustment would be possible by the conservative inherited self-regulation alone; contact must be a *creative transformation* [italics added]. On the other hand, creativity that is not continually destroying and assimilating an environment given in perception and resisting manipulation is useless to the organism and remains superficial and lacking in energy; it does not become deeply exciting, and it soon languishes.
>
> (Perls et al., 1951, p. 406)

This creative transformation is individual realisation or collective evolution.

> There is creative Evolution, and that real new entities have arisen in the universe, in addition to the physical conditions of the beginning. This is a universe of whole-making, not of soul-making merely. The view of the universe as purely spiritual, as transparent to the Spirit, fails to account for its dark opaque character ethically and rationally; for its accidental and contradictory features, its elements of error, sin and suffering, which will not be conjured away by an essentially poetic world-view. Holism explains both the realism and the idealism at the heart of things, and is therefore a more accurate description of reality than any of these more or less partial and one-sided world-views.
>
> (Smuts, 1987, p. 318)

The final net result is that this is a whole-making universe, that it is the fundamental character of this universe to be active in the production of wholes, of ever more complete and advanced wholes, and that the evolution of the universe, inorganic and organic, is nothing but the record of this whole-making activity in its progressive development.

> Creative Evolution seems to move forward by small steps or instalments or increments of creativeness. Why there should be this discontinuity rather than a smooth continuous advance we cannot say; we can but note the fact, which seems to be a universal phenomenon.... Thus the unit character of Action and Structure is reproduced in the unit character of Evolution and of nuclear change in the cell.
>
> (Smuts, 1987, p. 331)

> Holism is the presiding genius of this advance. It determines the direction of the advance, and it incorporates the new element of advance synthetically with the pre-existing structure. It thus harmonises the old and the new in its own unity; it synthesises Variation and Heredity; and by slow degrees and over enormous periods of time carries forward the creative process from the most simple, primitive, inorganic beginnings to the most exalted spiritual creations.
>
> (Smuts, 1987, p. 332)

> Now normally the *élan vital*, the life force, energises by sensing, by listening, by scouting, by describing the world – how is the world there. Now this life force apparently first mobilises the center – *if* you have a center. And the center of the personality is what used to be called the soul: the emotions, the feelings, the spirit. Emotions are not a nuisance to be discharged. The emotions are the most important motors of our behavior.... Now these emotions, or this basic energy, this life force.... these muscles are used to move about, to take from the world, to touch the world, to be in contact, to be in touch.
>
> (Perls, 1969b, pp. 63–64)

At the atomic level the need to be in touch or not plays itself out in a mirroring microcosm.

> The fundamental building blocks of the material world itself are fermions (for instance, electrons and protons), those 'antisocial' particles which

> prefer to keep themselves to themselves. Without bosons, fermions would seldom get together and build anything; without fermions, bosons would have nothing to draw into relationship and thus nothing with which to order and structure their own more complex coherence. From the very beginning, then, from the most primary level of what later becomes the material world and the world of consciousness, the building blocks of matter (fermions) and the building blocks of consciousness (bosons) are necessarily involved in a mutually creative dialogue.
>
> (Zohar, 1990, p. 206)

Fermions are particles that go round and round and do not like being with other particles. Bosons are friendly and like being connected. And the world is made up of these, who are struggling with the same kinds of problems with which we are struggling: contact and withdrawal, individuality and commonality, accommodation and assimilation.

> The tension between particles and waves within the wave/particle duality is a tension between being and becoming. Similarly the tension within ourselves between the I and the not-I, between keeping ourselves to ourselves and engaging in more or less intimate relationships is a tension between staying as we are and becoming something new. The key to both is quantum wave mechanics.
>
> (Zohar, 1990, p. 114)

> This ability to combine real individuality with definitive relationship is one unique and important result of looking at persons quantum mechanically. Neither individuality nor relationship is lost. Neither is more primary.
>
> (Zohar, 1990, p. 120)

Physis is Our Future

The question is, what is the inherent force that makes neurotic individuals want to get better and makes organisms evolve? Homoeostasis has advantages. Self-actualisation and evolution are hard work. Perls had a sense of this curative force of nature which facilitates the natural urge toward growth and realisation. 'In Aristotle, the "nature" [Physis]...of any individual thing or specific kind of thing is conceived as the immanent cause or self-active principle of its self-realisation, i.e. of its spontaneous growth and action' (Lovejoy and Boas, 1973, p. 450).

Zeno named this force 'Physis', the force of Nature, which eternally strives to make things grow and to make growing things more perfect. 'For the Stoics Physis is identified with god and the active principle, while for Epicureans it consists of atoms and void' (Edwards, 1967, p. 122). Many philosophers have since recognised this creative evolutionary force of nature which makes all things grow in an orderly and progressive way. For example, Physis can be seen as identical to the *élan vital* of Bergson (1965), who was such a strong influence on the early Perls. Physis also means 'to grow, to be, to become' (Guerriere, 1980, p. 100). This is the force that deals with people giving up soiling their nappies on the one hand, and on the other to building the United Nations, to bringing down the Berlin Wall, to ending the state of emergency in South Africa, to all the health and recoveries we have made in our individual lives. This is closely related to nature, the force of nature, the life force in every cell, the life force in the evolving universe.

> Hence the [Physis] of a thing, is its Being, its inner dynamism, the process in which it rises up, by which it surges forth and endures, because of which it emerges as what and how it is; its upsurgence, its presencing.... The matter at issue is the physis of all things: their Being, their emergence, their presencing.... Although physis is wont to hide itself, it manifests itself in multiple ways...all suggest a certain oneness in multiple things, a certain *coincidentia oppositorum* (coincidence of opposites).... Through the oneness proper to a cycle, the one physis manifest itself.
>
> (Guerriere, 1980, pp. 100, 102, 105)

Freud, in *Beyond the Pleasure Principle* (1961) expressed his doubt about the existence of such a general creative force, terming it 'a pleasing illusion'. He himself was none too sure at one time, however, that something like physis did not assist Ananke as the motive force in evolution. 'This appreciation of the necessities of life need not, incidentally, weigh against the importance of "internal developmental trends" if such can be shown to be present' (Freud, 1973, p. 400). He seemed to have much more conviction about the death instinct, and later he gave equal weight to Eros and Thanatos.

I believe Physis is the name people have been looking for in describing the life force. It is what I believe Maslow was looking for when he said there is a third force in psychotherapy. Physis is the belief that draws humanistic/existential people together because we believe there is a *prior* phenomenon of growth and healing than Eros and Thanatos. Life and Death are there, yes, but really, before that, we grow, develop; we evolve, we connect, we strive for greater and greater perfection, we move towards 'the good'. Perls et al. were, of course, in agreement with this, 'Man does not strive to be good; the good is what it is human to strive for' (1951, p. 335).

In these words they were again articulating a philosophical position very similar to that of the Stoics who were grappling with this thousands of years ago in the following way:

> A good bootmaker is one who makes good boots, a good shepherd is one who keeps his sheep well, and even though good boots are in the Day-of-Judgement sense entirely worthless and fat sheep no whit better than starved sheep, yet the good bootmaker or good shepherd must do his work

> well or he will cease to be good. To be good he must perform his function; ...in performing that function there are certain things that he must 'prefer' to others, even though they are not really 'good'. He must prefer a healthy sheep or a well-made boot to their opposites. It is this that Nature, or Physis, herself works when she shapes the seed into a tree or the blind puppy into a good hound. The perfection of the tree or the blind puppy is in itself indifferent, a thing of no ultimate value. Yet the goodness of Nature lies in working for that perfection.
>
> (Murray, 1915, p. 43)

> For the essence of Goodness is to do something, to labour, to achieve some end; and if Goodness is to exist, the world process must begin again.... Physis must be moving upward, or else it is not Physis.
>
> (Murray, 1915, p. 43)

What I would like to do over the next few years is to reintroduce ourselves to Physis, the life force, of which I believe we are the servants in psychotherapy. I believe that life force is in individual people and the task of psychotherapists and educators is to allow people to get back in touch with that inner force inside themselves. That is what the job is about, about letting people get back in touch with first nature. It is not taking over and doing it to them.

Physis is the force that drives the interplay between Individuality and Commonality – it is the creative life force which strives for increased wholeness and increased perfection through evolutionary processes of growth and change.

> We are part of an Order, a cosmos, which we see to be infinitely above our comprehension.... But in the rest of the world, we can see a moving Purpose. It is Physis, the word which the Romans unfortunately translated 'Nature', but which means 'growing' or 'the way things grow' – almost what we call Evolution. But to the Stoic it is a living and conscious evolution.... The direction was towards the perfection of each thing or species after its own kind.... If a man is an artist, it is his function to produce beauty.
>
> (Murray, 1915, p. 126)

Or if one is a bootmaker – to make good boots. On the Day of Judgement it hardly matters whether you made good boots, or you are chic, or fat or starving. But it matters that you were doing it well.

What is fascinating about Physis is that 'it' loves to hide. It flares up early in the pre-Socratic thinking. And then it goes underground. And then someone like Heidegger grabs hold of it; existentialists, gestaltists, and Physis flares up again. And then again it gets lost. Two decades later I stumble across it again: 'Physis! Yes! That explains...'.

Thus the cycle or spiral of creative evolution continues from Heraclitus through the 'self' of Perls, Hefferline and Goodman, to the modern gestalt of today.

> The matter at issue in Heraclitus is physis.... And correlative to the matter is a self-experience which is as deep as physis is comprehensive. The experience of physis is an experience of self for two reasons: (1) physis comprehends (encompasses) the self as it does everything else; and (2) the self is the locus where (for the human self) physis comprehends (understands) itself. Human experience is, in terms of physis, the self-experience of physis.
>
> (Guerriere, 1980, pp. 129–130)

The striving for growth, excellence and creative adjustment is just as real for the individual as for the system of psychotherapy that we call gestalt as for the planetary concerns that face our world today. I have studied the psyche and served the psychotherapy forums, gestalt or otherwise, in several countries for almost two decades. As we grapple with similar problems in the councils of gestalt psychotherapy among ourselves and with colleagues from other psychotherapy orientations (as we do at the United Kingdom Council for Psychotherapy), I would like to pass on to you the conviction of one of our direct grandfathers in gestalt, Jan Smuts:

> It has been my lot to have passed many of the years of my life amid the conflicts of men, in their wars and their Council Chambers. Everywhere I have seen men search and struggle for the Good with grim determination and earnestness, and with a sincerity of purpose which added to the poignancy of the fratricidal strife.
>
> But everywhere too I have seen that it was at bottom a struggle for the Good, a wild striving towards human betterment; that blindly, and through blinding mists of passions and illusions, men are yet sincerely, earnestly groping towards the light, towards the ideal of a better, more secure life for themselves and for their fellows. Thus the League of Nations, the chief constructive outcome of the Great War, is but the expression of the deeply-felt aspiration towards a more stable holistic human society. And the faith has been strengthened in me that what has here been called Holism is at work even in the conflicts and confusions of men; that in spite of all appearances to the contrary, eventual victory is serenely and securely waiting, and that the immeasurable sacrifices have not been in vain. The groaning and travailing of the universe is never aimless or resultless. Its profound labours mean new creation, the slow, painful birth of wholes, of new and higher wholes, and the slow but steady realisation of the Good which all the wholes of the universe in their various grades dimly yearn and strive for. It is the nature of the universe to strive for and slowly, but in ever-increasing measure, to attain wholeness, fullness, blessedness. The real defeat for men as for other grades of the universe would be to ease the pain by a cessation of effort, to cease from striving towards the Good.... Wholeness, healing, holiness – all expressions and ideas springing from the same root in language as in experience – lie on the rugged upward path of the universe, and are secure of attainment – in part here and now, and eventually more fully and truly.
>
> (Smuts, 1987, pp. 344–45)

References

BERGSON, H. (1965). *Creative Evolution.* London: Macmillan.

CLARKSON, P. (1989). *Gestalt Counselling in Action.* London: Sage.

DUBLIN, J.E. (1977). Gestalt therapy, existential-gestalt therapy and/versus "perls-ism". In: E.W.L. Smith (Ed.), *The Growing Edge of Gestalt Therapy*, pp. 124–150. Secaucus, NJ: The Citadel Press.

EDWARDS, P. (Ed.) (1967). *Encyclopaedia of Philosophy.* London: Collier-Macmillan.

FREUD, S. (1961). *Beyond the Pleasure Principle.* London: Hogarth Press. (Originally published 1920.)

FREUD, S. (1973). Some thoughts on development and regression – aetiology. In: A. Richards (Ed.) and J. Strachey (trans.), *Introductory Lectures on Psychoanalysis, the Pelican Freud Library,* Vol. 1, pp.383–403. Harmondsworth: Penguin. (Originally published 1916–17.)

FOX, M. (1983). *Original Blessing.* New Mexico: Bear and Co.

GLEICK, J. (1988). *Chaos: Making a New Science.* London: Heinemann.

GOOLD, F.E. (1964). *You Will Come Back.* Ontario, Canada: The Blavatsky Institute. (Originally published 1958.)

GUERRIERE, D. (1980). Physis, sophia, psyche. In: J. Sallis and K. Maly (Eds), *Heraclitean Fragments: A Companion Volume to the Heidegger/Fink Seminar on Heraclitus*, pp. 86–134. Alabama: University of Alabama Press.

JUNG, C.G. (1968). Archetypes of the collective unconscious. In: *The Collected Works,* Vol. 9, pp. 3–41, Part I, 2nd edn (R.F.C. Hull trans.). London: Routledge and Kegan Paul. (Originally published 1934.)

LEONARD, G. (1978). *The Silent Pulse.* New York: E.P. Dutton.

LEWIN, K. (1952). *Field Theory in Social Science: Selected Theoretical Papers.* London: Tavistock. (Originally published 1951.)

LOVEJOY, A. and BOAS, G. (1973). *Primitivism and Related Areas in Antiquity.* New York: Ferrar, Straus and Givaux.

LOVELOCK, J.E. (1979). *Gaia: A New Look at Life On Earth.* Oxford: Oxford University Press.

MACDONALD, A.M. (Ed.) (1972). *Chambers Twentieth Century Dictionary.* London: W. and R. Chambers.

MARCEL, G. (1952). *The Metaphysical Journal* (B. Wall, trans.). London: Rockliff. (Originally published 1927.)

MERLEAU-PONTY, M. (1962). *Phenomenology of Perception* (C. Smith, trans.). London: Routledge and Kegan Paul.

MURRAY, G. (1915). *The Stoic Philosophy.* London: G. Allen and Unwin.

PERLS, F.S. (1969a). *Ego, Hunger and Aggression.* New York: Vintage. (Originally published 1947.)

PERLS, F.S. (1969b). *Gestalt Therapy Verbatim.* Moab, UT: Real People Press.

PERLS, F.S., HEFFERLINE, R. and GOODMAN, P. (1951). *Gestalt Therapy: Excitement and Growth in the Human Personality.* New York: Julian Press.

PRIGOGENE, I. and STENGERS, I. (1984). *Order Out of Chaos.* London: Heinemann.

RESNICK, R. (1984). Gestalt therapy east and west: bi-coastal dialogue, debate or debacle? *Gestalt Journal,* 7 (1), 13–32.

RINZLER, D. (1984). Human disconnection and the murder of the earth.*Transactional Analysis Journal,* 14, 231–236.

RYCROFT, C. (1972). *A Critical Dictionary of Psychoanalysis.* Harmondsworth: Penguin. (Originally published 1968.)

SMUTS, J.C. (1987). *Holism and Evolution*. Cape Town, South Africa: N. and S. Press. (Originally published in 1926.)
WATSON L. (1974). *Supernature*. London: Coronet.
ZINKER, J. (1987). *Creative Process in Gestalt Therapy*. New York: Vintage.
ZOHAR, D. (1990). *The Quantum Self*. London: Bloomsbury.

Part III
Systemic Integrative Psychotherapy

Chapter 7 Systemic Integrative Psychotherapy With a Young Bereaved Girl

By Charlotte Sills, Petrūska Clarkson and Roland Evans

Referral and Contract

The family consisted of father and his two daughters, Gwen, age 21, and Ann, age 12. Gwen referred Ann to the agency because, a month after finding her mother dead in bed, Ann was still afraid to be alone upstairs in the house. She was also unable to cry or display any grief.

The therapists took a systems approach to this case which focused primarily on process rather than content. Consequently, they chose not to inquire in detail about the mother's history. They were told that she had had manic and depressive episodes for many years which had been worse since Ann's birth. In the week before her death, the mother had been moderately depressed and in bed with influenza.

Mother committed suicide by placing a plastic shopping bag over her head and fastening it around her neck with a white ribbon tied in a bow. There was no suicide note. The referred daughter, Ann, had returned home from school and found her mother dead in bed. Ann had screamed, and her father, just returned from shopping, had run upstairs and removed the bag while Ann watched. Since that time the girl had been unable to go upstairs alone because she was frightened that she would see her mother. She was also unable to sleep alone, and it was for this reason that her sister, Gwen, had become concerned for her. Gwen (who was 'happily divorced' from her husband, and not working) returned to the family home with her children.

At first individual psychotherapy seemed indicated, but an assessment visit suggested that a family therapy approach would also be appropriate. Although the girl's fear was certainly triggered by the traumatic experience of finding the mother, it seemed to be maintained by

From Sills, C., Clarkson, P. and Evans, R. (1988). Systemic integrative psychotherapy with a young bereaved girl. *Transactional Analysis Journal*, **18**, 102–109, with permission. Also published in French in *Actualités en Analyse Transactionelle*, **18**(2), 102–109.

the family's behaviour, which helped Ann remain incapacitated and kept her in the 'sick' role vacated by her mother. Thus, cohesion and equilibrium in the family were maintained following the catastrophic emotional and structural change brought about by the mother's suicide.

It was the therapists' assessment that family members were not grieving normally. The term 'normal bereavement' is intended to convey the process from initial shock, through the painful internalising of the reality of the loss, to the eventual 'letting go' – with the withdrawal of energy from the dead person so that it can be re-invested in the future. This process involves expressing thoughts and feelings related to the loss (Murray-Parkes, 1975; Worden, 1983). This family's reaction was characterised as 'not normal' because, since the suicide occurred, they had neither talked about the death, nor expressed strong feelings. The therapists thought that the family had elected the younger daughter as the 'identified patient' in order to help them resolve and cope with problems related to the mother's death.

The family said that the assessment visit was the first time they had talked together about the death since it had occurred. They readily and gratefully agreed to six 75-minute sessions, to take place in their home over six weeks with a male and a female therapist. The contracts were designed first to decrease Ann's fears so that she would be able to go upstairs alone and to sleep alone and, secondly, to provide an opportunity for the family to begin grieving.

The therapists decided on the following treatment strategy: sessions 1 and 2 would involve assessing the family system and its reinforcing modes of interaction. Sessions 3 and 4 would be concerned with interventions in the family system and facilitation of the grieving process. Sessions 5 and 6 would aim to facilitate resolution, re-integration of the family, and evaluation of the work done together.

Assessment (Sessions 1 and 2)

During these sessions father and Ann sat very close together on a settee. She either held his arm, or put it around her as she sucked her thumb. The furniture was arranged against two walls in such a way as to separate the settee and its occupants from everyone else. Gwen, the elder daughter, sat far away from the 'couple' and smoked throughout the session. Gwen tended to talk more than father or Ann, but avoided any reference to her own feelings. Her tone of voice was matter-of-fact and precise, yet suggestive of anger. The father was forthcoming and receptive, although reticent about showing emotion in front of his daughters. He seemed very sad. Ann did not participate spontaneously, only answering in monosyllables when questioned. In times of stress she snuggled closer to her father. Both father and elder daughter tended to answer for Ann and tried to protect her from intrusive questions.

Father and Gwen indicated that Ann had always been close to her father. She was a late child, born nine years after her sister. The parents had related fairly well apart from mother's continuing and worsening psychological problems. The elder sister had felt excluded at Ann's birth and had a stormy relationship with father. She had become pregnant at age fifteen and had left home to get married. She resented having to return in order to look after her father and sister. Gwen felt more like a mother to Ann; she was competent and adult in her role in the home.

In relation to the bereavement, none of the family had expressed any strong emotion to each other, other than their initial reactions to the death. At the funeral Ann told her father that she would not cry if he did not; there seemed to be an agreement not to upset each other. Gwen, on the other hand, said that she continually thought about her mother and graphically described how she had seen her 'frozen like a hunk of meat' in the morgue. She also pictured mother decomposing in her grave, and expressed anger and blame towards her father for letting her mother die.

A large funeral and wake consisting of maternal family members had taken place, but no one in the nuclear family told the extended family that the mother had committed suicide. They had all found this secrecy very stressful. In addition, they were expecting an inquest to take place and were concerned about possible publicity.

Many bereavement experts (Bowlby, 1975; Murray-Parkes, 1975; Ramsay, 1977) believe that the danger of a death being denied is considerably increased where the circumstances of the death are difficult. It was clear that this family was denying the death of the mother and avoiding their grief work. In transactional analysis terms, they were discounting the situation on the level of the existence of the problem (Schiff et al., 1975). The denial was supported and maintained by several factors:

1. Gwen's return to the family home to care for Ann filled the 'mother' slot in the family's group imago (Figure 7.1) such that the impact of mother's absence was greatly reduced. Note in both imagoes the symbiotic relationship between Ann and her father, and the peripheral slot occupied first by Gwen and then by her children.
2. The horrific details of the mother's death were vividly imprinted on the minds of Ann and her father. Killing herself as she had must have epitomised the worst of her manic *and* depressive behaviour. Such behaviour on the mother's part had given the situation a sense of everyday unreality. They had become accustomed to this sort of episode, for mother had often acted in an odd or embarrassing man-

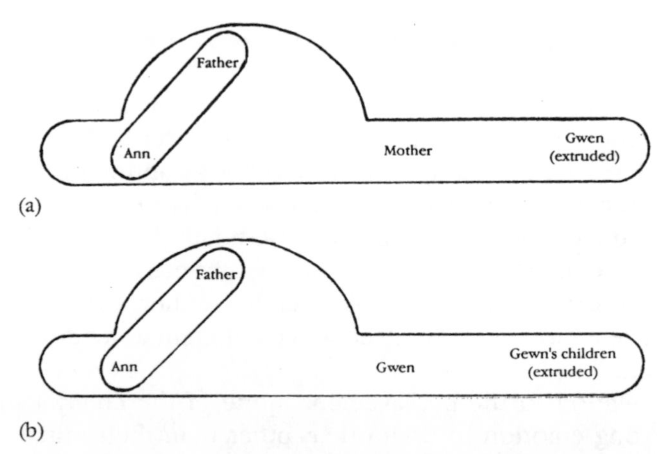

Figure 7.1. Family imagoes (a) before and (b) after the mother's death.

ner. Ann's fear of seeing her mother upstairs suggested a disbelief that mother was actually dead and gone. Gwen had her own horror picture from the morgue. It was imperative that they all shift to dealing with the real loss of a real person.

3. Not only was the 'secret' kept from the extended family and friends, but there was also a striking lack of overt communication in the family. Father and Ann 'spoke' to each other non-verbally by look or touch. Gwen was naturally reticent and was further isolated by her poor relationship with her father. No one was receiving the usual support necessary for a normal bereavement process (Murray-Parkes, 1975).
4. The enmeshed close relationship (Minuchin and Fishman, 1981) between Ann and her father had obviously long pre-dated the mother's suicide. Although Gwen wanted to return to her own home, it seemed likely that Ann's fears would necessitate father and daughter sleeping in the same room, something the therapists were concerned about because of the emotionally incestuous relationship that already existed between Ann and her father. At each session a heart-shaped cushion embroidered with the words 'True Love' sat on the settee between the pair; it seemed to encapsulate the psychological agreement between them.

The therapists formulated their understanding of the family system by adapting an integration of the cathexis material (Schiff et al., 1975) with the racket system (Erskine and Zalcman, 1979). This integration was part of a model first developed in 1985 by Sills and Salters (1991) as a tool for individual analysis and treatment planning. (For a transactional analysis-orientated description of family systems, see Massey, 1985.)

The formulation (Figure 7.2) shows how the family's relationships

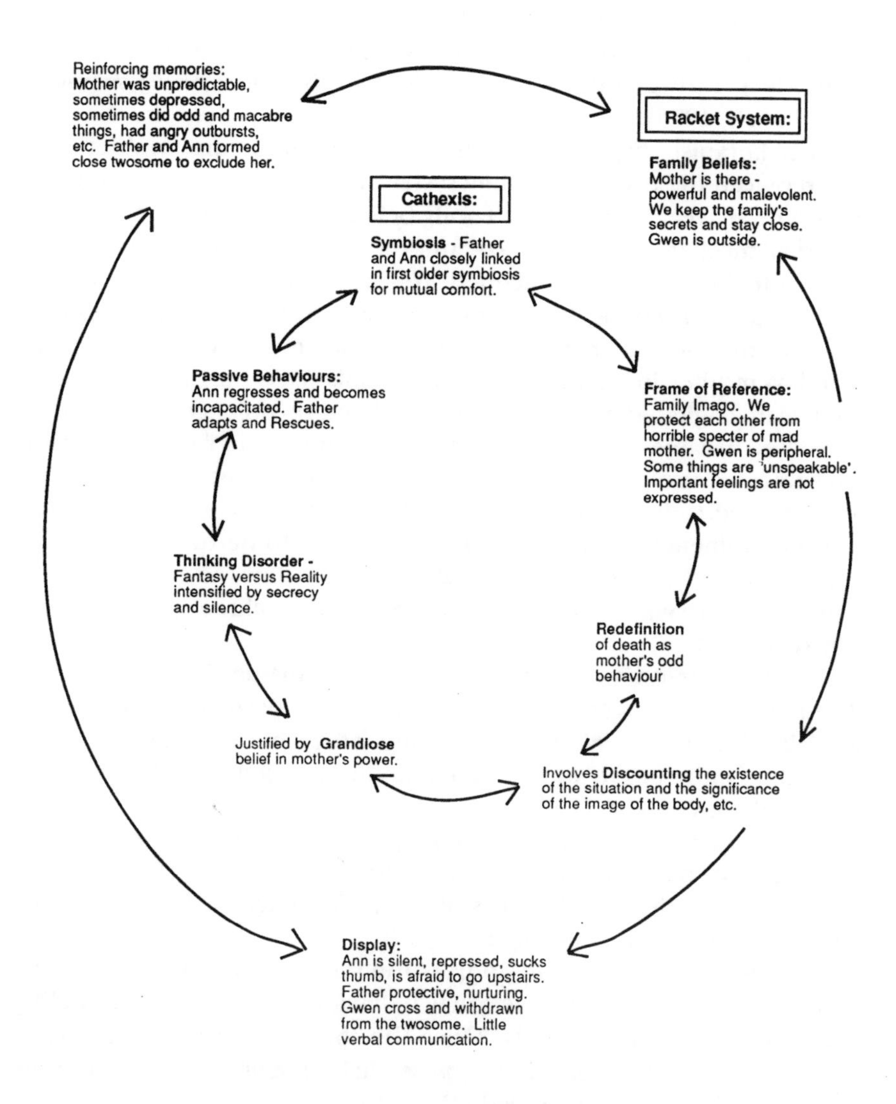

Figure 7.2. Integrative systemic analysis of Ann's family.

after the mother's suicide led to a self-perpetuating denial of the death. The close, exclusive relationship between father and Ann was caused by and also perpetuated the frame of reference which held that there was something fearful against which the family must protect itself, something which had to be excluded. This was the scary, malevolent 'presence' of the mother. She was not really dead (discount) because she had supernatural powers (grandiosity). These beliefs caused incapacitation in Ann (passive behaviours and display) and overnurturing on father's part. Both had fantasies about what mother's ghost might do. Everyone remembered both how scary and unpredictable mother could be and, of course, the day she was found in her bed (reinforcing memories). Father and Ann stayed close in their first-order symbiosis (Schiff et al., 1975).

The therapists hypothesised that this self-reinforcing symbiotic system replaced the pre-death family system which had grown since Gwen left home six years earlier. The family beliefs were that secrecy was vital and that mother, who was crazy, unpredictable, unhappy and critical, needed to be somehow contained. Nothing could be done to change the situation (discount) because mother was too depressed (grandiosity) and Ann and father were so close and loving. Ann and father pandered to mother in a patronising way (display). As they became closer, she became agitated and sometimes escalated to violence or incapacitation; they became even closer and kept further away from her, feeling angry and hopeless about her, but good about each other. They remembered (reinforcing memories) the other times mother was crazy, and they remembered how good it always felt to be together. Mother felt abandoned and remembered all the other times she felt like that. The symbiosis was maintained, mother was excluded, and no one talked about it.

The one person who did talk about the unnaturally close relationship between father and Ann was mother. She used to complain that she felt left out and unloved by Ann and father, but she was not heard. Later the family began to face this painful knowledge and experience profound guilt.

In brief process work it may not be possible or necessary to do a full family script matrix including drivers and injunctions. However, the concept of a script matrix can still be useful where it focuses on the programming component (Figure 7.3).

The therapists decided to address the system as it was visibly manifested in a pattern of interactional behaviour and expressed feeling (Palazzoli, 1975) (Figure 7.4). Once the therapists' understanding of the family system was formulated, possible interventions for each of the constituent factors were devised (Table 7.1).

The main objectives of therapy were:

1. To decrease Ann's fears and change her passive behaviour.
2. To strengthen the generational boundaries between Ann and her father and re-establish Gwen as a daughter and sister (Minuchin, 1978), thus addressing the original symbiosis which threatened to interfere with grieving and also to lead to potential incest problems.
3. To facilitate the bereavement process for family members and to emphasise in particular the first tasks of mourning, that is, to accept the reality of the loss and experience the pain of grief (Worden, 1983).

Table 7.1 Treatment plan – intervention in the family process

Systems constituents maintaining bomoeo-static balance	*Planned interventions*	
1. A. fears being alone / seeing her dead mother	Process	Create parental boundary. Father is invited temporarily to delegate parental role to therapist. Passivity confronted.
	Content	Therapist to use desensitisation with fearful behaviour.
2. Father has to be with A.	Process	Reduce A.'s need for father.
	Content	Facilitate catharsis, promote G.'s role in relation to the family.
3. G. gets left out /excluded	Process	Increase alliance between father and G.
	Content	Facilitate communication between father and G.
4. G. feels angry and jealous	Process	Increase G.'s status in the family.
	Content	Exploration and expression of G.'s feelings.
5. G. picks fight with father	Process	Establish appropriate closeness/ distance between G. and father.
	Content	Negotiation of contract.
6. Father and A. maintain enmeshed relationship	Process	Strengthen parental boundary.
	Content	Physically separate A. and father during sessions.
7. Father and A. communicate without words	Process	Establish appropriate boundary.
	Content	Facilitate explicit communication.
8. Secrets are kept/feelings are not expressed	Process	Establish separation of family members.
	Content	Facilitate expression of members' secrets, feelings and fantasies.
9. Reality is not accepted/ mother is not dead	Process	Confront reality.
	Content	Exercises emphasising that mother is dead

4. To facilitate more open and explicit communication between family members.

Because there were so few sessions available, interventions with multiple functions were chosen.

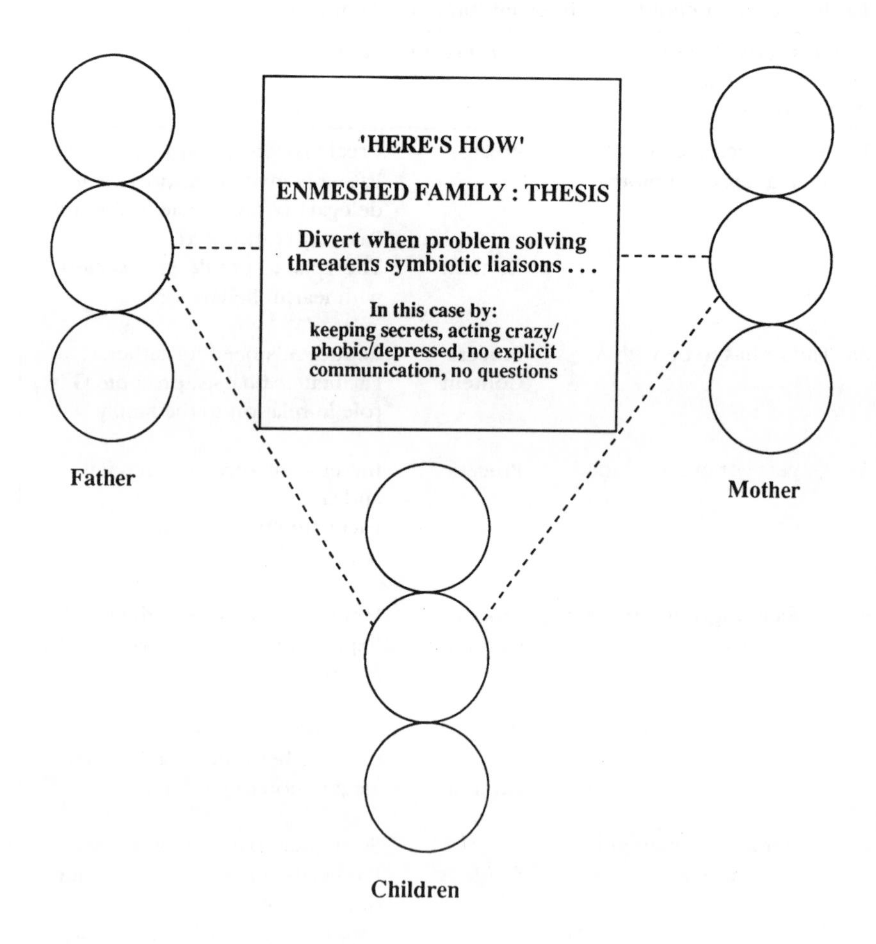

Figure 7.3. Script matrix with family system.

Intervention 1 (Session 3)

A discussion was held in which father and the therapist agreed on the following plan. A contract was made with Ann to use a desensitisation procedure to decrease her fear of seeing her dead mother (Ramsay, 1977). The male therapist accompanied Ann upstairs and into the parents' bedroom where the mother had died. Ann was encouraged to verbalise her fears using a subjective scale of 1–100; she was also taught breathing exercises to cope with anxiety. The male therapist role-played Ann's father removing the plastic bag from the dead mother's head while Ann watched (Ann's fear reached '200' at that point!). The process of expo-

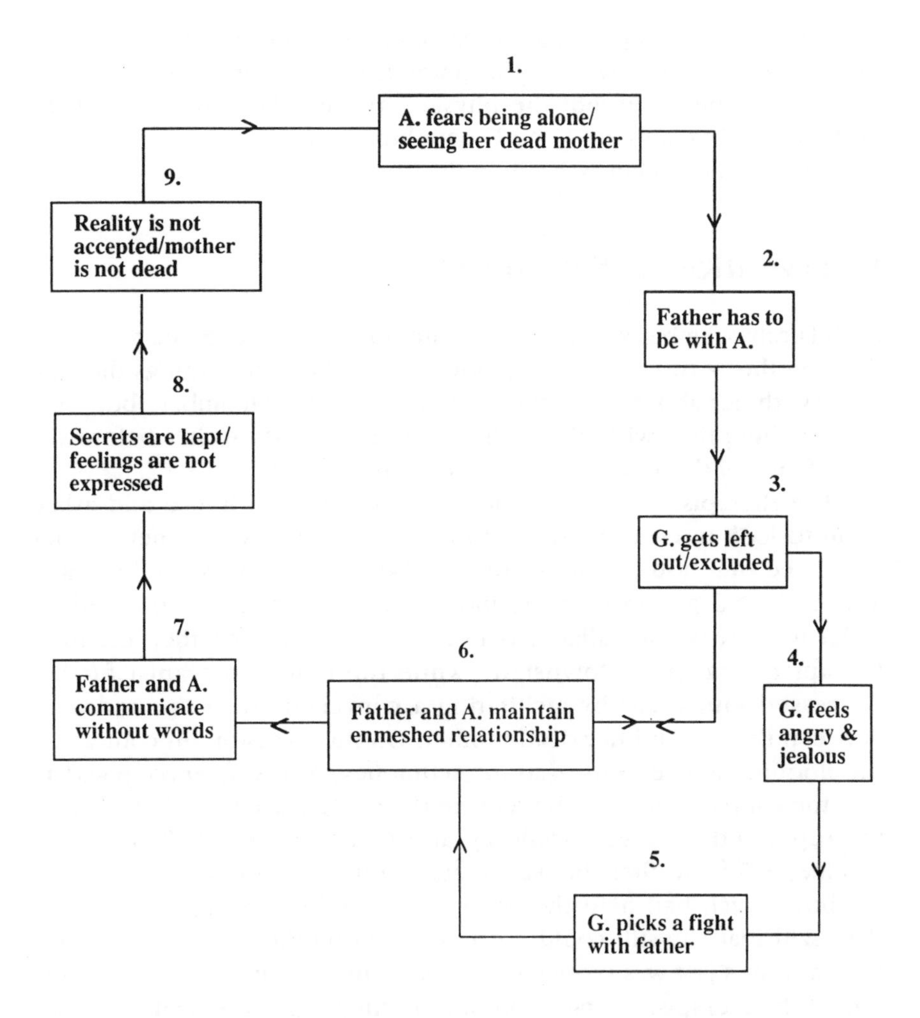

Figure 7.4. Family interaction/feeling patterns.

sure to the feared situation was repeated until the girl's fear had decreased significantly on the subjective scale. Paper and a pencil were then attached to the wall at the top of the stairs and she was told to note her subjective fear rating each time she passed in the days to come.

While this desensitisation process was taking place, the female therapist facilitated a discussion between the father and Gwen about their feelings towards the dead mother and confronted them on their dysfunctional communication. A written contract was agreed which set out what they wanted from each other and were willing to give in return. This included time to be spent together and with Gwen's children, sorting the mother's possessions together, and so on.

This intervention promoted each of the four objectives of the therapeutic sessions. However, in the opinion of the therapists, the family was still unable to accept the physical and psychological loss of the mother. During session 5, both daughters explicitly stated that they knew that their mother was still in the house.

Intervention 2 (Session 5)

Each family member was asked to write down statements related to the dead mother – three things they loved about her, three things they felt angry with her about, three things they wanted to remember about her, and anything they wished they had been able to say to her before she died. Some of these were shared during the session.

The therapists then took the family around the house and asked them to look in every room, cupboard, etc. and to state whether they could see the mother. Afterwards they went to the parents' bedroom and each said goodbye to the mother as if she were on the bed. In order to increase the alliance between Gwen and her father, the male therapist took them downstairs while the female therapist further addressed Ann's fear by facilitating a conversation in the bedroom between the girl and her dead mother. On this occasion, in contrast to the flooding and desensitisation techniques, Ann was encouraged to face the source of her fear by reliving the original scene and expressing the repressed feelings (Goulding and Goulding, 1979; Perls, 1969; Erskine, 1974). At first she was unable to do this. She mimed untying the bow which had held the bag in place and removing the bag. She then said that she still could not talk to her mother because she 'saw' that mother's jaw was crooked and her teeth and tongue were hanging out. At the therapist's suggestion Ann reached out and straightened her mother's face. Then she gazed at 'her mother' and burst into tears. She expressed her feelings of sadness and guilt that her mother had felt so unloved, as well as her own anger at being left alone so traumatically. Then she reversed roles (Perls, 1969), changing positions on the bed, and, as her mother, answered 'I know you loved me'.

Meanwhile father and Gwen were helped by the male therapist to explore how they expressed and communicated anger. This led to a discussion of how the mother had communicated anger and how they had responded to her. Both father and Gwen acknowledged their parts in maintaining the pre-death situation by not providing a more effective supportive environment for the mother.

The sessions were concluded by the therapists modelling the importance of explicit communication by giving positive and negative strokes to each other. The family then expressed the things they had both liked and disliked about their sessions. Throughout the sessions comments were made which were designed to increase both the boundaries between father and Ann and the sisterly links between Gwen and Ann. Some information about bereavement was given, and the therapists, wherever possible, were empathetic toward the family's feelings in order to encourage them to express and share them (Rogers, 1980).

Evaluation and Follow-up

By the end of the therapy it was noted that Ann looked less pale, contributed more to the sessions, and spent little time holding her father or sucking her thumb. The seating of the family changed spontaneously – Ann had rearranged the settee and chairs so that the grouping was more circular and she no longer sat close to her father. Her record of subjective fear showed a significant decrease over a two-week period as revealed in her subjective scores. During the first week there were no scores less than 50 and most were 80 to 100. By the end of the second week there were many scores of 20 and 30 and a number of zeros.

In the final session each member of the family expressed emotions appropriate to the bereavement process (Murray-Parkes, 1975): Ann cried deeply about her dead mother and showed feelings of anger and guilt, father was able to show his deep sadness, and although Gwen was not demonstrative, she acknowledged that she felt angry and guilty about her mother.

Each family member was able to communicate an evaluation of the sessions in a clear, honest and straightforward manner that was quite unexpected. They expressed gratitude and said that they knew that the whole family had been helped to change, not only Ann.

Follow up was conducted after two months by a conversation with their father. He said that Gwen had left the house to return to her own home, was functioning well, and visited them about twice weekly. Gwen and her father were getting on well, and the daughters had recently arranged a surprise party for their father.

Ann was sleeping alone in her own room and no longer asked to be accompanied up the stairs; she displayed an appropriate sense of boundaries by feeling discomfort at entering the parental bedroom. She had periods of sadness, but these did not interfere with her life. The father again expressed satisfaction with the outcome of the family sessions and felt that they had helped greatly to clear up Ann's problem.

Follow up after six months consisted of two conversations with Gwen, who said that things were continuing well. Ann was talking with friends about her mother, and they were being supportive. Gwen herself asked for details about a local single parents group.

Comment

A striking element in the success of this therapy was the importance of the therapists' ulterior messages involving the three Ps (Permission, Protection and Potency) (Crossman, 1966; Berne, 1972). Many of the interventions relied on the potency of the therapists. Traditionally, the therapist must be felt by the client to be more powerful than the Parent (Berne, 1961); in this case the therapists had to be powerful enough to promote the parental role of the father as well as to facilitate the 'exorcism' of the mother's traumatic and horrible death. The reality testing of checking for the mother in all the cupboards (the family said there was one that had not been opened since her death) was like a confrontation of her crazy, hostile power. The therapists had to lead the way in saying to the mother, 'You are no longer here. You are dead', in order for the family to believe this and start to grieve. Potency and protection were also essential for Ann to feel able to adjust her dead mother's horribly contorted face in her memory, and reduce her to ordinary proportions. Permission was offered – to talk about what the mother had done, to criticise her for it, to feel about it – to grieve. Protection was offered implicitly in the calm approach of the therapists, and explicitly in that the therapists were available to the family by telephone.

In this short-term psychotherapy, integrative principles were applied in the context of family systems theory. Using transactional analysis concepts, the therapists made a process formulation. They then designed interventions at the content level using techniques drawn from various theoretical models, including gestalt, bereavement therapy, and behavioural techniques. The therapists' aim was to unlock a stuck family system in order to allow the unfolding of the normal grieving process in this unhappy young girl.

References

BERNE, E. (1961). *Transactional Analysis in Psychotherapy.* New York: Grove Press.

BERNE, E. (1972). *What Do You Say After You Say Hello?* New York: Grove Press.

BOWLBY, J. (1975). *Attachment and Loss.* London: Pelican.

CROSSMAN, P. (1966). Permission and protection. *Transactional Analysis Bulletin,* **5** (19), 152–154.

ERSKINE, R. and ZALCMAN, M. (1979). The racket system. *Transactional Analysis Journal,* **9** (1), 51–59.

ERSKINE, R. (1974). Therapeutic intervention: disconnecting rubberbands. *Transactional Analysis Journal,* **4** (1), 7–8.

GOULDING, M.M. and GOULDING, R.L. (1979). *Changing Lives Through Redecision Therapy.* New York: Brunner/Mazel.

MASSEY, R.F. (1985). TA as a family systems therapy. *Transactional Analysis Journal,* **15** (2), 120–141.

MINUCHIN, S. and FISHMAN, H. (1981). *Family Therapy Techniques.* Cambridge, MA: Harvard University Press.

MURRAY-PARKES, J. (1975). *Bereavement: Studies of Grief in Adult Life.* London: Tavistock.

PALAZZOLI, M.S. (1975). *Paradox and Counter-Paradox.* Milan: Faltrinelli Editore.

PERLS, F.S. (1969). *Gestalt Therapy Verbatim.* Moab, UT: Real People Press.

RAMSAY, R.W. (1977). Behavioural approaches to bereavement. *Behavioural Research and Therapy,* **15**, 131–135.

ROGERS, C.R. (1980). *A Way of Being.* Boston: Houghton Mifflin.

SCHIFF, J.L. with SCHIFF, A.W., MELLOR, K., SCHIFF, E., SCHIFF, S., RICHMAN, D., FISHMAN, J., WOLZ, L., FISHMAN, C. and MOMB, D. (1975). *The Cathexis Reader: The Transactional Analysis Treatment of Psychosis.* New York: Harper and Row.

SILLS, C. and SALTERS, D. (1991). The comparative script system. *Institute of Transactional Analysis News,* **31**, 11–15

WORDEN, J.W. (1983). *Grief Counselling and Grief Therapy.* London: Tavistock.

Chapter 8
Systemic Integrative Psychotherapy

by Petrūska Clarkson and Phil Lapworth)
(Incorporating the Seven-level Model by Petrūska Clarkson)

Introduction

Systemic integrative psychotherapy deserves to be contextualised against the general philosophical and scientific background of the late twentieth century. It is against such a backdrop that the psychoanalytic, behavioural and humanistic/existential views of the nature of the person can be integrated by taking an inclusive perspective. This integrative psychotherapy approach, developed at metanoia Psychotherapy Training Institute, is facilitated by the recognition of *Physis*. Physis, first named by the ancient Greeks, is conceived of as a generalised creative force of evolution, both in human nature and psychotherapeutic endeavour. It is in this sense that systemic integrative psychotherapy has been developed at the Institute and remains in a constant process of creative evolution.

In this chapter the influence of contemporary currents in psychotherapy and psychotherapy research of discovering commonality, communication and integrative principles is briefly considered. Another major integrative principle addressed is that of the research evidence that effective psychotherapy is more a factor of the relationship between the client and the therapist than the particular theory espoused. Amongst other systems principles, the notions of wholeness, homeostasis and evolution in particular lead to a primary focus on the *relationship* as the most important vehicle of therapeutic change from an integrative perspective. I see the emphasis on the centrality of relationship as a major practical application of systems theory in psychotherapy. A systems approach is thus offered at one level as a metatheoretical perspective on psychotherapy (individual or family). At another level the systemic interplay between homoeostatic and

From Clarkson, P. and Lapworth, P. (1992). Systemic integrative psychotherapy. In: Dryden, W. (Ed.), *Integrative and Elective Therapy: A Handbook*, pp. 41–83. Buckingham: Open University Press, with permission.

evolutionary (developmental) mechanisms is also seen to apply to the psychological theory itself.

Five kinds of client/therapist relationship are identified which are hypothesised to be potentially present in any psychotherapy. This forms a primary framework for psychotherapeutic integration which incorporates several major different theories of therapeutic change. Four domains of variation (client, psychotherapist, time and environment) are discussed separately, but they are conceived of as mutually interacting, dynamically evolving systems. The larger systems of time and environment are conceived of as the containing matrix for the interplay of all the other systems.

I describe a seven-level integrative perspective as a holistic view of the person. This model is also useful as a classificatory and integrative conceptual tool for separating out different layers of knowledge (epistemological areas or universes of discourse) in psychology and psychotherapy. It acts both as a categorisation for different approaches as well as a tool for integration which depends not on the model itself but on the skilfulness of the integrator using it. This approach has also been found useful for psychotherapy integration at the concrete operations level or specific interventions level, providing a sorting tool for the multitude of interventions and strategies available to the integrating psychotherapist. I believe that psychotherapy integration is the task of each thinking and developing psychotherapist using singular or integrative theories, perspectives and tools gleaned from other workers, but essentially it concerns developing one's own individual integration with each unique therapeutic encounter. In this spirit, my colleague Phil Lapworth has contributed a case study which, although necessarily much abbreviated, reflects his own particular psychotherapeutic integration in practice.

The Background of the Times

The integration of psychotherapies is a growing movement throughout the world. For example, more psychologists now identify themselves as integrative than any other orientation in the USA, and in Britain and the rest of Europe, interest is also growing apace. This *Zeitgeist* reflects an increasing openness to communication, cross fertilisation and divergent creativity. Simultaneously, it reflects decreasing allegiance to orthodoxy, unilateral perspectives and certainty regarding 'the truth' of any one particular approach to human behaviour. Some of the background factors which influence this concern are the increasing levels of complexity of information in the human sciences from biology to economics to chaos theory (Gleick, 1988). There is a concomitant explosion in the very paradigms of thought such as are being discovered, articulated and indeed integrated in modern physics (Kuhn, 1970; Capra, 1982; Zohar, 1990).

At a collective global level, increasing openness to integration is reflected in some of the changes happening in different parts of the world. From Russia to Berlin to South Africa, apparently irreconcilable polarities are beginning to break down and the struggles between mutually exclusive positions on right and wrong are being superseded by the hard work of finding common ground, negotiation, compromise and possible mutual enhancement – or war. Alongside such developments comes also the chaos of cultural transitions and paradigm shifts in philosophy, science and psychology. Currently there is widespread questioning about basic frames of reference in the philosophical, biological and physical sciences, as well as in the arts. The notion of one 'truth' or a single solution to complex problems is being challenged in all the above fields. This appears to have led to a growing tolerance for multiple perspectives, often apparently paradoxical, for conceptualising the same problem. People may be discovering many different but equally viable ways of dealing with issues relating to differing universes of discourse.

Intellectual relativism and open-minded curiosity appear to be collective phenomena of late twentieth-century psychological and historical developments. This climate has been described as post-modern. It is in this cultural idiom that the pluralistic tolerance of different perspectives in integrative psychotherapy can most fruitfully grow. Lyotard (1984) defines the post-modern as suspicion or incredulity of meta-narratives – 'the grand narratives of the past' (traditional 'ultimate truths'). Postmodernism in art, architecture and literature embraces a heterogeneity that is opposed to consensus on the one hand and fascism on the other. It favours, rather, the coexistence of many different 'language games' (Wittgenstein, 1953). Its principle is the inventor's 'parology' – the invention of new knowledge. This is also the task of every individual integrative psychotherapist.

The problems facing the world on a macroscopic level, as well as psychotherapy on a microscopic level, have become too complex for many psychotherapists to continue to have unbridled faith in singular solutions or to insist on imposing such singular solutions on their trainees and colleagues. Economic pressure demands accountability from health services, insurance companies and psychotherapy providers. There is also accumulating research evidence that no one particular psychotherapy can be shown to be significantly more effective than another (Luborsky et al., 1975; Sloane et al., 1975; Bergin 1978). The fact that the investment of time, money and availability can vary considerably across psychotherapeutic approaches causes serious economic, theoretical and ethical concern (Norcross, 1986).

Theory

Common and integrative factors in psychotherapy

One of the primary reasons for the growth of interest and academic and clinical investment in integrative psychotherapy is the multiplication of so-called 'schools' of psychotherapy, with estimates ranging between 250 (Corsini, 1984) and 400. Yet since the Fiedler (1950) studies, no one approach to psychotherapy has been proved significantly better than another. (Fiedler found greater resemblances between senior practitioners of different schools than between trainees and such expert practitioners within the same school.) Rowan (1990) details the way different schools developed over time and also suggests that we are now in a period of integration rather than differentiation. Garfield (1980, 1982) is arguably the leading exponent of the view that certain therapeutic factors are common to most psychotherapeutic approaches. The factors he has identified as common across schools of psychotherapy are: the therapist/client relationship; interpretation, insight and understanding; catharsis; emotional expression and release; reinforcement in psychotherapy; desensitisation; relaxation; information in psychotherapy; reassurance and support; modelling; confronting one's problems; clarifying and modifying client expectancies, and providing both a credible therapeutic framework for the client's problems and a credible rationale for the psychotherapy.

Marmor (1982) identified the following seven elements that produce change in analytic treatment:

> (1) A basic matrix of a good patient–therapist relationship resting on both real and fantasied qualities that each brings to their work together.... (2) Release of emotional tension.... (3) Cognitive learning or the acquisition of insight.... (4) Operant conditioning, by means of subtle and often nonverbal cues of approval or disapproval, as well as by corrective emotional experiences in the relationship with the analyst. (5) Suggestion and persuasion, usually implicit, occasionally explicit. (6) Unconscious identification with the analyst, both conceptually and behaviorally. (7) Repeated reality testing and "working through".
>
> (p. 66)

The existentialist psychotherapist Yalom (1975) described 12 'curative' factors in effective group psychotherapy which overlap significantly with factors identified by Corsini and Rosenberg (1955). Different psychotherapies are thus seen by an increasing number of workers as deriving their potency from common factors.

Eysenck's (1952) challenge to prove the efficacy of psychotherapy has by no means been satisfactorily resolved, as has been shown in recent surveys of research literature in the field (Lambert, 1986). Few of us claim to be over-optimistic about the likelihood that future research will ever give us a reliable and valid statistical proof of permanent psychological change on all possible parameters acceptable to all psychotherapists. This will be particularly true if qualitative research methods are not encouraged.

> Research on psychotherapy outcome suggests that patients with a variety of problems are helped by many methods that may not have been put to the empirical test. The results of psychotherapy outcome research by no means suggest, however, that every participant gains from treatment to a clinically meaningful extent. The results are also compatible with the suggestion some clients may deteriorate during therapy.
>
> (Lambert et al., 1977)

Thus the question is by no means resolved. Furthermore, substantial numbers of psychotherapists, and many psychoanalysts, hold the view that the measuring instruments so far available to psychological researchers do not fit the complexity and subtlety of the effects thought to be achieved in psychotherapy. The more cognitive behaviour therapies, as represented in Lambert (1986), take the problem extremely seriously and many do diligent research. Humanistic-existential approaches have varied from participation in research statistically indicating high effectiveness (Bergin and Garfield, 1978) to the rejection of previous scientific paradigms and the positing of post-Newtonian scientific paradigms (Hawking, 1988; Merleau-Ponty, 1962; Rogers, 1986).

Thus what is at question is not only the reliability, the validity, consistency and coherence of the psychotherapies themselves, but also the attempts to subject these to scientific methods about which practitioners are still extremely divided. Thus, despite the apparent fact that psychotherapeutic approaches which take wide-angle perspectives on human beings could be investigated by researchers, the question still remains whether indeed an effective post-Newtonian paradigm can be or has been developed in psychology (Reason and Rowan, 1981).

Whatever its fruits, psychotherapy generally has taken almost 90 years to reach its present stage of accountability. This applies equally to the three established streams or lineages of theoreticians/clinicians originating from Freud, Moreno and Pavlov respectively. In some sense each one of these ideological 'grandfathers' can be seen as the primary three differentiated integrationists of their own time. However, the emergence of integrative psychotherapies as academic and clinical entities in their own right is comparatively recent, and already there are a large number of different forms of eclectic or integrative psychotherapy (Dryden, 1984). The first official association for integrative psychotherapy, SEPI (the Society for the Exploration of Psychotherapy Integration) was formed as recently as 1983, with the British Institute for Integrative Psychotherapy (BIIP), which is affiliated to International SEPI, being formed in 1987.

Psychotherapy integration therefore also needs to be placed in this historical context. In fairness it deserves to be given an equivalent number of decades as its historically older psychotherapeutic rivals, before the movement and its theories are judged as either unproven or unprovable. The value of theory is also by no means undisputed, even within ideological strongholds. From the Tavistock, Symington comments: 'The theories within psychoanalytic discourse have as much relation to psychoanalysis as a manual of sexual techniques have to being in love' (1986, p. 9). Utopian wishes for one finalised, true integrative psychotherapy with consistency, coherence, scientific rigour, conceptual clarity, practical value and aesthetic appeal, will probably have to wait a while to be satisfied. At least it may have to be postponed until any one approach to psychotherapy does reach such idealised criteria. In the meantime, workers for integration within or between schools are developing communicative bridges and developing frameworks which may perhaps come closer to excellence than any one close-minded paradigm affiliation (Dryden and Norcross, 1990). According to Smail:

> Because our experience of ourselves, other people, and of society...is infinitely more complicated...we cannot expect to quickly find a common language with which we can measure them. This demands a tolerance of different perspectives, a good will towards the experience of others, a patient groping after shared understandings, which will require a very different spirit from that in which psychological inquiry has largely been carried out in recent decades.
>
> (1978, p. 73)

The integration of psychotherapies, however, is not new. An analysis of any particular psychotherapy will invariably unearth some borrowed form, theory, concept or technique from another psychotherapy or related discipline. Freud, for example, originally integrated Breuer's technique of discussing emotional problems of patients under hypnosis, to bring about catharsis within his developing psychoanalytic theory. Even within the humanistic psychotherapies, which independently evolved in the tradition of the psychodramatic work of Moreno, substantial integration (with or without acknowledgement) can be found. To take another example, the notion of 'self-realisation' is anticipated in Aristotle (Lovejoy and Boas, 1973, p. 450). Integration is thus a process, a development, an evolution itself:

> In spite of many deviations and retrogressions the record is one of cumulative observation, with gradual *evolution of concepts* and clarification of thinking over more than 4,000 years. Traces of the evolutionary process survive in current psychiatric terminology, and the evolution has been in part a reflection of advances in knowledge.
>
> (Brill, 1967, p. 583; author's italics)

Views of the Person

The development of psychotherapies in the 20th century can be conceptualised in terms of the three major streams of thought that originated around the beginning of this century:

1. Those emanating from Freud which lead to the *psychoanalytic tradition* and its developments.
2. The *behaviourist tradition*, which can be traced back to the work of Pavlov (1928).
3. The *existential/humanistic tradition* which can be seen to emanate from the spirit and practice of Moreno, the psychodramatist and pioneering group psychotherapist (Greenberg, 1975).

A necessarily abbreviated summary here suggests that the psychoanalytic tradition emphasises the unconscious (Bowlby, 1980, 1985; Greenberg and Safran, 1987), drive theory (particularly Thanatos and Eros), transference and the repetition compulsion, ego psychology, object relations and, more recently, self-theory.

The behaviourist tradition emphasises the principles of learning reflexes and operant conditioning, models of reinforcement and scientific accountability, modelling, links between cognition and behaviour, and between emotion and cognition, as well as cognitive structures, schemas and scripts.

The humanistic/existential tradition can be characterised by a focus on existence, choice, autonomy, responsibility, anxiety, death, despair, freedom, values, potential for change, self-actualisation, social involvement and future orientation.

Maslow (1968) attached the term 'third force' to this latter grouping (p. iii). It can also be associated with a third force or drive in human behaviour – *Physis*. This has been defined as a generalised, creative 'force of Nature, which eternally strives to make things grow and to make growing things more perfect' (Berne, 1969, p. 89). The pre-Socratics conceived of Physis as the healing factor in illness, the energetic motive for *evolution* and *creativity* in the individual and collective psyche (Guerriere, 1980). Physis antedates Eros and Thanatos. It is conceived as more biological as it represents the evolutionary impulse inherent in every cell. It is also viewed as more spiritual as it implies that it is in the nature of the person and the planet to evolve creatively. Evolution is, of course, a *systemic* concept. This will be further discussed later in this chapter.

The three primary parent views of human beings (with the attendant value orientations and theories of each) are often seen as in contradiction or opposition to each other. The more the angle of the lens viewing human behaviour is narrowed, the more persuasive such differences can become. Alternatively, if one looks at them through a wide-angle philosophical lens, these three philosophical traditions could be seen as mutually complementary and enriching. A view of the person then emerges which arguably includes the person as a *learner* (behaviourism), the person as *reactor* (psychoanalysis), and the person as *creator* (humanistic/existential position). This is an integrative position based on inclusion, not exclusion. In practice this means that no one approach is believed to contain an exclusive claim to the 'truth' but that, between these different views, a more complete and fully-rounded appreciation of the human being can be construed.

Integration can then be conceived of as open and creative communication between these apparently conflicting and contradictory explanations of human beings (and how they think, feel, behave, grow and develop), and the coherently selective inclusion of useful and workable aspects of each (rather than the indiscriminate and total exclusion of one camp by another). Theories are understood as stories or metaphors used to make sense of ourselves, others and the world, not representing facts or truth in and of themselves (see the theoretical level of the seven-level model to be discussed later in this chapter).

Thus, though each of the above may have a story of human beings that differentiates one from the other, there are various themes or sub-plots that (as in all good stories) recur within each. There are naturally some common principles such as the recognition of human problems and life as process and development. Further, sometimes even the apparent oppositions can often be shown to be due to category confusion, not genuine contradiction (Ryle, 1973). Perhaps psychotherapy integration, even where apparent conflicts exist, becomes increasingly possible as we take some of the understandings from modern physics into a post-Newtonian psychology. Creativity (which is most needed in the work of healing) often emerges when apparently contradictory positions can be tolerated (Rothenberg, 1979). After all, even elementary particles 'seem to be waves on Mondays, Wednesdays and Fridays, and particles on Tuesdays, Thursdays and Saturdays' (Sir William Bragg quoted in Koestler, 1972, p. 52). Psychotherapists can perhaps grow scientifically minded enough to tolerate or even welcome similar conditions in our field.

The figure/ground concept of gestalt (Figure 8.1) can also be used to enable a mutually complementary perspective. This visual analogy makes it possible to see that two theories may be seen as incompatible in the sense of the assimilation, or merging, of one into the other. Although this may be the case from one point of view, it may be appear quite different from another point of view. It may also be necessary, more creative and useful, to focus alternately from one to the other of two, apparently mutually exclusive, perspectives. As in the gestalt figure/ground image where either two faces are seen or, alternately, a vase is seen, *both* may be needed if either are to be seen. In other words,

Figure 8.1. Gestalt psychology image of figure and ground (originally from ***Visuell wahrgenommene Figuren***, by Edgar Rubin. Köbenhaven: Gyldendalske Boghandel, 1921).

their meaning is revealed in the relationship. What may be seen, for example, from the object-relations perspective, as the depressive position incorporated into a person's later sense of guilt, may gain a useful counterbalancing view from a systems theory perspective of the need for a conscience within the social system. Neither need necessarily be exclusively true. One or the other may shed some light on the patient's pain. Both views may be true from alternating perspectives. Some integration may be reached if seen as part of a mutually reinforcing system – the person experiencing guilt as a result of intra-psychic processes may be encouraged to continue in this role for the sake of the larger system.

It is anticipated that in the turbulent and troubled psychological waters of the end of this century, communication may become more important than certainty, effectiveness more important than elegance for its own sake and intellectual and moral questioning of basic assumptions more important than adherence to a single *via integrata* (one true way of integration). The suggestion here is that we become more systemic, and metaphorically pull back the telescope that is solely directed at the behavioural planet (for example) and allow a wider-angle lens to include the other planets, the humanistic and the psychoanalytic in order to explore how they relate as a galaxy or *system* as a whole. This inclusivity necessitates a responsibility that is no longer to do with what is right or what is wrong, what is the truth and what is not the truth, but a responsibility to be able to explain why, when and how we select the theoretical constructs or the operational procedures that we do. Psychotherapy, like astronomy, is also a science. Therefore, as such, it needs to be teachable to others. Its practitioners need to be able to explain their thinking and their interventions in terms of what is important for a particular client at a particular moment, in particular circumstances, with a particular psychotherapist.

However, here is another application for the figure/ground gestalt. The vase of psychotherapy may be a science, but the faces of psychotherapy constitute an art. The psychotherapist responds at an intuitive level to the client and intervenes with perceptions and understandings which are seemingly mystical at times in their creativity and spontaneity, each forged anew in the existential moment of encounter between an 'I' and a 'You'. The changing figure/foreground perspective is thus also an image for the interplay between science and art, system and psyche, technology and intuition.

The possibility (philosophically as well as pragmatically) that there may be *three* drives, Eros, Thanatos and Physis, fuelling human lives and behaviourally interacting with the pervasive effect of conditioning, evolving and learning in relational systems may seem a simple enough proposition. However, it may take another 100 years to work it out. Of course much precision may be lost in taking a wide-angle view on the human condition. This macroscopic view needs to be complemented with attention to specific and smaller details. Naturally, what the microscope improves in terms of precision and minute observation, it loses in large-scale perspective. Different instruments (telescopes or microscopes) are also, of course, suitable for different purposes. Obviously, for reasons of space, the discussion here has to be indicative rather than exhaustive, invoking the reader's existing knowledge, imaginative powers and collegial cooperation.

Systemic Integrative Psychotherapy

Systemic integrative psychotherapy is currently defined as a personal, conceptual and experiential integration of values, theories, strategies and specific interventions within a psychotherapeutic relationship that is based on a systems perspective. It begins specifically with systems theory which describes natural systems (von Bertalanffy, 1969, for example) in terms of relationships, as well as the systemic context of psychotherapy as a process of *evolution over time*. A systemic approach is considered applicable to group, family or organisational contexts, but naturally also to individuals.

The *Shorter Oxford Dictionary* defines a system as 'a whole composed of parts in orderly arrangement according to some scheme or plan. A set or assemblage of things connected, associated, or interdependent, so as to form a complex unity' (Onions, 1973, p. 2227). On physical as well as psychological levels, living systems are made up of parts which themselves again constitute systems on a smaller scale (sub-systems). These are inevitably related to other systems in even larger organisations (supra-systems) which are hierarchically related. 'Thus the functional units on every level of the hierarchy are double-faced as it were; they act as whole when facing downwards, as parts when facing upwards' (Koestler, 1989, p. 287).

Beutler (1986) also suggested that 'Systems theory is another general theory that might possibly serve as a vehicle for communication and as an umbrella under which all therapeutic approaches could be described' (p. 97). It is a particularly useful approach to human behaviour and therapeutic change because:

1. As originally formulated by von Bertalanffy (1969) it does not necessarily imply adherence to any one particular philosphically based view of human beings.
2. It is an approach that focuses on wholes as wholes that are more than the sum of the component parts. This is different from the kind of holism that is sometimes the result of adding different levels of analysis, as in many theories that are confined to psychology alone.
3. It particularly facilitates clarity and efficiency in making decisions as to which strategies, and particularly which interventions, are likely to have the largest effect in the shortest period of time on the whole person.

Within the limited space available here, I can but suggest that systems principles can act as practice guidelines for understanding, choosing, sequencing and implementing minimal interventions for maximum effect, also in individual or group psychotherapy. Much explanation, qualification and interpretation of context and process have to be assumed here for the sake of brevity, and only some elements crucial to this discussion are highlighted. Despite great contributions, particularly in family therapy and organisational work, the rich literature in systems theory is yet to be mined to its fullest effect by current and future generations of clinicians in individual and group psychotherapy.

Systems theory is conceptualised by Cottone (1988) as metatheoretic to psychological theory. Depending on the level, it implies that even the way we view and interact with 'psychological evidence', ideological convictions or 'scientific knowledge' cannot be seen outside the ***relationship*** with our social linguistic, philosophical or personally pathological contexts. The observer can no longer be considered separately from the observed. A systemic integration as a finally achieved integration would be nonsense as the systemic approach mandates an ongoing dialogic relationship with any model, ***particularly*** itself (Maturana, 1980).

On a philosophical and theoretical plane, the systemic integrative approach considers that the integration of psychotherapies should therefore be a continually expanding and developing process whereby various theories, concepts and techniques are systematically employed within a clear framework to enhance the work between a particular psychotherapist and his or her client. Although it may be out of awareness, in a sense any psychotherapist (of singular, pluralistic or integrative persuasion) can be seen to be working within a systemic approach.

Whether or not it is conceptualised as such, psychotherapy is the work of facilitating and intervening as complex living systems.

Although systems are self-regulating, and thus involve homeostatic mechanisms, workers in the field from Hoffman (1981) to Teilhard de Chardin (1970) have also emphasised systemic *development*. From Goldstein (1939) to Fivaz (1980) there has been evidence that healthy living systems tend to re-organise at increasing levels of complexity and actualisation. Maruyama (1968) also studied systems and the evolution of systems in nature and society. Such evolution can be seen to be under the aegis of Physis in its guise as the evolutionary drive of Nature present in all living systems. 'The capacity of a system to evolve depends on an ability to move to more complex forms of differentiation and integration, greater variety in the system facilitating its ability to deal with challenges and opportunities posed by the environment' (Morgan, 1986, p. 47).

These principles may also be applicable to the evolution of psychology and psychotherapy as open systems which both seek to maintain homeostasis as well as facilitate their own evolution. (Such evolution may involve growth, decay or discontinuous second-order changes.) The originating developments of Freud, Pavlov and Moreno have evolved into the current rich diversity of approaches to psychotherapy. An emphasis on difference and disagreement even within 'schools' has often provided the spur to creative developments and the dissolution of outdated conceptual structures (Samuels, 1985). Conversely, an emphasis on difference may be restrictive, as Mahrer, an experiential psychotherapist wrote, 'It is always possible to emphasize *differences* in the larger theory of human beings, and these differences may be preserved and built up to prevent any real efforts at integration' (1989, pp. 66–7).

This is not only true between different approaches to psychotherapy, but also within a particular approach. For example, Rothstein, after comparing the expositions of six psychoanalytic theories (the approaches of Freud, Klein, Bion, Sullivan, Self, Object-relations and Lacan) commented as follows:

> Analysts employ theories to create the illusion that they have an answer, or the answer, in the therapeutic encounter, an encounter that is intrinsically filled with uncertainty. Theories provide models, or puzzle solutions, terms and procedures, all of which, if properly employed, enhance an analyst's self-esteem. In addition, theories are associated with traditions and institutions which further enhance the analyst's self-esteem as he works within them and provide both illusions of security and tangible benefits such as referrals. This institutionalisation of theory has contributed to an emphasis upon an exaggeration of differences and has interfered with more optimal communication between proponents of different points of view.
>
> (1985, pp. 129–130)

(This state of affairs is, of course, not unique to psychoanalysis, but may also apply to other psychotherapies.) The psychoanalyst Sandler's encouragement at one of the Workshops for Mental Health Professionals, recorded by Rothstein (1985), was to 'try to listen to what other people are saying'(p. 147). This has been echoed in Britain by Hinshelwood's comment on 'the hopeful atmosphere of integration in psychotherapy' (1989, p. 473). Pilgrim (1989) has also recommended that clinical psychologists in Britain embrace their own profession's rhetoric of 'successful eclecticism'. He is, of course, *not* referring to what Dryden has called 'haphazard eclecticism' (1984, p. 351). Lazarus disparagingly caricatured such eclectics with the phrase 'I use whatever makes sense to me and whatever I feel comfortable with' (1981, pp. 4–5).

Which particular theories, concepts or techniques a particular experienced psychotherapist chooses to integrate can only be done on an individual and personal basis. Only then can there be a true integration for that person, in relationship with his or her own approach to psychotherapy. People and their problems should come before theories or techniques. The latter surely exist to serve the former. Any humane and effective approach to psychotherapy – from psychoanalysis to gestalt – will hopefully honour this position. Systemic integrative psychotherapy is a process of considered integration rather than *ad hoc* or eclectic (in the worst sense) practice on the one hand, or rigid prescriptionism on the other. It takes place within a systemic and holistic framework. It has to be forged anew from the knowledge and experience of each individual clinician. The exposition here is not an attempt to 'provide' a final true integration. It is an attempt to provide a framework which may be helpful to experienced individual practitioners as they consciously and conscientiously *create* (rather than reproduce) a personally coherent system of applied integrative psychotherapy (whether it draws primarily from one theory base or twenty).

Four Domains of Variation

Any approach to psychotherapy has to account for at least four major domains of variation or difference. These are client variation, psychotherapist variation, variation over time and the variation in environment (Dryden, 1986). Figure 8.2 below schematically represents these domains of variation and their interaction (the overlap) by illustrating the relationship between client and therapist in the systemic context of time and space (environment).

The fact that the client and psychotherapist areas are shown as both separate and overlapping is intended to facilitate conceptual and practical differentiation between the personal *internal world* of each individual and their *interpersonal* world and acknowledge the importance

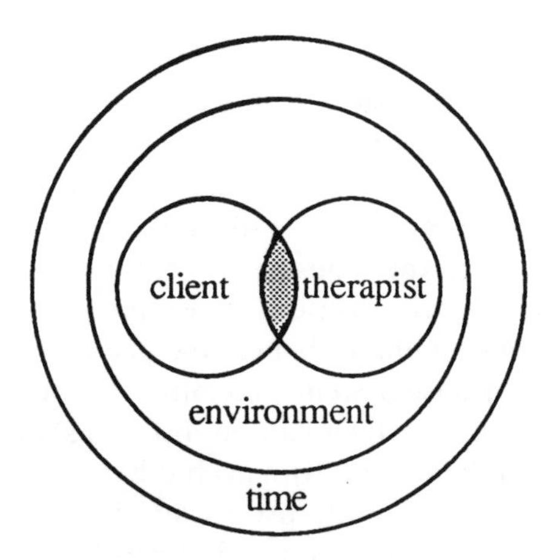

Figure 8.2. Domains of variation in psychotherapy.

and mutual interaction of *both*. The intra-psychic or internal world, of course, comprises fantasy, internal objects, representational systems and so on while the interpersonal world consists, for example, of communication, verbal and non-verbal transactions between people. Stern's (1985) account of an integrative perspective in terms of child development which accounts for both the internal and the interpersonal worlds of the human infant is here generalised to be used for psychotherapy integration, practice, training and supervision.

It is also central to a *systems approach* to understand that:

> Epistemologically, the things we see (people, objects etc.) exist only in relationship, and when analysed microscopically, they too, are best viewed as relationships. It is no secret in physics (Capra, 1975, 1982) that the closer we analyse some 'thing' the less it appears as a thing and the more it appears as a dynamic process (things in relationships). Consequently, relationships become a primary source of our knowledge of the world. This can be taken to the ontological extreme by stating that things do not exist...that, in fact, things ultimately *are* relationships.
>
> (Cottone, 1988, p. 360)

The client–therapist relationship system forms a natural unit throughout this discussion. It is within this matrix that the internal world of a person is externalised and becomes available for change. It is represented as the core of the psychotherapeutic system in Figure 8.2 (which is a cross-section of the summary diagram, Figure 8.4, p. 157). For the sake of discussion here, sub-systems are differentiated. However it is essential to keep in mind that all sub-systems are also all active, interacting, dynamic whole systems at other levels of analysis. Each element identified can also be studied as a complete system in itself.

Client variation

The individual client as a system, consisting of the interacting relationships between many sub-systems, is sometimes a less familiar perspective in the psychotherapeutic literature than family systems theory. However, in the same way that one distinguishes, biologically, the cardiovascular system from the digestive system, psychological systems of an individual person can also be differentiated and seen in mutual inter-relationship. For example, belief systems, self systems, value systems, autonomic response systems, cognitive construct systems (Kelly, 1955) etc. are all systems which can be distinguished from each other and treated in inter-relationship with each other.

Probably the most frequently used way of attempting to describe client difference in psychiatric and psychological circles is that of classic psychiatric diagnosis. Obviously this is an attempt to describe the idiosyncratic qualities of an individual taking into account larger patterns or frequently observed clusters of phenomena. Diagnosis attempts to describe what the person is presenting or what are the symptoms, syndromes, problems and concerns which the client is manifesting. There are many different systems of diagnosis, ranging from constructive use of DSM-III-R (*Diagnostic and Statistical Manual of Mental Disorders*, American Psychiatric Association, 1987), Kernberg's classifications (1984), diagnosis in terms of gestalt interruptions to contact (De Lisle, 1988), or Beutler's dimensions of symptom complexity, coping style, reactance level and focal theme (1986). According to Dryden (1984), any psychotherapy, and particularly an integrative psychotherapy, must take account of client variation by one or more of these (or newly created) means. Systemic integrative psychotherapy does not prescribe which diagnostic approach (from phenomenological description according to Minkowski (1970) to the World Health Organization's classification of mental disorders (1978)) must be used. It does require that an individual practitioner is familiar with such systems and is able to consistently use one or more of them with some relevance to their practice – if only to communicate with other colleagues.

For example, DSM-III-R diagnosis takes into account the psychiatric condition, the kind of personality, the individual's physical and psychosocial world as well as their functional capacities. While this gives it a descriptive power exceeding unidimensional classification systems, it retains a channel of communication with psychiatry. Whether or not a psychotherapist uses a standard diagnostic procedure, it will be expected that they use or develop some way of describing individual differences, and appreciating commonalities, between patients. Sensitively used in the hands of psychotherapists skilled in the healing uses of relationship, clarity of diagnosis does not necessarily *have* to impede the integrity of existential psychotherapy, but can be seen to be complementary and even humane (Clarkson, 1989c).

Assessment or diagnosis can also be seen as a way of describing how people present themselves in their existential world (Spiegelberg, 1972). This, of course, is a combination of their heredity and their past and current environment and is represented as such on the summary diagram, Figure 8.4 on p. 157. It is probably by now commonly accepted that 'nature' and 'nurture' interact as two major formative notions for regarding individual differences even though different workers ascribe greater or lesser importance to each. Modern child developmental theory (e.g. Stern, 1985) emphasises the interaction between nature and nurture with the child as the agent of the interaction. Both nature and nurture refer to the origins of present constellations of a person's behaviour, feelings and attitudes, whereas diagnosis refers to what they present or manifest.

Variables from nature refer to people's predispositions (e.g. to cancer or alcoholism), temperamental preferences (e.g. intensity of stimulation or time of rising), intellectual ceiling (IQ range) and physical talents or limitations (athleticism or lack of height), their introversion/extroversion typologies (whether from Eysenckian or Jungian perspectives), archetypal propensities, their cortical excitation/inhibition balance (which according to Eysenck (1968) affects the speed of conditioning or learning), their vulnerability quotient (Anthony and Cohler, 1987), their body type (Millon, 1969) and gender influences (from the biological determinism of Freud (1977) to feminist analyses (Mander and Rush, 1974; Eichenbaum and Orbach, 1983).

The influence of early environment, particularly the human care and interaction with the infant and child (from Bowlby, 1953 to Mahler et al., 1975) form a major portion of what constitutes psychological underpinnings for psychotherapy, particularly within the psychoanalytic and, to an important extent, humanistic/existential traditions. Here, nurture refers to the kind and extent of damage or adaptation due to the interaction between nature and nurture during developmental stages (whether conceived of in a Freudian or an Eriksonian (1977) paradigm) or developmental foci as in modern child development theories (from Stern, 1985 to Pine, 1985) which may later manifest in confusion, conflict or deficiency/effects of trauma.

The differentiation of detrimental effects of early childhood experience into the three foci of *confusion, conflict* and *deficit/trauma* was developed to aid clinicians in assessment and psychotherapy. It is more fully discussed elsewhere (Clarkson and Gilbert, 1990b). This conceptualisation has been found to have heuristic use – again for purposes of elucidation and improved understanding, not for finite exactitude. It posits three ways of thinking differentially about emphases in psychophysiological disturbance:

1. *Confusion*, which here refers to affective and cognitive confusion, for example, the approach of Beck et al. to depression (1979), irrational beliefs (Ellis, 1962), contaminations in transactional analysis (Berne, 1975), transference phenomena, delusions or disassociative phenomena (Watkins, 1976; Watkins and Watkins, 1986).
2. *Conflict* refers to the existence of internal conscious or unconscious conflict between different parts of the personality – however these may be conceived – from libidinal and antilibidinal ego (Fairbairn, 1952) to sub-personality conflicts (Rowan, 1990).
3. *Developmental deficits* refers to psychological lacks or injuries caused by deficient, abusive or over-protective parenting, either chronically or traumatically (Balint, 1968; Schiff et al., 1975), and consistent inadequate parenting (Sechehaye, 1951; Kohut, 1977) or *management of trauma* (Winnicott, 1958; Miller, 1985).

There is of course no absolute dividing line between using any of these three demarcation aids as the primary focus for psychotherapy; they naturally merge and overlap. However, at any one time, maximum therapeutic leverage and improved creative anticipation may be derived from whichever one the psychotherapist is using as 'figure' or focus.

Psychotherapist variation

Psychotherapists are people too. They have their idiosyncratic styles, qualities and preferences and personality traits which are obviously influenced by *all* the factors discussed under client variation. In addition, their choice of training and learned or developed skills and talents bear greatly upon their contribution to the psychotherapeutic encounter. Issues to do with transference and countertransference dynamics, for example, projective identification (Hinshelwood, 1989) and parallel process can be conceived of as belonging to the schematic overlap area between psychotherapist and client in Figure 8.2. The therapist of course also changes independently over time. Life issues such as pregnancy (Gottlieb, 1989), aging (Guy, 1987) and stress (Kottler, 1986) and/or increasing competency or disillusionment with the profession can be very powerful influences on the psychotherapy even though they may not directly have to do with an individual client.

There is a growing body of research, paying attention to the match between client and psychotherapist, which considers the influence of such factors as compatibility in terms of background, class, education and values (Garfield, 1986). Furthermore, an impressive body of research shows that one of the most overriding and influential factors in the outcome of psychotherapy is the relationship between psychotherapist and client (Frank, 1979; Hynan, 1981). In some discussions at the United Kingdom Council for Psychotherapy the following definition of psychotherapy has been used: 'The systematic use of a *relationship* between therapist and patient – as opposed to pharmacological or social methods – to produce changes in cognition, feelings and behaviour' (Holmes and Lindley 1989, p. 3). (The integrative dimensions of affect, behaviour and cognition were identified by Beutler in 1971.) It is the responsibility of the psychotherapist to use the relationship with the client ethically and productively for maximum healing. 'We are born of relationship, nurtured in relationship, and educated in relationship. We represent every biological and social relationship of our forebearers, as we interact and exist in a consensual domain called "society"' (Cottone, 1988, p. 363). It is for this reason that the client (or patient) in systemic integrative psychotherapy is thought of as always in relationship whether this be conceived of in object relations terms or in subject relations terms (as in existential approaches). In Figure 8.4 (p. 157) the centrality of relationship is diagrammatically carried through by showing the client in relationship to the therapist on every dimension.

An integrative psychotherapeutic framework of five possible modalities of client–therapist relationship has been identified by the author. It will be briefly summarised here as it forms the basis for the diploma training in integrative psychotherapy (Clarkson, 1992a). This framework is one means of intellectually and experientially engaging with the systemic complexity of the relationship matrix.

Firstly, in order for 'help' to be of use, a *working alliance* needs to be established in the first place. For example, patients actually have to take the medicine prescribed by their physicians. Research (e.g. Griffith, 1990) shows that this cannot at all be taken for granted. Greenson in psychoanalysis (1967) and Berne in transactional analysis (1975), among many others, have addressed the nature and use of this working alliance.

Secondly, there is the *transferential/countertransferential relationship* which is extremely well developed, articulated and effectively used within the theoretically rich psychoanalytic tradition and other approaches (Heimann, 1950; Langs, 1976; Racker, 1982; Cashdan, 1988; Clarkson, 1992b).

Thirdly, the *developmentally needed/reparative relationship* can be differentiated as another kind of relationship that is potentially present and needed in psychotherapy. (This is a traditional intervention in psychotherapy from Ferenczi (1980) to Fromm-Reichmann (1974), Kohut (1977), and Schiff and Day (1970).) Here the psychotherapist intentionally provides the corrective/reparative replenishing parental relationship (or action) in cases where the original parenting was deficient, abusive or over-protective. According to many, including Balint (1968), it needs to be differentiated from untherapeutic gratification. Balint differentiates between malignant and benign regression in psychotherapy.

Clearly, the therapeutically correct use of a developmentally needed reparative relationship (or interventions) should be carefully used in certain circumstances of benign regression.

Fourthly, particularly within the humanistic/existential tradition, there is appreciation of the *person-to-person relationship* or *real* relationship. This kind of therapist–client relationship is similar to what Buber called the 'I–Thou relationship' (1970). This has been retrieved and valued for its transformative potential in the psychotherapeutic arena *if* used skilfully and ethically (Rogers, 1961; Laing, 1965; Polster and Polster, 1974)). However there has always been, and there is again, growing recognition within psychoanalytic practice that the real relationship between analyst and analysand – following Freud's own example – is a deeply significant, unavoidable and potentially profoundly healing force also within the psychoanalytic paradigm (Archambeau, 1979; Malcolm, 1981; Klauber, 1986).

Finally, certainly within the Jungian tradition (Jung, 1969a) and also within the humanistic/existential perspective (Rowan, 1973), there is acknowledgement of the influence of the qualities that presently transcend the limits of our understanding ('There are more things in heaven and earth, Horatio, than are dreamt of in your philosophy' (*Hamlet*, I, scene V, v. 166)). However defined, some implicit or explicit recognition of the possibility, if not the existence, of a *transpersonal relationship* between healer and healed as it unfolds within the psychotherapeutic *vas* (container) is gradually beginning to gain more acceptance (see Chapter 2).

From a systemic integrative perspective these five forms of relationship in psychotherapy are all valid. Their intentional and informed use will of course depend on differences between individual patients and different phases in the psychotherapy over time. At any given moment in psychotherapy one of these relationships may predominate. For example, the development of the transference neurosis may appear to be antithetical to the furthering of the working alliance (Stone, 1961; Greenson, 1965 and 1967) or reparative intentions. Often, it is unlikely that two or more 'can be operative at the same moment. Which one is allowed to become figure, or focus, must depend on the nature of the psychotherapeutic task at a particular time with each unique patient. Other modes of therapeutic relationship may also be present but may be more in the background at a particular time' (see Chapter 2).

Variation over time

The psychotherapeutic relationship (whether it occurs in individual, family or group therapy) can only really be comprehensible in the context of time. This is a most important domain of variation in psychotherapy. People develop over time, and their relationships develop over time. The qualities and idiosyncrasies of both partners in the psychotherapeutic journey evolve only in the context of time.

Within a systemic appreciation of the role of time in psychotherapy, it can be conceptualised as ranging back (downwards) to the *past*, through the *present* and on (upwards) to the *future*. This vast expanse of time in an individual's life is potentially the very stuff of psychotherapy. However, the time of one psychotherapy session is of course a mere moment on this scale. This moment of meeting is represented in the summary diagram of Figure 8.4 (p. 157) by the 50-minute time span at the far right-hand side, as an example.

The relationship in the existentially alive *present* may be the working alliance or the person-to-person relationship (or both). As the relationship 'goes back into the *past*' and possibly becomes more 'regressive' it can be seen in terms of transference/countertransference or in terms of the developmentally needed/reparative (unfinished) relationship. As the relationship leaves the past and the present, it may begin to dwell more on what is conceivable as represented by the *future*. It may then take on more of a transpersonal nature.

Many psychotherapies have developed models which incorporate these dimensions of relationship over time in terms of developmental psychotherapeutic stages. For example, the cycle of gestalt formation and destruction can be applied to the developing relationship between psychotherapist and client which is, from the beginning, directed towards termination (Clarkson, 1989a). Similarly, general developmental stages have been identified by such workers as Lacoursière (1980) and need to be taken into account in group psychotherapy. What is required by the integrative psychotherapist is the awareness of the influence of changes over time and a repertoire for effectively negotiating these to the benefit of clients.

There are also stages in the learning process which can be noticed in successful psychotherapy. These seem to proceed through the stages of awareness, accommodation and assimilation. The author and a colleague developed this sequencing map from the learning phases described by Robinson (1974) as unconscious incompetence, conscious incompetence, conscious competence and unconscious competence (Clarkson and Gilbert, 1990a). *Awareness* refers to the first phase, which has to do with moving from unconscious incompetence to conscious incompetence. For example, a client may need to be made aware that negative thought patterns sustain depressive affect. *Accommodation* concerns the phase of moving from conscious incompetence to conscious competence. For example, instead of relying on the psychotherapist to interpret their dreams, the client learns how to use their dreamworld creatively as a key to self-understanding and personal growth. *Assimilation* here refers to the phase of psychotherapy whereby the client moves from conscious competence to unconscious competence; for example, when new feelings, attitudes and behaviours have become comfortably internalised. The patient who used to be phobic of public speaking, does so easily and well while in the assimilation phase without recourse to will-power, conscious use of 'technique' or undue self-consciousness. Similarly, the person who used to have a 'narcissistic personality disorder' develops enduring and mutually satisfying relationships with depth and spontaneity.

Environmental systems also change depending on the time-frame used. The current environment would include the setting and locality of the psychotherapy room, as well as the client's current life experiences within the family/social system and the present economic and political, national and international, local and global environment. This is the time and ecological system within which the individual exercises his or her existential responsibility. 'All quantum systems (most especially boson systems like ourselves) share this mechanism for creative self-discovery through a dialogue with their environment' (Zohar, 1990, p. 176).

As the environment 'moves back in time', it encompasses the environmental influences of both nurture and nature. Nature is placed further back in time and includes both inherited variables (temperament, physical attributes, perhaps archetypal predispositions etc.) as well as the presence of Physis (the life force which strives for healing, growth and actualisation). Nurture is placed subsequent to nature to represent the early influences of our childhood experiences which lead to later conflict, confusion or deficit. It is within the matrix of nurture and nature that individuals find the crucible for an autonomous life within their destiny. This is the context for consideration of what is known as object-relations influences and psychological development.

The aspirational environment represents the unknown and uncharted environment of the *future*, and involves that towards which the client (and the psychotherapist) may aspire, the goal towards which the psychotherapy may be directed or teleologically drawn, the self which the client may conceptualise or visualise. This kind of person-environment system is self-created or self-discovered, and concerns whatever the person understands of themselves and their world in terms of the future.

Space does not permit more than an indicative mapping of many of the conceptual areas which are hypothesised to be central to the theory and practice of systemic integrative psychotherapy. Precisely what an individual psychotherapist would choose to focus upon is left to the individual's training, experience, intellect, sensitivity and imagination. What is required, however, are viable and comprehensible ways of organising, managing and using our vast tracts of psychological data at a multitude of levels of similar and different orders. The interface between the patient and time is likewise not meant to be restrictive, but to invite consideration of the ways in which patients change over time. Of course the central over-arching area is the space (environment) where all these interact.

Variation in environment

Because the client is always seen as belonging to and influencing, as well as being influenced by, systemic relations, each of such dynamically alive systems can also be encountered in the psychotherapeutic relationship over time. 'In the systemic viewpoints...the relationship as the therapeutic context [or psychosocial environment] is fully recognised. The larger social system (represented by the service delivery system) and the client's system(s) of influence, e.g. the client's family, peer group and/or cultural group) are linked through the counsellor–client relationship' (Cottone, 1988, p. 367). Many psychotherapists are familiar with systems approaches to families (Hoffman, 1981), groups and organisations (Morgan, 1986) where the therapy is accomplished through interventions in the larger system. Group therapy, couples work or family therapy may well be the therapeutic setting of choice for a particular individual. Equally the individual therapist may work through the means of the systemic relationship between them.

Systemic variation must also take into account the surrounding social and physical environment including environmental stresses. A comprehensive perspective may include consideration of global events such as ecological breakdown, international unrest and of environmental factors such as the air we breathe and the food we eat. The immediate environment in which the psychotherapy takes place – that is, the consulting room, the clinic, the hospital or centre – its location, decoration, ease of access, the internal and external constraints – also has systemic implications. These can range from physiological disturbance (such as noise) to sociocultural effects (e.g. decor). Writers such as Rowan (1988), James (1983) and Douglas (1976), among others, have paid attention to such factors. Social class, race, disability, gender, sexual identity, religious belief, fashion, culture and cultural 'drift' for example, the increase in unemployment, homelessness, an increasing number of people over the age of 50, also need to be taken into consideration. Psychotherapy takes place within the larger context of the *Zeitgeist* (the spirit of the times). In the psychotherapy situation, journeying back to the client's childhood environment (e.g. the early nursing dyad or an extended family system) and forward to an aspirational future environment (d'Ardenne and Mahtani, 1989) is considered to be potentially as influential as what is in the current environment.

Practice

The parameters according to which a psychotherapist would develop, practice and sequence their behavioural strategies can clearly not be thoroughly addressed within the scope of this chapter and are well represented in extant psychotherapeutic literature. (*Strategies* are designed to eliminate, diminish, add, maintain, enhance, change or replace problematic cognitive, affective or physiological behaviours.) For example, one strategic parameter may concern a psychotherapist's *style*, which on the one hand may vary anywhere along the directive to non-directive continuum and on the other hand encompasses such individual qualities as warmth, wit, compassion and elegance. Another strategic parameter concerns the *arena* for the psychotherapeutic activity – individual psychotherapy, marital or family therapy, group psychotherapy, organisational consulting (e.g. in a residential home for the elderly), or a strategic impact on a collective or community (e.g. a group of teenage West Indian friends). Strategies are of course evolved from objectives, desires or *goals*. These may be articulated in terms of growth, 'cure' or adjustment or, as in Clarkson's paper (1989b) *evolutionary* change can be differentiated from *revolutionary* change. In any event it is vital to discriminate between different kinds of changes as outcomes of psychotherapy (Clarkson, 1988) so that both client and psychotherapist are working together towards the same objectives without getting involved in impossible or potentially destructive collusions.

Systemic integrative psychotherapy mandates a holistic view of the person. Such a view attempts to account for physiological, emotional, linguistic, sociocultural, rational, theoretical/metaphorical and transpersonal dimensions. These are seven conceptualised levels of human experience and behaviour which together are seen as constituting an integrative perspective on *the person as a whole*.

These seven levels also may be used as foci for psychotherapeutic theory, strategy or interventions. This is one of many maps found useful for the conceptualising and organising of levels of attention in psychotherapy or human experience. All psychotherapists, whatever their approach, probably develop maps or organising frameworks such as these as they develop and refine their own individual models of thinking about and practising psychotherapy.

Seven-level model

My model is published here at the insistence of colleagues and students who have found it valuable for integrating philosophical/theoretical *and* strategic/practical issues, both in psychotherapy itself and also for individual patients. It could be compared with Lazarus' BASIC I.D.

(1981) on the one hand, and with Wilber's (1980) on the other, although it was developed and taught at Pretoria University in 1975 before I had heard of either.

The five levels of psychotherapeutic relationship (discussed above) form the integrative framework for psychotherapist activity, and the psychotherapist's use of self in the process of systemic integrative psychotherapy (Clarkson, 1992a). The seven-level model offers both a *holistic view of the client as a person* in most aspects of human functioning, as well as a *comprehensive, integrative view of psychotherapy* with its multiplicity of emphases and applications to the person in the wider context of their existence.

The seven-level model was developed as 'an attempt to construct a thinking tool (or conceptual protractor) to provide a meaningful reference framework to deal with knowledge and experience in the widest possible wholistic fashion' (Clarkson, 1975). All seven levels are seen as coexisting. The healthy person will not develop one level chronically at the expense of another, but will tend to realise potential on all of these levels. Psychopathology can be conceived of in terms of a person's confusion, conflict or deficit between or within structures and dynamics at these seven levels. Attention to any one concurrently implicates all others in the system.

This model is epistemological in the sense that it implies different analytical techniques which define boundaries for the processes of knowing (Bateson, 1979). However, by ordering of knowledge (and ways of obtaining knowledge from the world in this way), different kinds of 'language games' (Lyotard, 1984) played in these different universes of discourse can be differentiated and evaluated. As a result it can help to clarify kinds of interventions or to sort techniques, particularly therapists' behaviours and concretely specific operations in order that the psychotherapy achieve the *behavioural impact* which is of eminent practical importance. Analysis of antecedents and consequences, or the archaeology of infantile object relations needs to be considered in terms of whether or not the person accomplishes the changes they desired – whether these concern insight into Oedipal conflicts (Freud, 1977), resignation to the depressive position (Klein, 1984), shouldering one's responsibility for being-in-the-world (Heidegger, 1949), or the ability to ask for a refund on faulty goods (Dryden, 1987).

The seven-level model is concerned with knowledge in two major ways. Firstly it can be used to differentiate how we obtain knowledge about the world using different levels of conceptualisation, different universes of discourse and different criteria for establishing validity, sense or 'truth' (epistemology in a philosophical sense). It is epistemological for the psychotherapist in the sense that people can sort their experiences in these different categories. Psychotherapeutic areas of knowledge, theories and procedures can also be discriminated by this means, and therefore it can be useful to guide the choice of concretely specific operations.

The seven-level model is a map rather than the territory; a map that can assist the psychotherapist practising in complex territory created in the face-to-face encounter of psychotherapist and client, and the life experiences brought by each into the psychotherapeutic arena. It is important to emphasise that it is a sorting device or a kind of protractor, to be used as a guide and measure of practice rather than a directive to dictate the psychotherapeutic journey. As it is less well known than some of the other component parts of systemic integrative psychotherapy, it requires a more, if vastly summarised, explanation. (For reasons of space, this discussion will exclude its epistemological and ontological implications for psychotherapy as a system.) It is presented here as an holistic view of the person as well as a major map usable as a integrative conceptual and practice-guiding tool for psychotherapists from many different orientations or to help a single psychotherapist order, prioritise and/or include a wide range of interventions which may complement or extend his or her usual range.

At no point is it to be conceived that one level is necessarily higher or better than another. It is thought that the healthy human being will be functioning well on *all these levels* simultaneously, with the biological at least as significant as any other. It is postulated that these 'universes' of discourse are frequently confused in the theory and in the practice of psychotherapy, leading to category errors, apparently irreconcilable difference and spurious contradictions.

The seven-level model can also be useful to assist in the incorporation of the great variety of specific operating procedures from different psychotherapies which are built on very different universes of epistemological discourse. It is suggested that these can be effectively used together, provided the practitioner is willing and able to discriminate between different perspectives (e.g. how to 'prove' a particular hypothesis within that theory) and to think for themselves at least within the four domains of variation outlined above. For example, integration may include other theoretical and strategic approaches such as gestalt body work, object relations, a developmental perspective, self theory and a phenomenological approach to diagnosis (Jaspers, 1963).

The seven levels are currently identified as:

1. Physiological
2. Emotional
3. Nominative
4. Normative
5. Rational
6. Theoretical
7. Transpersonal.

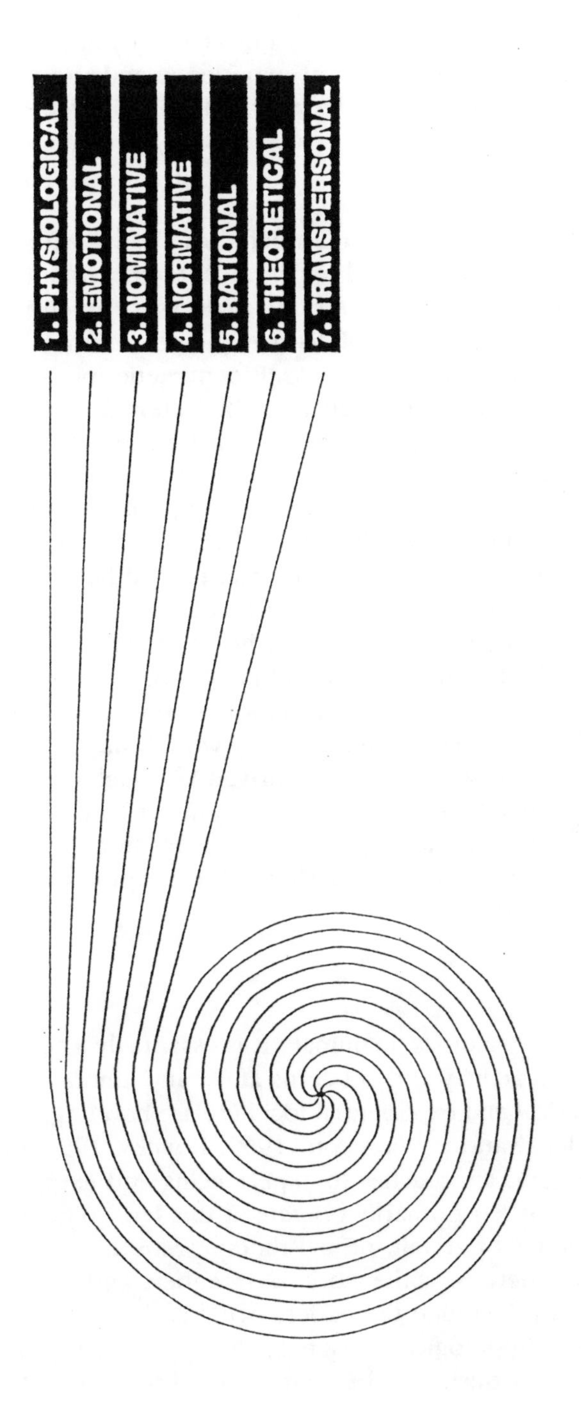

Figure 8.3. Diagrammatic representation of the seven-level model.

Under each heading below follows a brief, and by no means exhaustive, synopsis of possible aspects of experience and the psychotherapeutic approaches which may be emphasised at each level.

Level 1: physiological

This concerns the person as an 'amoeba' or 'body' with biological, physical, visceral and sensational experience, temperament, body type and predispositions. It concerns body processes, psychophysiology, sleep, food, physical symptoms of disease, the physical manifestation of anxiety and general sensory awareness. Bioenergetic and body-oriented approaches – the work of Reich (1972), Keleman (1985), Lowen (1969), and perhaps Wolpe (1961) – can be seen to be primarily focused on this level.

Methods of working primarily with the body, such as classical conditioning, desensitisation, breathing and relaxation techniques, can also primarily be located at this level. Sometimes psychotherapy at this level may be complemented with the use of medication, surgical intervention (e.g. plastic surgery), acupuncture, homoeopathy and osteopathy. Relaxation techniques (such as those of Jacobson, 1964) and breathing and body-posture procedures and techniques (such as those of bioenergetics) would also have a place here, as would massage (e.g. in the treatment of clients who are 'stroke-deprived') – which may be done by complementary health practitioners as an adjunct to psychotherapy – gestalt techniques for enhancing sensory awareness, and methods that emphasise the importance of breathing in psychological health and freedom from anxiety.

Level 2: emotional

This concerns the person as 'mammal'. It is essentially a preverbal area of experience and activity and concerns affect and emotion in psychology. The theoretical and experiential foci here are bonding, attachment, nursing, and deprivation (Winnicott, 1960; Bowlby, 1953 and Rutter, 1972). Theories and approaches to experiencing and expressing affect in psychotherapy often primarily operate at this level. The methodologies and techniques of gestalt, primal therapy, rebirthing, and prenatal work are relevant here, as is the work of Greenberg and Safran (1977).

At this level are included the experiencing and expression of affect over and above physiological presence; the person's fear, anger, sadness, joy, rage and despair. 'Resonance' phenomena and hypnotic induction procedures would probably be emphasised at this level of experience. This could include affective work towards the cathartic release of emotion (whether situationally current or archaic), the expression of emotion within the therapeutic relationship with the psychotherapist or group members and the expression of repressed emotion in the context of 'childhood scenes' (Miller, 1985). Specific therapeutic operations, such as focused expressive psychotherapy used by Daldrup et al. (1988), gestalt (e.g. polarity work), primal therapy (dealing with preverbal experience), psychodrama, bioenergetics, re-childing (Clarkson and Fish, 1988) and re-decision work of transactional analysis (Goulding and Goulding, 1979) could be located at this level (depending on how they are used). The use of visualisation techniques to influence psychophysiological conditions could be seen to operate primarily at this level (Rossi and Cheek, 1988).

Level 3: nominative

This concerns the person as 'primate'. Under this heading are included the awareness and labelling of experiences and the validation of experience through naming. Since at least the earliest biblical times people have known that the 'giving of names' develops 'dominion', ownership and the feeling of mastery over the existential world and the transformation of human experience. The naming of feelings and sensations, the naming of ego states (Watkins, 1976; Watkins and Watkins, 1986) and the naming of personified introjects, are relevant to this level. Those interventions described by Watzlawick et al. (1967, 1974) including the concept of second-order change in which reframing, making overt the covert, utilising resistance and paradoxical interventions play a part, belong here. The work of Enright (1980) on the renaming of symptoms in gestalt, Haley's (1963) and Erickson's (1967) paradoxical and strategic interventions are also approaches which centralise the nominative level of enquiry. All these approaches emphasise the transformative potential of 'what things are called'.

The naming and labelling of experience according to psychotherapeutic orientation would also come under this heading. For example, it would include the 'top-dog/underdog' of gestalt therapy, the 'placator/blamer/computer/distractor' of Satir's family therapy (1967), the 'archetypes' of Jungian analysis (Jung, 1968, 1969a), the sub-personalities of psychosynthesis (Assagioli, 1971) and other approaches (Rowan, 1990) and the 'Parent/Adult/Child' of transactional analysis all provide labels in order to assist understanding. Other approaches used here include neurolinguistic programming, the awareness phase of the gestalt cycle, phenomenology (e.g. Merleau-Ponty, 1962), Rogers' (1986) reflective process, empathic attunement (Rowe and Mac Isaac, 1989) and reframing (Bandler and Grinder, 1982). The naming and labelling of experience under the headings of diagnostic categories (whether the kind of assessment refers to reactance levels, feeling or thinking function (Jung, 1944), borderline personality organisation, or failure at the rapprochement stage (Mahler et al., 1975)) could also be seen as basically belonging here.

Level 4: normative

This concerns the person as social animal. It refers to norms, values, collective belief systems, societal expectations. Strategies and interventions from this level would tend to deal with facts, knowledge of attributes and practices regarding people as 'cultural beings' – the tribe, the group, the community. This level corresponds to the psychoanalytic notion of the super-ego or equally, the borrowed egos of Federn (1977) or Parent egos of Berne (1975). Statistical and cultural norms are affected by individual differences and the concept of 'consensual reality'. Glasser's reality therapy (1965), the cathexis approach (Schiff et al., (1975), and Peck (1978), all deal in important ways with norms and values. The values clarification movement (Simon et al., 1972) also provides major contributions to psychological thinking and intervention at the normative level. This level attends to the relation between the individual and the group, and how culture is built and ecology maintained. It also underpins cross-cultural considerations in psychotherapy, for example the role of cultural pressures in addictions and compulsions (Orbach, 1978).

Both statistical and cultural norms are included at this level. It refers to the measurements by which we assess some of the 'oughts' of our belief-systems, how to do things, what things mean in our culture, what is the 'usual' and what the 'unusual'. This is not to suggest that psychotherapy plays a normative role in the sense of encouraging conformity or providing further oughts; rather it looks at norms in terms of their appropriateness, usefulness and application in specific circumstances. Although the acceptance of some norms may be useful in certain circumstances, psychotherapies differ in how much they emphasise aims such as autonomy, integration, growth, awareness and self-actualisation. These can challenge and transcend many cultural and societal 'norms'. (The 'stiff upper lip' norm of the white British male, for example, or the 'apartheid' norm of white South Africa – both are contradictions of health, integration, well-being and growth and as such will be refuted in an approach to psychotherapy in which everyone is held equally to have worth, value, freedom of expression and dignity.)

Child development material could be used here as a model of normal developmental needs in the light of which cultural and familial norms can be examined. Transactional analysis procedures such as self re-parenting (James, 1974) and spot re-parenting (Osnes, 1974) can be used to work with identified deficits. Clearly the social environment acts as a reinforcing system in terms of stimulus/response interactions both for the group's need for cohesion and the individual's need to belong to the group.

Level 5: rational

This concerns '*Homo sapiens*' – the person as thinker. This layer of knowledge and activity includes thinking, making sense of things, examination of cause and effect, frames of reference, working with facts and information and reading skills. 'Reality testing', developing rationality, experimentation (e.g. Kelly's (1955) enquiring man model), form the ways by which knowledge is gained or experience differentiated on this level. Approaches particularly relevant here are: rational-emotive therapy (RET)(Ellis, 1962) which provides three stages to assist in disputing irrational beliefs, namely, defining, distinguishing and debating (Dryden, 1987); aspects of cognitive therapy (Beck et al., 1979, 1985); 'insight' in most psychotherapies; and decontamination work in transactional analysis (Berne, 1975).

In transactional analysis this level is dealt with by decontamination of the Adult ego state (Berne, 1975), differentiating between Parent prejudices and beliefs, Child magical thinking and delusions and the clear factual thinking of the Adult, in order for psychotherapy of each distinct ego state to be possible. Here transactional analysis develops basic psychoanalytic theory where the ego is seen as the reality-testing function according to Federn (1977) and Weiss (1950) and similar to the objective ego of Fairbairn (1952).

Level 6: theoretical

This level throws into relief the person as 'storyteller' – as a meaning maker, making sense of human experience through symbolism, story and metaphor. This is based on the notion of theoretical plurality and relativity: theories can be seen as 'narratives' – stories that people tell themselves – interesting, exciting, depressing, controlling, useful and relative but no one forever true. 'Theories' are in a different logical category from that of facts. Both in psychological theory and individual experience, it is important to separate these where possible. It is, for example, quite likely that the psychological theories or explanations that we have developed to support the empirical evidence accumulated by science at the rational level, may be 'mistaken' and, in time, replaced by other (better?) theories (Kuhn, 1970).

The history of science can certainly tell many such tales. The theories, explanations, metaphors and stories that humans have created in order to explain why things are as they are and why people behave as they do are included at this level. The many and varied psychotherapies each provide their own narratives or stories to explain people's behaviour and to create ways of changing it. Moreover, the Oxford philosopher Farrell pointed out (1979) that each story in psychotherapy tends to manufacture material which will fit it.

Psychoanalysis has several stories (Freud, Winnicott, Klein, Lacan, Kohut), behavioural therapy has others and humanistic psychotherapy has yet several others. Within these are further stories or metaphors which may be very different or very similar, overlap or interface, but all of which attempt to make some sense of our human experience. Thus at this level it may be useful for the client to use stories from one or more of the humanistic psychotherapies in order to gain clarity or a frame of reference that makes sense of a particular problem or aspect of therapy. It is also possible to integrate part-stories from the other schools of psychotherapy, for example, 'modelling' theory from behavioural therapy may usefully explain how parental messages may be given or reinforced at a non-verbal level. Or self theory from the psychoanalytic and Jungian traditions may enrich our understanding of the development of the self and assist in identifying confusion (e.g. where parts of the self are denied, repressed, disowned or split off), conflict (e.g. the real self and false self) and deficit (e.g. the interpersonally developed self lacking adequate object-relationships for healthy development). What is required though is that the ideological convictions of 'true beliefs' at level 4, the normative (in the absence of consensually accepted factual evidence at the rational level), are differentiated from the possible theoretical explanations that become attached to them. Theories are to be judged by criteria other than facts or normative beliefs.

Level 7: transpersonal

This refers to the epistemological area concerned with people as 'spiritual beings'. Beyond rationality, facts and even theories are the prescient regions of dreams, altered states of ecstatic consciousness, the spiritual, the metaphysical, the mystical, the existentially paradoxical, the unpredictable and the inexplicable. Religion both experientially and theoretically impacts psychological perspectives. It is represented in several approaches to psychotherapy and human development, for example the influence of Eastern philosophies (Fromm, 1960), and the creation-centred spirituality of Fox (1983). Also included at this level are those experiences that may be described as the surreal, the transcendent and the synchronous.

At this level belongs Jung's work on archetypes and the collective unconscious (1968), much of his approach to dreams and symbols (1977), as well as transpersonal psychotherapies such as psychosynthesis, gestalt and sectors of transactional analysis which include a spiritual dimension within their parameters. Perhaps even included are tools for human healing and evolution derived from the 'I Ching' (Wilhelm, 1988), the tarot, transcendental meditation, yoga, taoism and Tai Chi. Vaughan writes, 'The spiritual quest is, above all, a search for truth.... Truth can become a strong force for healing once the commitment is made. In psychotherapy, telling the truth about experience is an essential part of the process, but its relevance to spiritual well-being is rarely recognised' (1985, pp. 20–21).

In Chapter 2, this spiritual healing force within the therapeutic relationship itself is recognised in several approaches to psychotherapy. For example, Archambeau (1979) implies that the mutual unconsciousnesses of partners transform their relationship beyond that of the I–Thou relationship to something greater than the sum of its parts, something that happens in the 'between' of the relationship (the 'third self' of James and Savary, 1977).

The physical, body-process considerations of level 1 may *seem* unrelated, but what links these and all the other levels is that they are precisely the levels at which we experience ourselves and our environment, and the relationship between the two. Such an holistic approach to the client is essential to our integrative psychotherapy training. All aspects of our human experience can find inclusion under these seven levels (if not, we need to find other means). This conceptual structure has provided a useful framework for assessing, selecting, focusing and enhancing the work of several generations of psychotherapists by the integration of relevant theories and procedures from various models of psychotherapy. One of the strategies for psychotherapy integration recommended by Mahrer (1989) – that of *concretely specific working therapeutic operations* – can be facilitated by using a model such as the one presented here. In other words, integration is comparatively eased when it has to do with what psychotherapists do with clients at the basic nuts-and-bolts level, what they say to the clients or instruct them to do, in order to attain some change, reinforcement or response. This may include (using some of Mahrer's examples) clarifying the role of the patient, providing information on therapeutic arrangements, telling the patient how to focus attention, inviting the patient to express themselves with more feeling, drawing the patient's attention to the therapist–patient relationship, and so on. Millions of interventions or techniques on each of the seven levels (which are based on different epistemologies) can be divided into different types, as in Heron's six-category intervention analysis (1990) and Rowan's (1973) model.

Depending upon the required outcome, these interventions will have differing styles, foci, intentions and will be paced, timed and weighted in intensity differently at different points in the psychotherapy. Using this strategy for psychotherapy integration, it generally follows that, for example, the integration of some aspects of cognitive–behaviour therapy with psychoanalysis (Fonagy, 1989) becomes more workable because of the inclusion that is possible at the concretely specific operating procedures level of integration. 'This rich pool of operating procedures is part of the public marketplace. Any therapist, regardless of approach, can obtain operating procedures from this public pool. No therapeutic approach has exclusive rights of ownership over any of these operating procedures' (Mahrer, 1989, p. 81).

It is likely that most psychotherapists in the course of training, supervision, personal psychotherapy, through attendance at conferences and psychotherapy workshops, and seeing other psychotherapists at work, have accumulated a valuable resource of specific operating procedures that can be integrated into psychotherapeutic work. In this sense, whether acknowledged or not, every learning, developing, questing psychotherapist is probably an integrator.

Summary Diagram and the Case Study (Figure 8.4)*

Client example

This case example clearly does not represent the totality of the client's psychotherapy, as only certain highlights can be indicated within the available space. The seven-level model may be a more unfamiliar conceptualisation than the other major parameters; so this case study takes a vertical view of the psychotherapy in its terms, rather than the more usual chronological progression. Of course each psychotherapy, however we attempt to describe it, in fact diverts, converges, winds and unwinds through chronological and existential time, environmental systems and relationship dimensions in unique and unrepeatable configurations.

Introduction to client

Susan, a school counsellor, entered psychotherapy three years ago, aged 29. During the first meetings with her male psychotherapist, she was very nervous and avoided any eye contact. She was often sad, depressed and had very low self-esteem. She felt inadequate in friendships and potential sexual relationships due to finding it difficult to get close to people. She spoke of loathing herself as a person and particularly disliking her body, which she described as fat.

The psychotherapist's response to Susan was one of warmth and an

*By Phil Lapworth.

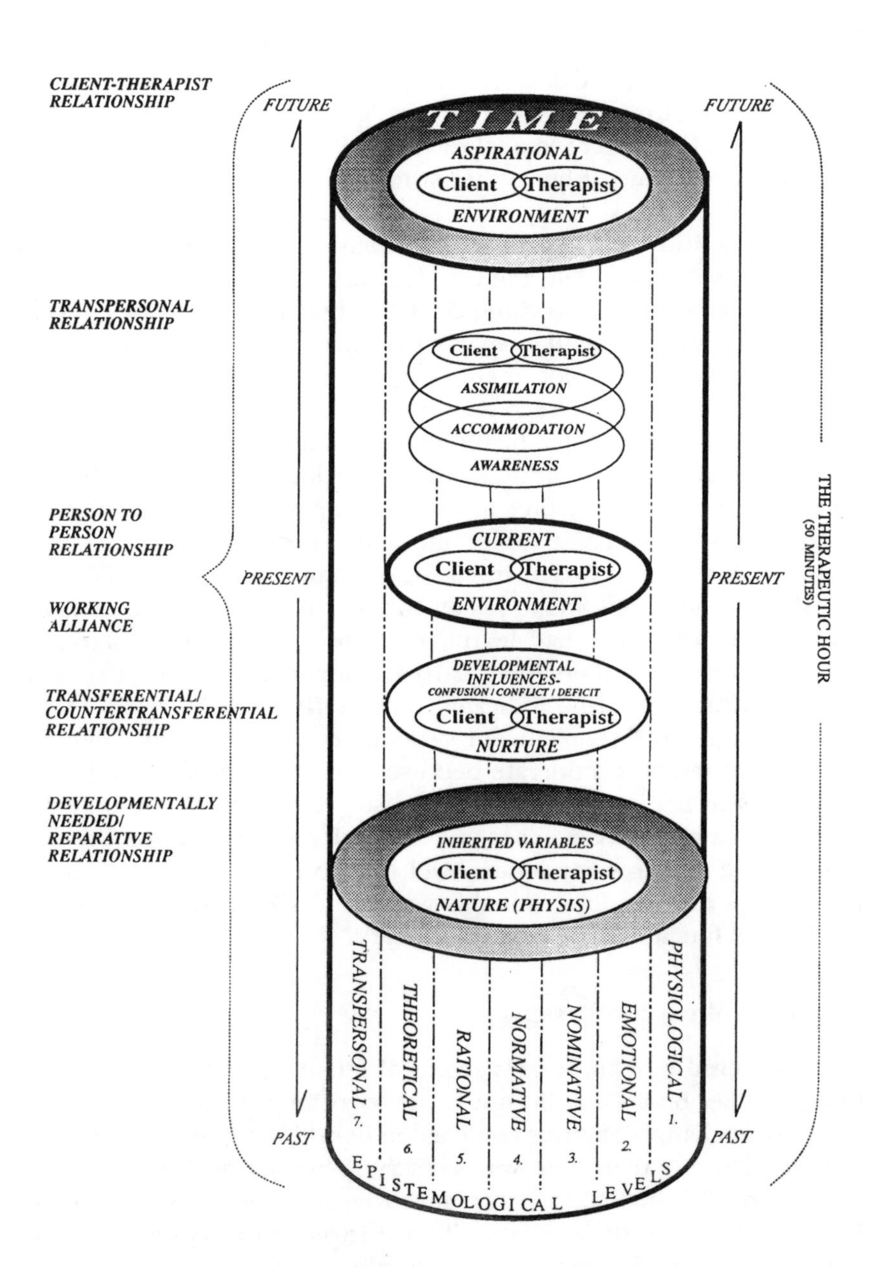

Figure 8.4 Summary diagram.

intuitive feeling that they could work together well. They agreed upon weekly individual psychotherapy in order to provide a regular arena in which to explore and change, through the one-to-one relationship, her self-image and self-loathing – crucial aspects reinforcing her feeling depressed. They also discussed the possibility of her entering a psychotherapy group when the time was appropriate in order to allow exploration of her interpersonal relationships including her rivalry with women who reminded her of her sister and her feeling of inadequacy in relation to others. A psychotherapy group would also provide her with opportunity and a safe space to experiment and practise new behaviours with both male and female peers.

Susan came from a working-class family in the north of England. Her mother was a forceful woman who was constantly critical of Susan. Her father was an odd-job man, often absent from home, in trouble with the law and having 'secret' affairs with women. Her younger sister was born with a congenital hearing loss. Because of this, the sister was the centre of attention and affection, particularly favoured by dad. Susan spent much of her time as a child living with her maternal grandparents who she felt cared for her more than her parents.

In thinking about Susan in classical diagnostic terms (DSM-III-R), she showed no symptoms to justify any psychiatric diagnosis on axis I. The way in which she had learnt to relate interpersonally indicated avoidant personality traits (on axis II) accompanied by chronic stomach tension (which could be indicated on axis III). Axis IV refers to psychosocial stressors (her current systemic context and environment). These were rated as moderate because of discord in her current relationship with her boyfriend. She was also rated as moderate on axis V in terms of a global assessment of her functioning, as she was currently functioning at a low moderate level due to her flattened affect and poor social relationships, but this was not particularly different from her level of functioning in preceding years.

Summary of psychotherapy

Susan entered psychotherapy aware of feeling depressed, not liking herself or her body. She did not know why she was feeling as she was nor how to change. She was confused in her thinking and feeling about herself, believing that there was something 'wrong' with her. The psychotherapist's initial warm acceptance towards Susan helped in establishing a therapeutic working alliance in which Susan's wants and needs were identified and clarified. Further, this enabled the development of the other four dimensions of psychotherapeutic relationship which at various later stages become catalytic media for change.

Over the course of her time in psychotherapy Susan became aware of how her childhood experiences influenced her self-esteem. Lack of empathic attunement and mirroring as an infant had left her with a fear of closeness and precarious sense of self and self-support. As she became conscious of how neglected her 'inner child' had become, she gradually understood how she perpetuated similar experiences in the present – for example, in her rivalrous feelings towards her favourite sister. She had also early in childhood introjected her mother's constant and destructive criticism of herself. In cognitive behavioural terms, this criticism became the incessant refrain of her self talk, or she constantly experienced a persecuting bad object. After some time she also allowed into her awareness the previously repressed experience of being sexually abused by her grandfather. She associated this with her fear of closeness, her lack of trust and her feeling of 'wrongness'. Though painful, this knowledge helped Susan unravel some of the confusion she had had about herself and enabled her to relive and work through those repressed unconscious childhood feelings and fantasies that had been interfering with her healthy adult functioning.

Accommodation and assimilation of this knowledge of her experience involved exploring and resolving the resultant inner conflicts, for example, between such polarities as feeling/non-feeling, love/hate, closeness/distance, creative/destructive and libidinal/anti-libidinal forces. Thus her inner conflicts also illuminated where her deficiencies lay and where focus needed to be given in terms of nurturing, self-care, recognition of skills, successes and achievements. The psychotherapist enabled her to develop a more nurturing and benign internal Parent to take care of the needs of her inner Child. She was used to forming relationships with friends and colleagues where she looked after the lame ducks. This was the way in which she maintained the deprivation from her early family in her current environment.

The transference, however, did not remain positive throughout the psychotherapy. The group experience re-stimulated Susan's childhood experiences with her father and her sister. She felt rivalrous with other women in the group and rejected by the psychotherapist. This was worked through by open confrontation, exploration, discussion and current reality testing. She grew in taking responsibility for herself from asking for her needs to be met in the group to experimenting to being more demanding with her friends.

Towards the termination of her therapy, Susan re-entered a negative transference with her therapist, again feeling unloved and unwanted. In fact she repeated most of her former psychotherapy issues at an even more intensive and acted-out level of transference before finally resolving the hurt resultant of her rejecting father, her critical mother and preferred sister. This later negative transferential period was one to which the psychotherapist could respond by containing her negative feelings while continuing to accept her and allowing Physis and her psyche to do battle.

Subsequent to this 'regression' (a common phenomenon towards the end of therapy) Susan has increased her self-esteem enormously by visualising and aspiring towards a conceivable self unfettered by destructive introjects. She is more spontaneous, appropriately trusting and clear in what she feels and what she thinks. She has increased her circle of friends and allows herself to be emotionally and physically close as she chooses. She thoroughly and appropriately mourned the termination of her relationship with the psychotherapist. She has begun training for a new career and has ended her psychotherapy in a spirit of resolution of the past, satisfaction with the present and optimism for the future.

Some of the psychotherapy with Susan will now be highlighted and explored in terms of the seven levels of experience as used in practice.

Level 1: physiological

Using Rowe's definition (1988) Susan would be described as an 'introvert', her 'preference' being for the progressive development of her individuality in terms of clarity, achievement and authenticity. She is a fast learner and very much an 'ideas' person who emphasises the importance of control and keeping things in order. Bearing in mind the desirability of creating a better balance between introversion and extroversion, Susan's preference for thoughts and ideas was a 'way in' to further work concerning her more extrovert desires, in particular wanting to make more satisfying contact with others.

It was important in working with Susan and her concern about her body that the possibility of any medical explanation (e.g. thyroid problems) be eliminated by medical consultation, before moving on to approaches at other levels (e.g. cultural norms in level 4). Interventions of a dietary nature were decided against, having made sure that overeating and unhealthy eating were not a part of the problem. Thus it was decided not to intervene at this level but to explore the issue at other levels.

In her second year of psychotherapy, the working alliance between client and psychotherapist was well established. A positive transferential relationship developed until Susan accessed the memory of her sexual abuse by grandfather of which she had been unconscious until this time. The positive transferential relationship here appears to have intensified Susan's underlying conflict between wanting to be close and being scared to be close. Her stomach tension had increased and did not respond to any anxiety-reducing interventions at this level until the trauma of her sexual abuse had been brought into consciousness. In other words, her stomach pain appeared to be a somatisation of the trauma.

Her breathing became very shallow for several weeks. Relaxation techniques were used as a coping strategy to deal with this physiological response while working at other levels (namely, emotional, nominative and normative). Bioenergetic breathing techniques and body postures were used to release repressed emotions and muscular 'holding' subsequent to the trauma.

It was noted that Susan's breathing pattern in general was to breathe out more than she breathed in. This was experienced by her as a reflection of her belief in a world that could not support her and where sustenance was in short supply. She inhabited an existential world in which she felt required to 'give out' in order to survive. Of course, this had been true when she was a child in her family. Correction of her breathing pattern by direct instruction from the psychotherapist was an intrinsic part of the updating of her experience of the world. Deficit during childhood, originating with her birth when she was induced two weeks prematurely due to septicaemia, delivered by forceps and needed oxygen (delivered by mask) in her first few hours of life, required reparative experiences – containment, acceptance and permission to live. The psychotherapist would pay close attention to her breathing and, at times when it was clear that Susan's intake of breath was shallow, would facilitate her to breathe in more and regulate her out-breath to provide a more balanced and self-supportive pattern.

In connection with this 'world view' and in the service of liking herself and getting close to others, Susan was encouraged to experiment with varying degrees of physical closeness to others in the psychotherapy group. She gradually began to experience these bodily sensations and contacts, such as touching hands, as both pleasurable and safe. In other words, over time, beginning with awareness of the need for contact, she has allowed herself to accommodate her need for closeness and contact and is moving through to the assimilation of such needs by getting close to others in a more spontaneous way. This has helped to bring about a shift in her view of her body as well as a shift in her view of the world: a significant step for someone whose only experience of physical closeness was with her grandfather who later abused her.

Level 2: emotional

At times when it would have been more appropriate and useful to feel angry or scared, Susan resorted to crying as a defensive means to cutting-off from others. It was not a loud 'relief' crying but a withdrawn, almost sulky sadness. At such times, the psychotherapist suggested that Susan explore any possible anger she might be feeling, for example: 'Supposing there was something you might be angry about, what would it be?'. When encouraged to express it she moved out of her sad, withdrawn state into an energetic mode in which she was more able to actively deal with her problems in the past and in the present. The expression of anger can be seen as moving into her authentic feeling (true self) and out of her inauthentic adaptation (false self) (Winnicott, 1958) – the means by which she had maintained past frames of reference in the here and now. In gestalt terms, the expression of her anger in response to figures from the past can be seen as 'closing' the gestalts that have remained incomplete, or which resulted in fixated, repetitive, physio-affective and behavioural patterns.

The focus of therapy for several months was one of allowing Susan to get in touch with her memories and feelings connected with being sexually abused. She contacted the 'frozen child' (Winnicott, 1958) within herself. Miller's (1983) understanding of the importance for the abused person of re-experiencing the trauma (bringing the past into the present) now with the reparative support of a witness and ally became very significant for Susan. Feeling safe and supported by the psychotherapist in the relationship they had built up over time, and trusting of the other group members, she eventually chose to re-experience the scene of abuse within the psychotherapy group (a source of several allies and witnesses) with the psychotherapist at her side. During this therapeutic work, Susan re-experienced her original terror (connected with the stomach tension referred to at the physiological level). She moved through this to express other feelings repressed at the time of the original trauma. This included anger, which she abreacted with loud shouts and self-protective pushing and hitting of the soft furniture, sadness, disgust and despair expressed in loud sobs and physical shaking, until at the end of the work she expressed a joyous relief, expressed by laughter, in the present. In this way she contacted her true self – not an object used by others but an autonomous person with a full emotional response, unlike the passive false self adaptation within which she felt almost deserving of abuse. Thus, within a safe and supportive current environment and trusting relationships, Susan was able 'to go back in time' to her childhood environment to heal the trauma of abuse. A period of mourning followed (as she worked through the loss of this special relationship with her grandfather, however painful it had been) until she could psychologically assimilate it over time.

Level 3: nominative

Naming is one way of working through confusion in order to resolve conflicts. It was fundamental to Susan's recovery that she name the perpetrator of her abuse in childhood. She had to do this in order to 'let go' of his 'possession' of her in the present and thus allow herself to be close to others. This can be seen in terms of awareness, accommodation and assimilation of the trauma which clearly did not happen all at once but was developed in the therapeutic environment and the psychotherapeutic relationship at several levels.

By naming her grandfather, she was able to take her own power by re-experiencing the event and resolving it within her psyche. For Susan, it was also important that she name her experience as 'abuse'. This was difficult to accept – 'How could someone who loves me abuse me?' But accepting that she was abused, helped put responsibility back with her grandfather where previously she had felt 'bad' or 'wrong' or 'guilty'.

The chronic stomach tension noted on axis III DSM-III-R was also primarily dealt with in a nominative way. In fact, it was by naming the physical sensation in her stomach as 'fear' that Susan was eventually able to access the experience of her sexual abuse. In gestalt terms, Susan moved through the sensation stage (stomach tension) of the gestalt cycle to awareness (naming of fear) which led to the mobilisation of her energy to appropriately protect herself or seek protection (the reparative relationship with her therapist) in order to take action (re-experiencing) and seek the origin through contact (re-decision) and eventual satisfaction (resolution) in order to withdraw from a now satisfactorily closed gestalt.

Level 4: normative

Susan used her body-shape as a 'reason' for not being close to others. This belief may have served a protective role at some stage but in reality it was more Susan's withdrawal and distancing behaviour that prevented closeness. The psychotherapist suggested looking at cultural norms within our society (Wolf, 1990). Together they observed that slimness is a requirement of the media while 'real' people come in a multiplicity of shapes and sizes. This helped Susan to take steps towards 'enjoying owning and being in my body so that I enjoy the experiences of massage, swimming, sex, clothes and other body-linked experiences' which she did by attending body-work sessions, joining in physical activities within the group and photographing herself.

Susan's avoidance of eye-contact was confronted in a normative way by the psychotherapist. He explained that it is an evolved cultural norm to make some eye contact while speaking. So, after some time in therapy when Susan failed to make eye contact, he would bring this to her attention and encourage her to experiment with looking at him. Such interventions as 'This is how I know you are talking to me' or 'This is how I know you are in contact with me as I speak to you' have encouraged this normative aspect of communication. The awareness, accommodation and assimilation process is naturally played out around single interventions, such as an interpretation in a single session, as well as over the longer period of an entire psychotherapy.

The normative level was particularly important within the developmentally needed/reparative relationship with the psychotherapist. Where deficit and trauma had been the originating problems, Susan received various permissions and corrective messages from various ages and stages of development. This was achieved through empathic attunement, modelling, repetition and reassurance and through other familiar re-parenting procedures. For example, towards the end of the second year of psychotherapy, having well established an open and trusting relationship, Susan spent about 15 minutes of each session sitting close by the psychotherapist's side while the rest of the group continued their work. During this time the psychotherapist affirmed her right to be there and told her that her inner Child's needs were OK with him, in order to normalise her need of closeness and attention which had been made 'abnormal' by her father's selective and preferential relationship with her sister.

Clearly, later in her psychotherapy and with termination in sight, the person-to-person relationship between psychotherapist and client increasingly became the norm while the reparative relationship became the exception.

Level 5: rational

For Susan, work at this level primarily took place within the working alliance with her psychotherapist – the relationship within her current psychosocial environment. It included the following rationalisations using techniques including interrogation explanation, information, illustration, persuasion, confirmation, even exhortation in dealing with areas of confusion. This process involved the confrontation of discounting behaviours and re-definitions from transactional analysis along with the three-stage cognitive change techniques of RET to assist in disputing Susan's irrational beliefs, namely:

1. Distinguishing between rational and irrational beliefs.
2. Debating with Socratic questioning.
3. Defining to help her make increasingly accurate definitions.

The following statements summarise the reality gains Susan made at this level.

- That she did not inherit congenital deafness was fortunate but in no way was it her fault that her sister contracted the disease.
- That she did not deserve to be ignored by her father. He did not ignore her because she was 'bad'. All children need care and attention from their parents to grow healthily.
- That her grandfather's sexual abuse of her was wrong. She was not the guilty one. She did nothing to be ashamed of. She was the victim of the situation, not the perpetrator.
- That her mother was unkind and critical of her because of her own inadequacies, not Susan's.

- That it is safe to trust some people and to be close to them.
- That some men do not only get close to women for sex.
- That parents and grandparents are responsible for their children while they are young. Children are not responsible for their parents or grandparents.

Level 6: theoretical (metaphorical)

In the course of her psychotherapy and through her own wide reading, Susan became increasingly 'psychologically minded'. She became familiar with transactional analysis's script theory, RET's theory of the perpetuation of psychological disturbance by negative beliefs in response to negative events, gestalt's 'fixed gestalts' at points around the 'cycle' and some object-relations theory. Suffice it to say that, in the course of her psychotherapy, Susan accepted at the very least the basic theoretical principle that events in the past have influenced the way she feels, thinks and behaves today (the 'nurture' theory). In the following extract Susan is thinking through her experiences on this theoretical level, and interpreting her current behaviour in the light of her past experience.

> What do I need to be forgiven for that I'm often so ashamed and humiliated by criticism? I remember the constant criticism of my mother. I especially remember this excruciating feeling of embarrassment when, having not even entered the High School entrance exam, my mother lied to a friend of hers that the grammar school uniform I was wearing was, in fact, the High School uniform. Of course, the friend knew better and challenged her on it. I wanted to disappear. That's what I've been doing up to now – trying to make myself invisible and unnoticeable and disappear in the face of perceived criticism from others which is really the mother in my head. In my therapy, I'm standing up to her, I'm telling her how embarrassed I was, how cruel she was, how hurt I felt and how I hated her for her constant criticism. I'm standing up to her for the first time and I'm not afraid of her. I feel strong and powerful. I do not disappear in the face of criticism. I stay in the present. I am healing my childhood.

In a similar way, the past was brought into the present through the transferential relationship. It is impossible in a few lines to do justice to this vital aspect of the psychotherapy. Suffice it to say that the transference was used in the re-working of her relationship with both her father and mother. At times the psychotherapist was seen and responded to as the idealised and wished-for father, at others he was seen and responded to negatively as the original withholding and rejecting father (or the cruel and critical mother). At other times, Susan felt identified with what she perceived as the 'needy child' of the psychotherapist.

The psychotherapist's countertransference ranged from experiencing feelings towards Susan of protective caring (and using this in a 'good-enough' rather than 'perfect' reparative way) to dismay when Susan oft-repeated a negative transference which attempted to devalue and destroy the good work she was doing in her psychotherapy. The latter took a lot of working through: the psychotherapist needing to tread a narrow path between interpreting, confronting or simply accepting the negative transference while remaining unrejecting and uncritical of Susan. He responded to her projection of a needy child onto him by understanding her desire to look after him as disguised information as to how she wanted to be looked after herself.

Bringing unconscious or subconscious material to consciousness by the interpretation of dreams was also useful in understanding Susan's past. Before therapy, Susan rarely remembered her dreams. Her psychotherapist asked her to speak to her subconscious and ask it to help her retain her dreams in consciousness – since then she has dreamt many dreams, and kept a rich and fascinating dream diary. For example, she dreamt of looking over a wall at people having fun until she is soaked by a wave of black water. She dreamt she had been given a new party dress which she spilt something on and stained. Her friends said it didn't show but she tried to get rid of it, failed, and missed the party.

Susan saw both these dreams as symbolising her difficulty with intimacy. She understood the wall and the stain as barriers that she used to employ against closeness. The wave of black water she associated with her fear of being close and of being overwhelmed by emotions if she allowed herself to feel them. She felt the stain as her belief that there was something wrong with her. When others accepted her, they were 'fools' not to see it. Susan says, 'I was "stained" by my childhood experiences but instead of blaming myself and trying to scrub them out, I'm finding that time and caring have faded the stains. My self-compassion is transforming the stain into part of the new pattern I am creating.'

Level 7: transpersonal

The transpersonal relationship between Susan and her psychotherapist, so hard to describe, is based upon a genuine, mutual, high regard and acceptance (developed over shared time) that transcends the other definable relationships that have occurred in the course of the psychotherapy.

This relationship was 'felt' implicitly as existing in the 'between' of the relationship – the relationship between the unconscious of the psychotherapist and the unconscious of the client – those moments of being-together in a dimension which is impossible to articulate exactly (Clarkson, 1990). It was, along with a shared belief in change, in a true self and in transformation, a powerful healing force within the psychotherapy.

The inexplicable and the synchronous have also played their part in Susan's psychotherapy. On her birthday, following a psychotherapy session where she had talked of her fear of 'standing on my own two feet', she twisted her ankle. She had twisted her ankle once before on her fifth birthday and at that time had suffered emotional as well as physical hurt by being ignored. Though regretting her injury, Susan took heart in the very different environment (with caring friends) in which she now exists and two nights later was given further symbolic encouragement from her subconscious when she dreamt she was being presented with an award at the school at which she works. Two other staff were awarded toys. She was awarded, to her delight and much applause, a pair of running shoes.

Finally, an even more inexplicable and synchronous event happened towards the end of her psychotherapy, when Susan was disturbed at repeating some transferential attitudes towards her psychotherapist. At the point at which she was complaining that she didn't know what to do, a picture she had drawn of a magician which was on the consulting room wall, revolved quite slowly until the magician came to rest upside down. It can be seen as an example of synchronicity (the acausal connecting principle identified by Jung (1969b). Though quite accepting of the message, Susan appropriately (considering the wish-fulfilling magical nature of the former transference) remained unimpressed by the form of this 'instruction' from the cosmos.

Conclusion

In the course of this chapter, including an illustrative case example, an attempt has been made to describe and clarify the complexities of developing a systemic integrative approach to psychotherapy. Variations and dimensions within the psychotherapeutic field have been outlined as necessary considerations for this task. Hopefully, what the reader is left with is a useful framework for further exploration so that, together, we may better serve the people we aspire to serve and improve communication with each other as practising psychotherapists.

References

AMERICAN PSYCHIATRIC ASSOCIATION (1987). *Diagnostic and Statistical Manual of Mental Disorders*, 3rd edn, revised. Washington, DC: American Psychiatric Association.

ANTHONY, E.J. and COHLER, B.J. (Eds) (1987). *The Invulnerable Child.* New York: Guilford Press.

ARCHAMBEAU, E. (1979). *Beyond Countertransference: The Psychotherapist's Experience of Healing in the Therapeutic Relationship.* PhD dissertation. San Diego: California School of Professional Psychology.

D'ARDENNE, P. and MAHTANI, A. (1989). *Transcultural Counselling in Action.* London: Sage.

ASSAGIOLI, R. (1971). *Psychosynthesis: A Manual of Principles and Techniques.* New York: Viking.

BALINT, M. (1968). *The Basic Fault: Therapeutic Aspects of Regression.* London: Tavistock.

BANDLER, R. and GRINDER, J. (1982). *Reframing: Neuro-Linguistic Programming and the Transformation of Meaning.* Moab, UT: Real People Press.

BATESON, G. (1979). *Mind and Nature: A Necessary Unity.* London: Wildwood House.

BECK, A.T., RUSH, A.J., SHAW, B.F. and EMERY, G. (1979). *Cognitive Therapy of Depression.* New York: Guilford Press.

BECK, A.T., EMERY, G. and GREENBERG, R.L. (1985). *Anxiety Disorders and Phobias: A Cognitive Perspective.* New York: Basic Books.

BERGIN, A.E. and GARFIELD, S.L. (Eds) (1978). *Handbook of Psychotherapy and Behavior Change,* 2nd edn. New York: Wiley.

BERGIN, A.E. (1978). The evaluation of therapeutic outcomes. In: A.E. Bergin and S.L. Garfield (Eds), *Handbook of Psychotherapy and Behavior Change*, pp. 217–270, 2nd edn. New York: Wiley.

BERNE, E. (1969). *A Layman's Guide to Psychiatry and Psychoanalysis.* London: André Deutsch.

BERNE, E. (1975). *Transactional Analysis in Psychotherapy.* London: Souvenir Press. (Originally published 1961.)

BERTALANFFY, L., VON (1969). The theory of open systems in physics and biology. In: F.E. Emery (Ed.), *Systems Thinking*, pp. 70–85. Harmondsworth: Penguin.

BEUTLER, L.E. (1971). Attitude similarity in marital therapy. *Journal of Consulting and Clinical Psychology*, 99, 298–301.

BEUTLER, L.E. (1986). Systemic eclectic psychotherapy. In: J. C. Norcross (Ed.), *Handbook of Eclectic Psychotherapy*, pp. 94–131. New York: Brunner/Mazel.

BOWLBY, J. (1953). Some pathological processes set in motion by early mother–child separation. *Journal of Mental Science,* 99, 265.

BOWLBY, J. (1980). *Attachment and Loss: Vol. 3, Loss*. London: Hogarth Press.

BOWLBY, J. (1985). The role of childhood experience in cognitive disturbance. In: M.J. Mahoney and A. Freeman (Eds), *Cognition and Psychotherapy.* New York: Plenum Press.

BRILL, H. (1967). Nosology. In: A.M. Freedman and H.I. Kaplan (Eds), *Comprehensive Textbook of Psychiatry*, pp.581–589. Baltimore, MD: Williams and Wilkins.

BUBER, M. (1970). *I and Thou* (W. Kaufmann, trans.). Edinburgh: T and T Clark. (Originally published 1923.)

CAPRA, F. (1975). *The Tao of Physics.* London: Wildwood House.

CAPRA, F. (1982). *The Turning Point: Science, Society and the Rising Culture.* London: Wildwood House.

CASHDAN, S. (1988). *Object Relations Theory: Using the Relationship.* New York: W.W. Norton.

CLARKSON, P. (1988). Script cure? – A diagnostic pentagon of types of therapeutic change. *Transactional Analysis Journal,* **18**, 211–219.

CLARKSON, P. (1989a). *Gestalt Counselling in Action*. London: Sage.

CLARKSON, P. (1989b). Metaperspectives on diagnosis. *Transactional Analysis Journal,* **19**, 45–50.

CLARKSON, P. (1992a). Systemic integrative psychotherapy training. In: W. Dryden (Ed.), *Integrative and Eclectic Therapy: A Handbook*, pp.269–295. Milton Keynes: Open University Press

CLARKSON, P. (1992b). Transference and countertransference in TA. In: *Transactional Analysis Psychotherapy: An Integrated Approach*, pp.148–174. London: Routledge.

CLARKSON, P. and FISH, S. (1988). Rechilding: creating a new past in the present as a support for the future. *Transactional Analysis Journal*, **18**, 51–59. (Originally published in Spanish translation 1986.)

CLARKSON, P. and GILBERT, M. (1990a). The training of counsellor trainers and supervisors. In: W. Dryden and B. Thorne (Eds), *Training and Supervision for Counselling in Action*, pp.143–169. London: Sage.

CLARKSON, P. and GILBERT, M. (1990b). Transactional analysis. In: W. Dryden (Ed.) *Handbook of Individual Therapy in Britain*, pp.199–225. Milton Keynes: Open University Press.

CORSINI, R. (1984). *Current Psychotherapies*. Itasca, IL: F.E. Peacock.

CORSINI, R. and ROSENBERG, B. (1955). Mechanisms of group psychotherapy: processes and dynamics. *Journal of Abnormal and Social Psychology*, **51**, 406–411.

COTTONE, R.R. (1988). Epistemological and ontological issues in counselling: implications of social systems theory. *Counselling Psychology Quarterly*, **1**, 357–365.

DALDRUP, R.J., BEUTLER, L.E., ENGLE, D. and GREENBERG, L.S. (1988). *Focused Expressive Psychotherapy: Freeing the Overcontrolled Patient*. London: Cassell.

DE LISLE, G. (1988). *Balises II: A Gestalt Perspective of Personality Disorders*. Montreal: Le Centre d'Intervention Gestaltiste, Le Reflet.

DOUGLAS, T. (1976). *Group Work Practice*. London: Tavistock.

DRYDEN, W. (1984). Issues in the eclectic practice of individual therapy. In: W. Dryden (Ed.), *Individual Therapy in Britain*, pp. 341–363. London: Harper and Row.

DRYDEN, W. (1986). Eclectic psychotherapies: a critique of leading approaches. In: J.C. Norcross (Ed.), *Eclectic Psychotherapy: An Introduction and Overview*, pp. 353–375. New York: Brunner/Mazel.

DRYDEN, W. (1987). *Counselling Individuals: The Rational–Emotive Approach*, London: Taylor and Francis.

DRYDEN, W. and NORCROSS, J.C. (Eds) (1990). *Eclecticism and Integration in Counselling and Psychotherapy*. Loughton: Gale Centre.

EICHENBAUM, L. and ORBACH, S. (1983). *Outside In...Inside Out – Women's Psychology: A Feminist Psychoanalytic Approach*. Harmondsworth: Penguin.

ELLIS, A. (1962). *Reason and Emotion in Psychotherapy*. New York: Lyle Stuart.

ENRIGHT, J. (1980). *Enlightening Gestalt: Waking Up from the Nightmare*. Mill Valley, CA: Pro-Telos.

ERICKSON, M.H. (1967). *Advanced Techniques of Hypnosis and Therapy*. New York: Grune and Stratton.

ERIKSON, E. (1977). *Childhood and Society*. London: Triad Granada. (Originally published 1951.)

EYSENCK, H.J. (1952). The effects of psychotherapy: an evaluation. *Journal of Consulting Psychology*, 16, 319–324.

EYSENCK, H.J. (Ed.) (1968). *Handbook of Abnormal Psychology*. London: Pitman Medical Publishing.

FAIRBAIRN, W.R.D. (1952). *Psycho-analytic Studies of the Personality*. London:Tavistock.

FARRELL, B.A. (1979). Work in small groups: some philosophical considerations. In: B. Babington Smith and B.A. Farrell (Eds), *Training in Small Groups: A Study of Five Methods*, pp. 103–115. Oxford: Pergamon Press.

FEDERN, P. (1977). *Ego Psychology and the Psychoses.* London: Maresfield Reprints. (Originally published 1953.)

FERENCZI, S. (1980). *Further Contributions to the Theory and Technique of Psycho-Analysis.* London: Maresfield Reprints. (Originally published 1926.)

FIEDLER, F.E. (1950). A comparison of therapeutic relationships in psychoanalytic, nondirective and Adlerian therapy. *Journal of Consulting Psychology,* 14, 436–445.

FIVAZ, R. (1980). Une evolution vers l'impasse? *Polyrama,* Ecole Polytechnique Fédérale de Lausanne, **45**, 9–11.

FONAGY, P. (1989). On the integration of cognitive-behaviour theory with psycho-analysis. *British Journal of Psychotherapy,* **5**, 557–63.

FOX, M. (1983). *Original Blessing: A Primer in Creation Spirituality.* Santa Fe, NM: Bear and Co.

FRANK, J.D. (1979). The present status of outcome studies. *Journal of Consulting and Clinical Psychology,* 47, 310–316.

FREUD, S. (1977). Three essays on sexuality. In: A. Richards (Ed.) and J. Strachey, (trans.), *The Pelican Freud Library, Vol.* 7, pp. 33–170. Harmondsworth: Penguin. (Originally published 1905.)

FROMM, E. (1960). *Psychoanalysis and Zen Buddhism.* London: Allen and Unwin.

FROMM-REICHMANN, F. (1974). *Principles of Intensive Psychotherapy.* Chicago: University of Chicago Press. (Originally published 1950.)

GARFIELD, S.L. (1980). *Psychotherapy: An Eclectic Approach.* New York: Wiley.

GARFIELD, S.L. (1982). Eclecticism and integration in psychotherapy. *Behavior Therapy,* 13, 610–623.

GARFIELD, S.L. (1986). An eclectic psychotherapy. In: J. C. Norcross (Ed.), *Handbook of Eclectic Psychotherapy,* pp. 132–162. New York: Brunner/Mazel.

GLASSER, W. (1965). *Reality Therapy.* New York: Harper and Row.

GLEICK, J. (1988). *Chaos: Making a New Science.* London: Heinemann.

GOLDSTEIN, K. (1939). *The Organism,* Book 6. New York: America Books.

GOTTLIEB, S. (1989). The pregnant psychotherapist: a potent transference stimulus. *British Journal of Psychotherapy,* **5**, 287–299.

GOULDING, M.M. and GOULDING, R.L. (1979). *Changing Lives Through Redecision Therapy.* New York: Brunner/Mazel.

GREENBERG, I.A. (Ed.) (1975). *Psychodrama: Theory and Therapy.* London: Souvenir Press. (Originally published 1974.)

GREENBERG, L.S. and SAFRAN, J.D. (1987). *Emotion in Psychotherapy: The Process of Therapeutic Change.* New York: Guilford.

GREENSON, R.R. (1965). The working alliance and the transference neuroses. *Psychoanalytic Quarterly,* 34, 155–181.

GREENSON, R.R. (1967). *The Technique and Practice of Psychoanalysis,* Vol. 1. New York: International Universities Press.

GRIFFITH, S. (1990). A review of the factors associated with patient compliance and the taking of prescribed medicines. *British Journal of General Practice,* **40**, 114–16.

GUERRIERE, D. (1980). Physis, sophia, psyche. In: J. Sallis and K. Maly (Eds). *Heraclitean Fragments: A Companion Volume to the Heidegger/Fink Seminar on Heraclitus,* pp. 87–134. Tuscaloosa, AL: University of Alabama Press.

GUY, J.D. (1987). *The Personal Life of the Psychotherapist.* New York: Wiley.

HALEY, J. (1963). *Strategies of Psychotherapy.* New York: Grune and Stratton.

HAWKING, S. (1988). *A Brief History of Time.* London: Bantam Press.

HEIDEGGER, M. (1949). *Existence and Being.* Chicago: Henry Regnery. (Originally published 1929.)

HEIMANN, P. (1950). On countertransference. *International Journal of Psychoanalysis,* **31**, 81–84.

HERON, J. (1990). *Helping the Client: A Creative Practical Guide.* London: Sage.

HINSHELWOOD, R.D. (1989). *A Dictionary of Kleinian Thought.* London: Free Association Press.

HOFFMAN, L. (1981). *Foundations of Family Therapy: A Conceptual Framework for Systems Change.* New York: Basic Books.

HOLMES, J. and LINDLEY, R. (1989). *The Values of Psychotherapy.* Oxford: Oxford University Press.

HYNAN, M.T. (1981). On the advantages of assuming that the techniques of psychotherapy are ineffective. *Psychotherapy: Theory, Research and Practice,* **18**, 11–13.

JACOBSON, E. (1964). *Anxiety and Tension Control: A Psychobiologic Approach.* Philadelphia: Lippincott.

JAMES, J. (1983). Cultural consciousness: the challenge to TA. *Transactional Analysis Journal,* **13**, 207–216.

JAMES, M. (1974). Self-reparenting: theory and process. *Transactional Analysis Journal,* 4 (3), 32–39.

JAMES, M. and SAVARY, L. (1977). *The New Self: Self Therapy with Transactional Analysis.* Reading, MA: Addison-Wesley.

JASPERS, K. (1963). *General Psychopathology* (J. Hoenig and M.W. Hamilton, trans.). Chicago: University of Chicago Press. (Originally published 1913.)

JUNG, C.G. (1944). *Psychological Types* (H.G. Baynes, trans.). London: Trench Trubner.

JUNG, C.G. (1968). Archetypes of the collective unconscious. In: *The Collected Works,* Vol. 9, Part 1, 2nd edn, pp.3–41. London: Routledge and Kegan Paul. (Originally published 1934.)

JUNG, C.G. (1969a). Psychology and religion. In: *The Collected Works,* Vol. 11, 2nd edn pp.3–106. London: Routledge and Kegan Paul. (Originally published 1938.)

JUNG, C.G. (1969b). Synchronicity: an acausal connecting principle. In: *The Collected Works,* Vol. 8 (2nd edn) pp.417–519. London: Routledge and Kegan Paul. (Originally published 1952.)

JUNG, C.G. (1977). Symbols and the interpretation of dreams. In: *The Collected Works,* Vol. 18, pp.185–266. London: Routledge and Kegan Paul. (Originally published 1961.)

KELEMAN, S. (1985). *Emotional Anatomy: The Structure of Experience.* Berkeley, CA: Center Press.

KELLY, G.A. (1955). *The Psychology of Personal Constructs.* New York: W. W. Norton.

KERNBERG, O.F. (1984). *Severe Personality Disorders: Psychotherapeutic Strategies.* New Haven, CT: Yale University Press.

KLAUBER, J. (1986). Elements of the psychoanalytic relationship and their therapeutic implications. In: G. Kohon (Ed.), *The British School of Psychoanalysis: The Independent Tradition,* pp.200–213. London: Free Association Books.

KLEIN, M. (1984). *Envy, Gratitude and Other Works.* London: Hogarth Press and Institute for Psychoanalysis. (Originally published 1957.)

KOESTLER, A. (1972). *The Roots of Coincidence.* London: Hutchinson.

KOESTLER, A. (1989). *The Act of Creation.* London: Arkana. (Originally published 1964.)

KOHUT, H. (1977). *The Restoration of the Self.* New York: International Universities Press.

KOTTLER, J.A. (1986). *On Being a Therapist.* San Francisco: Jossey-Bass.

KUHN, T.S. (1970). *The Structure of Scientific Revolutions,* 2nd edn. Chicago: University of Chicago Press.

LACOURSIERE, R. (1980). *Life Cycle of Groups.* New York: Human Sciences Press.

LAING, R.D. (1965). *The Divided Self.* Harmondsworth: Penguin.

LAMBERT, M.J. (1986). Implications of psychotherapy outcome research for eclectic psychotherapy. In: J.C. Norcross (Ed.), *Handbook of Eclectic Psychotherapy,* pp.436–462. New York: Brunner/Mazel.

LAMBERT, M.J., BERGIN, A.E. and COLLINS, J.L. (1977). Therapist-induced deterioration in psychotherapy. In: A.S. Gurman and A.M. Razin (Eds), *Effective Psychotherapy: A Handbook of Research,* pp.452–481. New York: Pergamon Press.

LANGS, R. (1976). *The Bipersonal Field.* New York: Jason Aronson.

LAZARUS, A.A. (1981). *The Practice of Multimodal Therapy.* New York: McGraw-Hill.

LEVINSON, D.J. (1978). *The Seasons of a Man's Life.* New York: Ballantine.

LOVEJOY, A. and BOAS, G. (1973). *Primitivism and Related Areas in Antiquity.* New York: Ferrar, Strauss and Giraux.

LOWEN, A. (1969). *The Betrayal of the Body.* New York: Collier-Macmillan.

LUBORSKY, L., SINGER, B. and LUBORSKY, L. (1975). Comparative studies of psychotherapies: is it true that "Everybody has won and all must have prizes"? *Archives of General Psychiatry,* **32**, 995–1008.

LYOTARD, J.F. (1984). *The Postmodern Condition: A Report on Knowledge,* (G. Bennington and B. Massumi, trans.) Manchester: Manchester University Press.

MAHLER, M.S., PINE, F. and BERGMAN, A. (1975). *The Psychological Birth of the Human Infant.* London: Hutchinson.

MAHRER, A.R. (1989). *The Integration of Psychotherapies: A Guide for Practicing Therapists.* Ottawa: Human Sciences Press.

MALCOLM, J. (1981). *Psychoanalysis: The Impossible Profession.* New York: Knopf.

MANDER, A.V. and RUSH, A.K. (1974). *Feminism As Therapy.* New York: Random House.

MARMOR, J. (1982). Change in psychoanalytic treatment. In: S. Slipp (Ed.) *Curative Factors in Dynamic Psychotherapy.* New York: McGraw-Hill.

MARUYAMA, M. (1968). The second cybernetics: deviation-amplifying mutual causal processes. In: W. Buckley (Ed.) *Modern Systems Research for the Behavioral Scientist.* Chicago: Aldine.

MASLOW, A. (1968). *Toward a Psychology of Being,* 2nd edn. New York: Van Nostrand.

MATURANA, H.R. (1980). Biology of cognition. In: H.R. Maturana and F.J. Varela *Autopoiesis and Cognition: The Realization of the Living.* Boston, MA: D. Reidel. (Originally published 1970.)

MERLEAU-PONTY, M. (1962). *The Phenomenonology of Perception* (Colin Smith, trans.). London: Routledge and Kegan Paul.

MILLER, A. (1983). *The Drama of the Gifted Child and the Search for the True Self.* London: Faber and Faber.

MILLER, A. (1985). *Thou Shalt Not Be Aware: Society's Betrayal of the Child* (H. and H. Hannum, trans.) London: Pluto Books. (Originally published 1981.)

MILLON, T. (1969). *Modern Psychopathology: A Biosocial Approach to Maladaptive Learning and Functioning.* Philadelphia, PA: W.B. Saunders.

MINKOWSKI, E. (1970). *Lived Time* (N. Metzel, trans.). Evanston, IL: Northwestern University Press. (Originally published 1933.)

MORGAN, G. (1986). *Images of Organization.* Beverly Hills, CA: Sage.

NORCROSS, J.C. (1986). Eclectic psychotherapy: an introduction and overview. In: J.C.

Norcross (Ed.), *Handbook of Eclectic Psychotherapy*, pp.3–24. New York: Brunner/Mazel.

ONIONS, C.T. (Ed.) (1973). *The Shorter Oxford English Dictionary*, 3rd edn. Oxford: Oxford University Press.

ORBACH, S. (1978). *Fat Is a Feminist Issue.* London: Arrow.

OSNES, R.E. (1974). Spot-reparenting. *Transactional Analysis Journal*, 4 (3), 40–46.

PAVLOV, I.P. (1928). *Lectures on Conditioned Reflexes*, (W.H. Ganff, trans.). New York: International Publishers.

PECK, S. (1978). *The Road Less Travelled: A New Psychology of Love, Traditional Values and Spiritual Growth.* New York: Simon and Schuster.

PILGRIM, D. (1989). The rise and rise of clinical psychology *Changes*, 7, 44–6.

PINE, F. (1985). *Developmental Theory and Clinical Process.* New Haven, CT: Yale University Press.

POLSTER, E. and POLSTER, M. (1974). *Gestalt Therapy Integrated.* New York: Vintage. (Originally published 1973.)

RACKER, H. (1982). *Transference and Countertransference.* London: Maresfield Reprints. (Originally published 1968.)

REASON, P. and ROWAN, J. (Eds) (1981). *Human Inquiry: A Sourcebook of New Paradigm Research.* Chichester: Wiley.

REICH, W. (1972). *Character Analysis*, 3rd edn. New York: Simon and Schuster.

ROBINSON, W.L. (1974). Conscious competency – the mark of a competent instructor. *Personnel Journal*, 53, 538–539.

ROGERS, C.R. (1961). *On Becoming A Person: A Therapist's View of Psychotherapy.* London: Constable.

ROGERS, C.R. (1986). *Client-Centered Therapy.* London: Constable.

ROSSI, E.L. and CHEEK, D.B. (1988). *Mind–Body Therapy: Ideodynamic Healing in Hypnosis.* New York: W.W. Norton.

ROTHENBERG, A. (1979). *The Emerging Goddess.* Chicago: University of Chicago Press.

ROTHSTEIN, A. (Ed.) (1985). *Models of the Mind: Their Relationships to Clinical Work.* Madison, CT: International Universities Press.

ROWAN, J. (1973). *The Reality Game.* London: Routledge.

ROWAN, J. (1988). Counselling and the psychology of furniture. *Counselling: Journal for the British Association of Counselling*, 64, 21–24.

ROWAN, J. (1990). *Subpersonalities: The People Inside Us.* London: Routledge.

ROWE, C.E. and MACISAAC, D. (1989). *Empathic Attunement: The 'Technique' of Psychoanalytic Self Psychology.* Northvale, NJ: Jason Aronson.

ROWE, D. (1988). *The Successful Self.* London: Fontana.

RUTTER, M. (1972). *Maternal Deprivation Reassessed.* Harmondsworth: Penguin.

RYLE, G. (1973). *Dilemmas: The Tarner Lectures, 1953.* Cambridge: Cambridge University Press.

SAMUELS, A. (1985). *Jung and the Post-Jungians.* London: Routledge and Kegan Paul.

SATIR, V. (1967). *Conjoint Family Therapy.* Palo Alto, CA: Science and Behavior Books.

SCHIFF, J. and DAY, B. (1970). *All My Children.* New York: Pyramid Publications.

SCHIFF, J.L. with SCHIFF, A.W., MELLOR, K., SCHIFF, E., SCHIFF,S., RICHMAN, D., FISHMAN, J., WOLZ, L., FISHMAN, C. and MOMB, D. (1975). *Cathexis Reader: Transactional Analysis Treatment of Psychosis.* New York: Harper and Row.

SECHEHAYE, M. (1951). *Reality Lost and Regained: Autobiography of a Schizophrenic Girl, with Analytic Interpretation by M. Sechehaye* (F. Urbin-Ralson, trans.). New York: Grune and Stratton.

SHAKESPEARE, W. (1951). *The Complete Works*, P. Alexander (Ed.). London: Collins.

SIMON, S.B., HOWE, L.W. and KIRSCHENBAUM, H. (1972) *Values Clarification: A Handbook of Practical Strategies for Teachers and Students.* New York: Dodd, Mead and Co.

SLOANE, R.B., STAPLES, F.R., CRISTOL, A.H., YORKSTON, N.J. and WHIPPLE, K. (1975). *Short-term Analytically Oriented Psychotherapy Versus Behavior Therapy.* Cambridge, MA: Harvard University Press.

SMAIL, D.J. (1978). *Psychotherapy: A Personal Approach.* London: J.M. Dent.

SPIEGELBERG, H. (1972). *Phenomenology in Psychology and Psychiatry.* Evanston, IL: Northwestern University Press.

STERN, D.N. (1985). *The Interpersonal World of the Infant.* New York: Basic Books.

STONE, L. (1961). *The Psychoanalytic Situation.* New York: International Universities Press.

SYMINGTON, N. (1986). *The Analytic Experience: Lectures from the Tavistock.* London: Free Association Books.

TEILHARD DE CHARDIN, P. (1970). *The Phenomenon of Man.* London: Fontana. (Originally published 1955.)

VAUGHAN, F. (1985). *The Inward Arc.* Boston, MA: New Science Library.

WATKINS, J.G. (1976). Ego states and the problem of responsibility: a psychological analysis of the Patty Hearst case. *Journal of Psychiatry and Law,* Winter, 471–489.

WATKINS, J. G. and WATKINS, H. H. (1986). Hypnosis, multiple personality and ego states as altered states of consciousness. In: B. B. Wolman and M. Ullman (Eds) *Handbook of States of Consciousness,* pp. 133–158. New York: Van Nostrand Reinhold.

WATZLAWICK, P., HELMICK BEAVIN, J. and JACKSON, D.D. (1967). *Pragmatics of Human Communication: A Study of Interactional Patterns, Pathologies and Paradoxes.* New York: W.W. Norton.

WATZLAWICK, P., WEAKLAND, J.H. and FISCH, R. (1974). *Change: Principles of Problem Formation and Problem Resolution.* New York: Norton.

WEISS, E. (1950). *Principles of Psychodynamics.* New York: Grune and Stratton.

WILBER, K. (1980). *The Atman Project: A Transpersonal View of Human Development.* Wheaton: Theosophical Publishing House.

WILHELM, R. (trans.) (1988). *The I Ching.* London: Routledge and Kegan Paul. (Originally published 1951.)

WINNICOTT, D.W. (1958). *Collected Papers: Through Paediatrics to Psychoanalysis.* London: Tavistock.

WINNICOTT, D.W. (1960). *The Maturational Processes and the Facilitating Environment.* London: Hogarth.

WITTGENSTEIN, L. (1953). *Philosophical Investigations.* Oxford: Blackwell and Mott.

WOLF, N. (1990). *The Beauty Myth.* London: Chatto and Windus.

WOLPE, J. (1961). The systematic desensitization treatment of neuroses. *Journal of Nervous and Mental Disease,* **132**, 189–203.

WORLD HEALTH ORGANIZATION (1978). *Mental Disorders: Glossary and Guide to Their Classification.* Geneva: WHO.

YALOM, I. (1975). *The Theory and Practice of Group Psychotherapy,* 2nd edn. New York: Basic Books.

ZOHAR, D. (1990). *The Quantum Self.* London: Bloomsbury.

Part IV
Transference and Countertransference in Psychotherapy and Supervision

Chapter 9
Through the Looking Glass: Explorations in Transference and Countertransference

Introduction

From both Greek and Latin the word *transference* means 'to carry across'. The phenomenon of 'carrying across' qualities from what is known (based on past experience) to what is analogous in the present has probably always been a feature of human psychology. Such processes occur between husband and wife, teacher and pupil, citizen and state functionary. Thus it is important to recognise that transference and countertransference in this sense are ubiquitous and necessary components of any learning processes. *They occur whenever emotions, perceptions or reactions are based on past experiences rather than on the here-and-now.*

The subject of transference involves an astonishing variety of contradictions, ambiguities and connotational disputes. The number of 'types' of transference and related phenomena also decreases or increases depending on the author and the method of classification used.

It is this author's view that apparent theoretical inconsistencies are often the result of confusions about definitions, which are herein reviewed. This chapter presents a practical map for use by transactional analysts and other psychotherapists. It is effective when used as a tool in supervision (from self or supervisor) and not as an analytic disturbance to the development of the transference modality in the psychotherapeutic relationship. Of course, the map is not the territory. It has been found effective for planning or anticipating directions in treatment or helping the psychotherapist understand the situation better when there are intractable difficulties or unrelenting plateaux.

From Clarkson, P. (1991). Through the looking glass: explorations in transference and countertransference. *Transactional Analysis Journal*, 21 (2), 99–107, with permission.
This and Chapter 10 are abbreviated segments from *Transactional Analysis: An Integrated Approach* by P. Clarkson (1992). London: Routledge. The author is grateful to Jenny Mackewn for editorial assistance.

Transference, of course, is only one of several therapeutic relationships potentially present between patient and therapist in psychotherapy. It is to be differentiated from the working alliance, the reparative/developmentally needed relationship, the real (I–You) relationship and the transpersonal relationship (see Chapter 2).

Transference Phenomena: Definitions and Types

In Freudian psychoanalysis, transference was originally regarded as an unfortunate phenomenon which interfered with the process of psychoanalysis (Freud, 1958; originally published in 1912). Later, however, Freud (1955; originally published in 1920) saw it as an essential part of the psychotherapeutic process and indeed one of the cornerstones of psychoanalytic practice. Fairbairn (1952), Klein (1984) and Winnicott (1975) assumed that patients' responses in the transference relationship were valid evidence on which to base their theories about the origin of object relations in infancy.

Definitions of Transference

Rycroft (1972) defined transference as:

> 1. The process by which a patient displaces on to his analyst feelings, ideas, etc., which derive from previous figures in his life; by which he relates to his analyst as though he were some former object in his life; by which he projects on to his analyst object-representations acquired by earlier introjections; by which he endows the analyst with the significance of another, usually prior, object. 2. The state of mind produced by 1 in the patient. 3. Loosely, the patient's emotional attitude towards his analyst.
>
> (p. 168)

According to Racker (1982), Freud denominated as transference all the patient's psychological phenomena and processes which referred to the analyst and were derived from other previous object relations. Therefore in one usage it refers to all feelings of the patient towards the psychotherapist which are transferred from past relationships. The *phenomenological time* of transference is thus the past replayed in the present as if it were the present. The *phenomenological shape* of transference is the fantasised externalisation of an internal relationship between the individual and one or more others. (Manor (1992) relates this to intrapsychic and external transactional object relations.) These others represent significant relationships of the individual's past (such as the mother/infant dyad, the child/parental couple triad, the child/family group, or the child/teacher/peer relationship).

Transference is thus that anticipatory pattern of relationship which the individual seeks to replicate with significant others, regardless of his or her individual, unique qualities experienced at that moment. Transference thus is that relational pattern people carry with them from situation to situation. The other person is not freely met for the first time, but is more often met through a screen on which the person is projecting his or her own particular movie.

This chapter concentrates on dyadic transferential relationship patterns, leaving the triadic and group transferential phenomena for later discussion. However, the same analytic map presented here can be easily extrapolated to fit triadic or group transferences.

Transference is one of the primary mechanisms by which human beings learn from their past relationships to anticipate how to behave in future relationships. For many people, past object relationships have been traumatic or strained (Pine, 1985) and they carry the pattern of these learned relationships into their present lives and future as well as into the psychotherapeutic relationship. Therefore, until the transference is resolved, the *anticipated other* remains psychologically unchanged as the script process unfolds outside Adult awareness.

> The decisive part of the work is achieved by creating in the patient's relation to the doctor – in the 'transference' – new editions of the old conflicts; in these the patient would like to behave in the same way as he did in the past, while we, by summoning up every available mental force in the patient compel him to come to a fresh decision.
>
> (Freud, in Racker, 1982, p. 46)

Regardless of whether the psychotherapist intentionally attempts to present a blank screen or not, workable transference phenomena occur with sufficient duration and intensity necessary in most therapeutic relationships for effective psychotherapy to take place.

Perspectives on Transference

Although the terms 'complementary' and 'concordant' are used by Freud (1955) and Racker (1982) to describe forms of countertransference rather than transference, they are used here to describe several other kinds of transferential phenomena. Novellino (1984) appeared to use the term 'conforming identification countertransference' (p. 63) in the same way that Racker (1982) used 'concordant countertransference', but he retained the use of 'complementary identification countertransference' (p. 84). The terms 'abnormal' and 'normal' were used by Winnicott (1975) in relation to countertransference. This chapter suggests that the terms 'facilitative' and 'destructive' are better suited to these phenomena, and it extrapolates their use to other categories of transference phenomena in the psychotherapeutic and supervisory relationship.

Also introduced in this context are Lewin's (1963) terms *proactive* and *reactive* to designate whether the subject of the discussion originates the stimulus (proacts) or responds (reacts) to a stimulus from the other. Because the psychotherapeutic space belongs essentially to the patient, the psychotherapist's proactivity is usually, although not always, viewed as detracting from the primary task – enhancing the patient's autonomous proactivity.

It is important to remember throughout the following discussion that transferential or countertransferential stimuli may be verbal or non-verbal. According to Berne's (1961) third rule of communication the ulterior or psychological level will generally determine the outcome. The mechanism by which this occurs is probably a form of hypnotic induction (Conway and Clarkson, 1987). Under the circumstances described in their paper, ulterior messages (communications) can have the force of hypnotic inductions when a person's Adult is decommissioned. Script decisions often influence or interfere with integrated Adult functioning (good contact with current reality). Therefore, whomever (analyst and/or patient) is not in Adult may very well be influenced *outside awareness* to feel or act in ways consistent with the other's script expectations. This corresponds with and explains the idea of projective identification: 'A complex clinical event of an interpersonal type: one person disowns his feelings and manipulatively, *induces* [italics added] the other into experiencing them' (Hinshelwood, 1989, p. 200).

Watkins (1954) also speculated on the similarities between trance and transference, enumerating several ways in which psychoanalytic procedures *induce* changes of consciousness resembling trance induction. Unlike the intimates of patients who have been *role played into* the patient's games, psychotherapists who have been through their own personal psychotherapy are trained to remain with Adult in the executive while doing psychotherapy. Thus they can notice the transferential projections and expectations in the ways they react to the patient, using such information to benefit the patient. Such *objectivity* necessitates considerable self-knowledge, regular supervision, and interpersonal satisfactions outside psychotherapeutic work.

Categories of Patient Transference

Complementary transference

In this form of transference, the patient seeks completion of the symbiotic relationship. In a complementary transference towards the projected Parent of the psychotherapist, the patient projects the actual or fantasised past historical parent onto the psychotherapist. For example, the patient expects the psychotherapist to humiliate him/her in the same way as their historical parent did. Alternatively, the patient may hope for an idealised fantasy parent based on their childhood wishes.

In another variation of complementary transference, the patient projects the actual or fantasised past Child ego state(s) of the parent onto the psychotherapist. For example, the patient takes care of the psychotherapist's Child by protecting him or her from the patient's rage, or behaves in a way similar to the punitive parenting that the patient introjected from his or her own abusive parent(s).

Because of the nature of the psychotherapeutic relationship, projections onto the Child of the psychotherapist will tend to be of second-order structural symbiotic kind. That is, as it is not the patient's function to take care of the psychotherapist, but vice versa, it is usually based on fantasy, for example, that the psychotherapist needs to be taken care of because he or she is frightened. Equally, an impaired psychotherapeutic relationship may arise, for example, when the therapist inappropriately shows vulnerability or makes demands on the patient for such caretaking. To avoid the despair of realising and reliving the failure of the original parents, the patient may move into the complementary Child-to-Parent transference.

Concordant transference

This form of transference occurs when the patient projects his or her own past Child onto the psychotherapist in an attempt to find identification. For example, the patient imagines that the psychotherapist feels sad and lonely whereas the patient's historic Child is grieving for an early parental abandonment. In this form of transference, the patient may experience both self and psychotherapist as equally helpless. People with a narcissistic personality disorder often use this form of transference, particularly in the beginning of psychotherapy. 'I see in you, my psychotherapist, the ways you are like me.' So in a sense, this kind of patient experience has similarities to the mirroring or twin transferences of Kohut (1977). Either complementary or concordant transference may contain potentials or elements of destructive or facilitative forces.

Destructive transference

This describes the patient's acted out or fantasised destructive past as manifested in the psychotherapeutic relationship. Of course, this only refers to occasions when third-degree games are played to the pay-off point and does not refer to the therapeutic use of destructive feelings and fantasies. It specifically refers to behaviour that exceeds the boundaries of the psychotherapeutic contract and that can no longer be dealt with in the psychotherapeutic arena. Such acting out of second- or third-degree games – such as homicide, suicide or transference psychosis – effectively destroys the psychotherapeutic contract and often represents a script payoff or conclusion. Such destructive acting-out makes management procedures (hospital admission or daily supervision, for example) extraneous to the psychotherapeutic relationship necessary.

Facilitative transference

It is important to differentiate normal or healthy transference phenomena from other types of transference. The patient in this case may transfer (carry over) onto the current psychotherapeutic relationship a temperamental preference or style on the basis of what has been effective for him or her in the past . An easy-going phlegmatic patient, who has a temperamentally slower pace (Eysenck and Rachman, 1965) may prefer a psychotherapist of a similar temperament. This is not necessarily pathological.

This facilitating form of transference does not fit the definition of script. It may represent productive learned patterns from the past which are transferred into the present with a successful outcome. As these patterns are not self-limiting (as scripts are) but, rather, self-actualising or aspirational (see Chapter 4), they should not be pathologised, but seen as the possible basis for choosing a compatible partner in the psychotherapeutic journey. However, they are technically transferential in the sense that they are transferred from past affective relationships, not newly formed in the here-and-now.

Figure 9.1 summarises this chapter for the sake of comparison, clarity and overview. It would be most useful for the reader to look only at one segment at a time after a particular topic has been discussed. The figure brings together the different kinds of transference and countertransference in a comprehensive way. It also adds brief (because of limitations of space) explanations in transactional analysis terms.

Countertransference Phenomena: Definitions and Types

Rycroft (1972) defined countertransference as

> 1. The analyst's TRANSFERENCE on his patient. In this, correct, sense, countertransference is a disturbing, distorting element in treatment. 2. By extension, the analyst's emotional attitude towards his patient, including his response to specific items of the patient's behaviour. According to Heimann (1950), Little (1951), Gitelson (1952), and others, the analyst can use this latter kind of countertransference as clinical evidence, i.e. he can assume

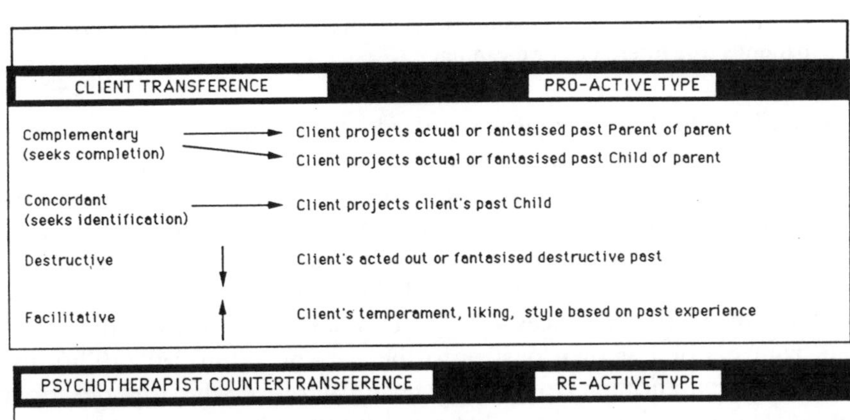

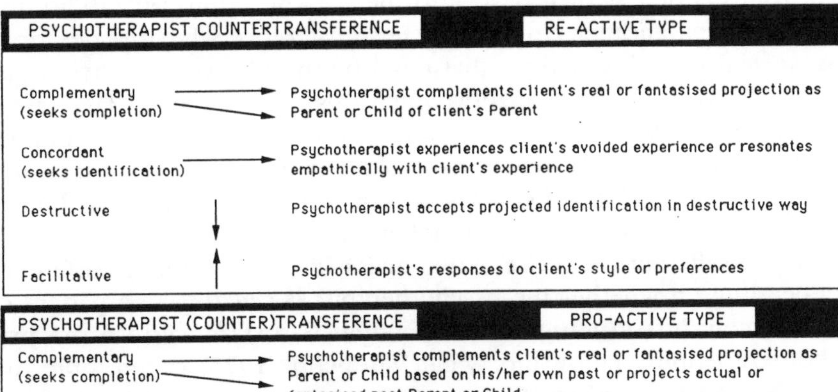

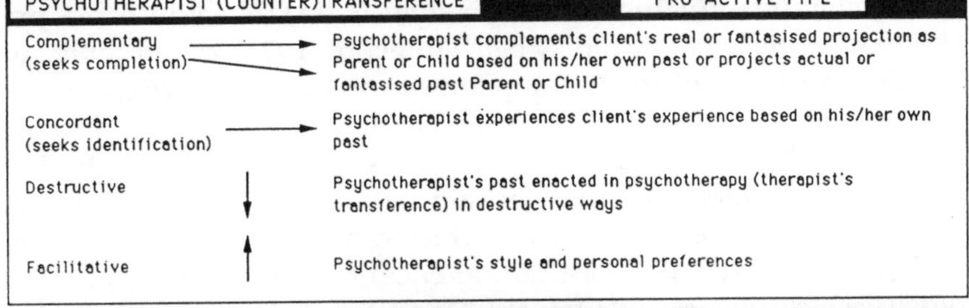

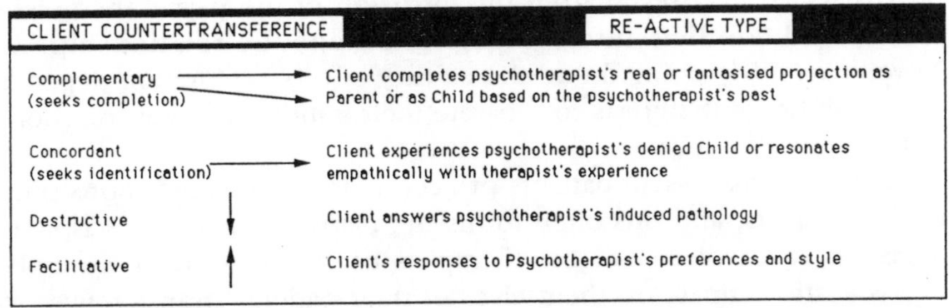

Figure 9.1 Summary of transference and countertransference. Diagonal arrows are used in relation to complementary transferences to indicate the psychological inequality of the complementary relationships; horizontal arrows visually demonstrate concordance or identification; downward arrows allude to the destructiveness of unhealthy transference and its possible relationship to the force of Destrudo (Weiss, 1950; Berne, 1969); the upward-pointing arrows represent the aspirational arrow possibly related to Physis, the generalised creative urge that reaches upward out of the individual's past experiences towards the transformative potential inherent in human nature (Berne, 1969, p. 89).

> that his own emotional response is based on a correct interpretation of the patient's true intentions or meaning.
>
> (p. 25).

As can be seen from Rycroft's standard definition, there are two major categories of countertransference: one constituting the analyst's transference onto the patient, and the other the analyst's responses to the patient. Winnicott (1975) defined as abnormal countertransference 'those areas that arise from the analyst's past unresolved conflicts that intrude on the present patient' (p. 175). In a sense these are the psychotherapist's transferences – the psychotherapist is transferring material from his or her own past onto the patient. Winnicott (1975) also differentiated another type of countertransference which he described as normal – those reactions that describe the idiosyncratic style of an analyst's work and personality, which this author sees as facilitative. Winnicott (1975) also identified a category he called 'objective countertransference.... Those reactions evoked in an analyst by a patient's behaviour and personality...[which] can provide the analyst with valuable internal clues about what is going on in the patient' (p. 195).

I also differentiate between two major kinds of countertransference depending on whether the psychotherapist is *reacting to* a patient or proactively *introducing his or her own transference* into the psychotherapeutic relationship. What Winnicott (1975) called 'objective countertransference' (p.195) is referred to here as *reactive countertransference* to emphasise that the psychotherapist is reacting accurately or objectively to the patient's projections, personality and behaviour in the psychotherapeutic relationship. Winnicott's (1975) 'abnormal countertransference' (p.195) is referred to here as *proactive countertransference* (psychotherapist transference) to emphasise the potential pitfalls which may result from the intrusion of the psychotherapist's unresolved conflicts into the psychotherapeutic relationship. As Novellino (1984) pointed out, the efficacy of this exploration depends on the ability of therapists to separate their issues from their reactions to the patient's issues.

As already discussed, patients project their script expectations onto their therapists, and this often forms the matrix from which script redecisions can evolve. Whether therapists use the emotional, symbolic or associative impact on themselves of their patients' transferences to benefit the patients (reactive countertransference), or as a vehicle for enacting their own historically determined relationship patterns (proactive countertransference), is largely determined, not by a psychological perfection, but by integrated Adult awareness of self and the impact of the other.

Understanding and feeling the impact and nature of the transferences or projective identifications which patients attempt to elicit from the psychotherapist provides very useful information if the therapist's

Adult is unimpaired. With a fully functioning Adult, therapists can avoid being pulled into their patients' script dramas and can remain available to experience these dramas (not being a mirror-like projective screen) while at the same time the 'integrated personality' (Federn, 1977, p. 218) maintains conscious awareness and control.

Reactive Psychotherapist Countertransference

Complementary reactive countertransference

The psychotherapist complements the patient's real or fantasised projection (as Parent or Child of the patient's parent) by responding with the feeling probably experienced by the original parent. For example, the therapist responds to the patient's projection of his or her overnurturing mother by feeling the urge to rescue.

Concordant reactive countertransference

The therapist experiences the patient's avoided experience or resonates empathically with the patient's experience. For example, after a session the therapist feels unaccountably and uncharacteristically despairing; although the patient talked about her brother's death, she did not let herself experience her corresponding emotions, and the therapist is left with the weight of the unexpressed feeling.

Destructive countertransference

The therapist accepts the projected identification out of awareness and acts on it in an unhealthy way. For example, the patient sees the therapist as her neglectful mother: the therapist responds by forgetting appointments and going on holiday without giving the patient due notice; the patient's expectation acts as a subliminal, hypnotic induction to the therapist who responds outside his or her awareness. It is the therapist's responsibility to be aware of such indications and use them therapeutically, not destructively.

Facilitative countertransference

It is again important, as Winnicott (1975) indicated, to differentiate countertransference that is normal, healthy and even possibly facilitative for the patient. It is natural to feel affection for a lovable patient, appreciative of a creative patient and respect for a humble one. Such feelings may be based on one's past experiences of patients. Withholding emotional responses to the healthy self-expressions of one's patients can make the process of psychotherapy quite barren and may lead us to neglect important opportunities for enhancing creative capacities and reinforcing healthy behaviour patterns.

Proactive Psychotherapist Countertransference

Complementary proactive countertransference

This describes the process whereby the therapist brings into the therapeutic relationship his or her script transferences, projections and expectations based on his or her past experiences. This is usually considered to be unhelpful and is frequently destructive to the therapeutic process. Of course therapists are not perfect and are on their own personal journeys of self-discovery and self-development. That personal script issues, suppressed feelings or avoided sensitivities may be present in psychotherapists at work, cannot be denied. Whether or not these are in awareness, acknowledged, owned, worked through, supervised, humbly accepted or truly transformed is what makes the difference between unconscious exploitation and helpful empathy for the human struggle.

Complementary proactive countertransference occurs when the psychotherapist complements (or completes the gestalt of) the patient's real or fantasised projection as Parent or Child based on the psychotherapist's own past, or projects the actual or fantasised past Parent or Child. For example, the psychotherapist may behave in a withholding, passive, and coldly analytical way in response to the patient's neediness, not because this is therapeutically appropriate but because this is the way the therapist was treated by his or her parents.

Concordant countertransference

The psychotherapist experiences the patient's experience based on the therapist's own past. For example, the therapist assumes that the patient feels guilty about injuring a schoolfriend in the same way as he or she did when younger. The patient may or may not have a similar experience, and such identification needs from the psychotherapist may be unhelpful or actively hindering to the therapy process.

Destructive proactive countertransference

The psychotherapist enacts (or acts out) his or her own past in the psychotherapy in ways that are destructive or limiting to the patient's welfare. This, of course, is identical to what would be understood by Rycroft (1983) as the psychotherapist's transference in the broad sense, that is, of transferring relationship patterns from the past into current relationships; or in the narrow sense, in other words, the feelings engendered toward the analyst based on transferring relationship patterns or expectations from the patient's (or in this case, the psychotherapist's) past. For example, a young psychotherapist may expect that an older patient will find fault with him in the same way as the therapist's father did; he may then reject the patient at the first sign of negativity. Alternatively the psychotherapist may transfer his or her own suicidal tendencies on to the patient and if the patient is obliging and, for example, needs a parent for whom sacrifice is necessary, the patient may commit suicide, in a sense, for the psychotherapist/parent. English (1969) refers to the hot potato (or episcript) as passed from parents to children. In addition, this author believes that it can be passed from psychotherapist to patient.

Facilitative proactive countertransference

This form of countertransference is based on the unavoidable and probably necessary existence of the psychotherapist's individual style and personal preferences. For example, the psychotherapist may enjoy working with people with creativity problems rather than control issues. What makes this transferential and not based on a newly created Adult discovery in the here-and-now, is the fact that the therapist assumes this on the basis of his or her past experiences. Thus he or she may disallow himself or herself the potential delights of working with patients who are controlling.

Reactive Patient Countertransference

Every psychotherapist will no doubt occasionally introduce proactive countertransference elements – that is, the psychotherapist's self-generated issues – into the psychotherapy. For example, a therapist may come to a session late as a result of a traffic accident and the resulting snarl-up. Naturally, patients respond to such events and to the psychotherapist's demeanour, possibly in archaically determined ways that are more reactive to the therapist's past than to their own.

I also identify another form of countertransference: the patient's reactive countertransference to the therapist's introduction of his or her own material. Technically this is not the patient's transference because it is not based on his or her past material, but is elicited from the patient by the therapist's abnormal or proactive countertransferences. Just as patients can induce therapists to respond/react in ways that are script reinforcing by means of the hypnotic induction of ulterior communications, so too, can therapists project onto their patients or even affect them by means of projective identification.

Langs (1985) and Casement (1985) have repeatedly addressed the many ways in which the patient provides the psychotherapist with feedback, supervision, and active attempts to 'heal' the therapist. However, when neither is aware of this collusion, therapeutic progress may be undermined or destroyed. Searles (1975) also suggested the idea that the patient needs to heal his or her psychotherapist. Alternatively, the patient may try very hard to be a good patient because the therapist needs children who work hard but never achieve success.

The choice of the word countertransference is to indicate that it is 'counter' to a transference, and to recognise and allow for the fact that the patient may be responding to material based on the psychotherapist's past in the psychotherapeutic relationship.

Complementary patient countertransference

The patient may react complementarily by completing the psychotherapist's real or fantasised projection as Parent or as Child based on the psychotherapist's history or recent past. For example, a patient who does not have issues about taking care of parents may find that he or she is invited or induced to take care of the psychotherapist when the psychotherapist is experienced as tired, burnt-out or fragile. The importance of differentiating this form of response to psychotherapist-induced reaction lies in *not* attributing projection to the patient. He or she is *correctly* perceiving the therapist's emotional states as they impinge upon the therapy.

Good therapeutic management of this form of patient countertransference involves identifying what both the psychotherapist and the patient bring into the psychotherapy room, without blaming or attributing causality to the pathology or projection of the patient. The therapist is responsible for separating out such elements from the psychotherapeutic relationship and taking preventative or corrective action through, for example, further analysis and/or additional supervision.

Concordant patient countertransference

Concordant patient countertransference happens when, for example, the patient identifies with the psychotherapist's denied Child or resonates empathically with the psychotherapist's experience, whether or not those feelings or experiences are valid for the patient. A patient may sense the psychotherapist's fear of violence, based on the psychotherapist's unresolved issues about a violent childhood home; in resonating with these feelings, the patient avoids sharing his or her feelings of violence or murderous rage towards the therapist, fearing that the therapist could not cope with it. This process is frequently at work with patients who, with a second or third psychotherapist, begin to talk about issues that they could not share with the first. According to Miller (1985), such avoidance may also be based on the patient protecting the Parent/therapist from dealing with his or her own feelings of abandonment or abuse.

Destructive patient countertransference

This refers to particularly damaging acted-out patterns between psychotherapist and patient which are primarily based on the therapist's pathology. In such cases the therapist's transference may induce pathological responses of an extreme nature, such as 'going mad for the psychotherapist,' which allows the therapist to avoid dealing with his or her own madness while dealing with the patient's madness.

Facilitative patient countertransference

This form of patient countertransference involves the patient's natural responses to the psychotherapist's style and way of being. After a long and intimate therapeutic relationship which leads to productive changes in a patient's life, he or she may feel fondness and affection for certain qualities of the therapist. An example would be a particularly apt use of metaphor or a clarity of thinking and expression which is not countertherapeutic but based on an appreciation of the particular attributes of the helper.

Conclusion

The meanings of transference and countertransference have been explored and refined in this chapter by means of comparison, contrast and clarification. The understanding and application of these various forms of transference and countertransference in psychotherapeutic and supervisory settings using transactional analysis will be further developed in the next chapter.

References

BERNE, E. (1961). *Transactional Analysis in Psychotherapy.* New York: Grove Press.

BERNE, E. (1969). *A Layman's Guide to Psychiatry and Psychoanalysis.* London: André Deutsch.

CASEMENT, P. (1985). *On Learning from the Patient.* London: Tavistock.

CONWAY, A. and CLARKSON, P. (1987). Everyday hypnotic inductions. *Transactional Analysis Journal,* **17** (2), 17–23.

ENGLISH, F. (1969). Episcript and the "hot potato" game. *Transactional Analysis Bulletin,* **8** (32), 77–82.

EYSENCK, H.J. and RACHMAN, S. (1965). *The Causes and Cures of Neurosis.* London: Routledge and Kegan Paul.

FAIRBAIRN, W.R.D. (1952). *Psychoanalytic Studies of the Personality.* London: Tavistock.

FEDERN, P. (Ed.) (1977). Ego psychological aspect of schizophrenia. In: *Ego Psychology and the Psychoses,* pp. 210–226. London: Maresfield Reprints. (Originally published 1949.)

FREUD, S. (1955). Beyond the pleasure principle. In: J. Strachey (Ed. and trans.), *The Standard Edition of the Complete Psychological Works of Sigmund Freud,* Vol. 19, pp. 1–64. London: Hogarth Press. (Originally published 1920.)

FREUD, S. (1958). The dynamics of the transference. In: J. Strachey (Ed. and trans.), *The Standard Edition of the Complete Psychological Works of Sigmund Freud,* Vol. 12, pp. 97–108. London: Hogarth Press. (Originally published 1912).

GITELSON, M. (1952). The emotional position of the analyst in the psychoanalytic situation, *International Journal of Psychoanalysis,* **33**, 1–10.

HEIMANN, P. (1950). On countertransference. *International Journal of Psychoanalysis,* **31**, 81–84.

HINSHELWOOD, R.D. (Ed.) (1989). *A Dictionary of Kleinian Thought.* London: Free Association Books.

KLEIN, M. (1984). *Envy, Gratitude and Other Works.* London: The Hogarth Press and Institute for Psychoanalysis.

KOHUT, H. (1977). *The Restoration of the Self.* New York: International Universities Press.

LANGS, R. (1985). *Workbooks for Psychotherapists,* Vols 1–3. Emerson, NJ: Newconcept.

LEWIN, K. (1963). *Field Theory in Social Science: Selected Theoretical Papers.* London: Tavistock.

LITTLE, M. (1951). Countertransference and the patient's response to it. *International Journal of Psychoanalysis,* **32**, 32–40.

MANOR, O. (1992). Transactional analysis, object relations and the systems approach: finding the counterparts, *Transactional Analysis Journal,* **22** (1), 248–259.

MILLER, A. (1985). *Thou Shalt Not be Aware: Society's Betrayal of the Child* (H. and H. Hannum, trans.). London: Pluto Books. (Originally published 1981.)

NOVELLINO, M. (1984). Self-analysis of countertransference in integrative transactional analysis, *Transactional Analysis Journal,* **14** (1), 63–67.

PINE, F. (1985). *Developmental Theory and Clinical Process.* New Haven: Yale University Press.

RACKER, H. (1982). *Transference and Countertransference.* London: Maresfield Reprints. (Originally published 1968.)

RYCROFT, C. (1972). *A Critical Dictionary of Psychoanalysis.* Harmondsworth: Penguin.

SEARLES, H.F. (1975). The patient as therapist to his analyst. In: P.L. Giovacchini (Ed.), *Tactics and Techniques in Psychoanalytic Therapy,* Vol II, pp. 95–151. New York: Aronson.

WATKINS, J.G. (1954). Trance and transference. *Journal of Clinical and Experimental Hypnosis,* **2**, 284–290.

WEISS, E. (1950). *Principles of Psychodynamics.* New York: Grune and Stratton.

WINNICOTT, D.W. (1975). Hate in the countertransference. In: D.W. Winnicott, *Through Paediatrics to Psychoanalysis,* pp. 194–203. London: Hogarth Press and the Institute of Psycho-Analysis.

Chapter 10
Further through the Looking Glass: Transference, Countertransference and Parallel Process in Transactional Analysis Psychotherapy and Supervision

Introduction

Berne (1975) saw scripts as belonging in the realm of transference phenomena:

> They are derivatives, or more precisely, adaptations of infantile reactions and experiences. But a script does not deal with a mere transference reaction or a transference situation; it is an attempt to repeat in derivative form a whole transference drama, often split up into acts, exactly like the theatrical scripts which are intuitive artistic derivatives of these primal dramas of childhood.
>
> (p. 116)

In psychotherapy such as transactional analysis, transference may be allowed, invited, resolved, temporarily interrupted, avoided or minimised, depending on the patient's diagnosis and needs, and the nature of the psychotherapeutic contract. The extent to which transactional analysts recognise and use transference phenomena depends very much on their training and personal experience of psychotherapy. However, it is clear that, in the terms we are using here, the transactional analyst is frequently dealing essentially with the transferential encoding of the individual's life drama when he or she does script work (Novellino, 1984; Moiso, 1985).

In classical psychoanalysis, the analyst was conceived of as a *mirror* for the patient (Freud, 1973, p. 118). The therapist's detachment gave the patient the space to externalise the internal conflicts and the therapist's

---

From Clarkson, P. (1991). Further through the looking glass: transference, countertransference and parallel process in transactional analysis psychotherapy and supervision. *Transactional Analysis Journal*, **21** (3), 174–183, with permission.

job was to analyse and interpret the transference. Kernberg (1982) uses the term *genetic interpretation*, which is here understood to refer to the historic origins of transferential phenomena. He distinguished between such genetic interpretations and those that dealt with the transference as it affected the psychotherapeutic relationship. Thus the transference manifestation was dealt with, but not necessarily through a genetic interpretation. For example, rather than saying 'You're angry with me the way you used to be angry with your mother when you experienced her as withholding', the analyst would acknowledge the patient's anger in the here-and-now and reflect back that it seemed exaggerated. This approach developed in response to the danger of interpretations being experienced as persecutory. Moiso (1985) used a similar example to illustrate his approach to transference, which he called a psychodynamic transactional analysis therapy. 'Therapist: "Maximillian, you are not only discounting me professionally, but you are destroying the image of me that you carry within yourself. Don't do that and ask for what you want".' (p. 200)

Masterson (1985) and Kernberg (1982) claim that it is essential for the analyst to focus on the external circumstances of the patient and do some teaching of life management skills to enable the patient to be available for psychotherapy. Many Kleinians and Freudians would consider such interventions antitherapeutic in that anything that focuses on reality and not on the relationship between analyst and patient is considered to interfere with the analysis. Kernberg and Masterson believe, as do I, that the patient's present circumstances are legitimate, and indeed, an essential field for investigation and intervention.

Transactional analysts range in theory and practice across a broad spectrum. On the one hand, there are the Gouldings, who have stated:

> We prefer, usually, not to invite a transference, although of course we do use ourselves. We are much more likely, however, to endeavor to keep out of the work, and to let the patient do his work against himself, by setting up dialogues, by keeping I–Thou transactions going, by saying 'any more?' instead of 'tell me'. Thus we hope that the patient, instead of resisting us, will resist himself, recognise the impasse when he gets to it, and either break through or stay stuck at the point of impasse. We prefer that he battle against his own internal Parent, instead of with his transferred 'parent', us.
>
> (Goulding and Goulding, 1978, p. 210)

On the other hand there are Moiso, Novellino and Clarkson who intentionally and actively work with the transference. Schiff et al. (1975) wrote: 'Our policy is to accept the patient's investment of power (transference) to the extent we believe it is possible to utilise that power for their welfare' (p. 102). Their re-parenting approach uses a replacement model of reparative therapeutic relationship, a radical departure from many other forms of psychotherapy. Alongside the transference/

countertransference relationship, there are also the person-to-person relationship, the working alliance and the transpersonal relationship in therapy.

In Chapter 2, the elements of the reparative/developmentally needed relationship were reviewed. Although mention was made of entering the symbiosis (Robinson, 1974), the re-parenting is *not* transferential because it is specifically different from what happened before and is therefore not transferring from the past. It is neither 'undoing' (Freud, 1937, p. 43) nor understanding, neither insight nor re-decision: it is replacement. It may be that replacement work of this kind is inadvisable, potentially damaging and probably not genuinely possible until the transferential space has been cleared. Moiso (1985) wrote that re-decision work, re-parenting and two-chair work can be damaging at the beginning of therapy, when the transference is still very much in evidence.

Allowing the Transference

If the patient's development was arrested at an unresolved symbiotic stage, he or she will tend to project those unresolved developmental issues and expectations into the psychotherapeutic relationship. If patients failed to separate self from mother, they cannot see the psychotherapist as separate. The arrested or rudimentary self requires a symbiotic partner and will create one according to its expectations, regardless of what the therapist does or does not do. Thus the therapist can only allow the phenomena and concentrate on how to work with it creatively, with the goal of eventually resolving the transference.

There is sometimes a misunderstanding that *games* in transactional analysis treatment must be stopped at all costs even at the first con (invitation to the game). This is sometimes deleterious because the patient learns superficial adaptation or obedience to the psychotherapist's rules rather than engaging in a psychotherapeutic relationship. According to Berne (1968, p. 134), it is often more important to allow the game or transferential projection (which provides the fuel for the game) to unfold, providing in the process evidence that allows both patient and therapist to recognise the pattern as well as material for analysis. This makes denial more difficult and helps in the development of a common language for referring to these patterns. For example, a patient with a parent that was homicidal, judgmental and critical, weak or ill probably fears that the therapist will use, abuse, or neglect him or her. One possible strategy that is particularly useful in the earlier stages of psychotherapy is for the psychotherapist temporarily to accept this kind of transference. The patient can then be invited to explore and experience it in detail, including physical, emotional, behavioural, and cognitive manifestations. In the safe context of the therapeutic relationship, the patient can do this without the response that would usually occur in the outside world, where people tend to respond to the game invitations and thus reinforce the experienced 'truth' of the transferred expectation. Once the unfinished business or transference is fully alive and clear, the patient, supported by the therapist, can compare present evidence with the patient's archaic expectations and learning, developing in the process skills in self-analysis, and generalising that can eventually lead to resolution of the transference.

Inviting the Transference

In most cases the therapist does not have to be a mirror in order for the patient to enter into a transference relationship. The therapist's simple presence in the consulting room is usually enough to create a potentially transferential space. This is borne out by the ubiquitousness of transferential phenomena in everyday relationships – including between marital partners, who are often least likely to mirror each other. The difference in the therapeutic situation is *not* the difficulty of eliciting the transference, but the opportunity to understand it and work through it.

However, some patients apparently do not develop transference either because there is no need to or because they resist due to an inability or unwillingness to engage. In the first case, the patient sees the psychotherapist clearly and is able to get on with the task. For example, this occurs in some forms of short-term psychotherapy or with specific contracts, where a mild benign transference may operate with no harm and endless beneficial results – the kind of warmth that is potentially transferred to teachers and doctors who have been helpful.

Without this type of positive transference there is little hope for successful human relationship. It is a moot point whether this should technically be defined as transference if it is not based on earlier positive experiences transferred from past people onto the present person without any evidence that such feelings are warranted. It is more accurately described as a realistic expectation based on knowledge of the reliability of the person's own judgment and intuition. In transactional analysis terms we are talking about integrated Adult functioning and reality testing skills. If someone consults a therapist, he or she expects that the therapist will be helpful; this is based on a reasonable expectation that specially trained people will have the skills they claim to have. So, in such instances, this may be all that is necessary for the task of psychotherapeutic change, and it may *not* be necessary to enter a transferential relationship. This may be because the person did not have particular difficulty with a parent in the past, or because the person had already resolved the tendency to project transferentially.

In the second case, there are people who may not appear to enter the transference because they are unable or unwilling to engage, and avoid doing so through the use of defence mechanisms, for example intellectualising or rationalising. An example is a patient in group psychotherapy who comments in a throw-away manner, 'Of course I should be jealous because Joe is getting the attention, and I probably felt that way about my younger brother'. This could be resistance to the sibling transference which is then even more secure because it is so thoroughly denied or repressed out of awareness. The therapist may choose to confront such a rationalisation or denial and invite the patient to slow down and allow sensation and feelings, to breathe and re-own the emotion, and thus relive the earlier ego states. This can happen through regression, hypnosis or spontaneous reactivation of an earlier ego state.

Some examples of transference-inviting questions are: 'How do you feel as you say that to me?' 'How do you feel about me?' 'What do you think when I say that?' 'How am I like your mother?' 'What do you imagine I might do next? I imagine you think I will reject you? Tell me.' Inviting the transference can be done passively (by being a mirror) or actively (by displaying emotion or behaviour similar to that which the patient is projecting, for example, being late for an appointment with a patient who fears abandonment, and saying 'This is what you were afraid would happen, and now it has happened'). Sometimes there is so little uncontaminated Adult available that almost whatever the psychotherapist does, says, or is (or is not), is used by the patient to confirm projections.

Another kind of resistance to the transference is displayed by people who have a more schizoid adaptation. Of course for such people it is technically transferential *not* to have a genuine interpersonal relationship, as this is probably what happened to them as children. People did not relate to them in ways that were beneficial to their growth, or sometimes did not relate to them at all. Parents may have been over-invasive, neglectful or abusive of them or their siblings. They are, perhaps, transferring a fear that the psychotherapist may be as invasive or abusive as the original parent, and their withdrawal is part of the transferential relationship. The psychotherapist respects their withdrawal. But it is sometimes necessary and humane to enter into the relationship and to risk approbation or fear in order to make the beginnings of a human, person-to-person relationship. Such patients can then begin to learn when and how to trust and how to protect themselves appropriately without cutting off from nourishing human contact.

Temporarily Interrupting the Transference

Sometimes it is necessary and desirable to interrupt a fully developed transference. For example, when a patient is totally taken up with rage or grief towards the end of a session, the therapist might remind the person that there are only 10 minutes left and ask him what he or she needs before leaving. In doing so the therapist is calling upon the patient's integrated Adult functioning and strengthening the working alliance. If the patient insists upon seeing the therapist in an unrealistically negative way (based on past expectations of neglect or abuse), the therapist may decide to refuse to play the game and to help the patient to cathect Adult. The psychotherapist may, for example, remind the patient of their real relationship or working alliance by saying: 'You are not trapped by me or with me. You are paying for a service and you are free to stop paying me for this service, if it is not to your satisfaction. This is different from when you were a child and you couldn't leave your parents' home.'

If the patient is so completely gripped by rage (due to the transferred expectation that the therapist cannot help him or her) that they threaten to leave, the therapist may talk to the patient's Adult self by reminding him, 'You have an opportunity now to work this through with me. The chances are that if you don't, you will continue to find or make other similar situations again and again. You can walk out on me now but you will walk on with the same problem in the future.'

Avoiding or Minimalising the Transference

It is not really possible to avoid transference completely but it can be minimised by ignoring the game, analysing the game, commissioning the Adult, establishing Adult-to-Adult contracts, reality testing, and so on.

For example, sometimes when a patient is overwhelmed by feelings evoked by the transference, the therapist may intervene by working with someone else in the group and letting the first patient cry until he or she is better able to think. The therapist may or may not make this explicit by saying what the patient is doing and why.

In another case, a patient was angry with his therapist because she had scheduled such a late appointment. By going through their diaries and re-discovering some restrictions on the patient's as well as her own time, the therapist went over the facts, and appealed to common sense, their working alliance, and the patient's mutual responsibility for making arrangements for appointments.

Humorous exaggeration can be made of the patient's transferential moan, 'Oh, no one loves you, not even your therapist!', or humorous confrontation: 'Of all my patients, your success is the one most likely really to damage me, is that it?' Humour obviously needs to be used with care, and only where a relationship is already established and the therapist has some evidence of the patient's ability to tolerate teasing.

Refusing the parental role is another option. For example, if a patient asks the therapist's permission in a child-like way, the therapist can respond 'What is stopping you?', that is, the therapist refuses to be the granter of permission, and encourages the re-establishment of the Adult-to-Adult working alliance. The therapist can also show how other patients are a resource, as well as referring patients to other patients for their support, and by using other group members to attract transference.

It is important that trainers and supervisors minimise the transference in their relationships with trainees and supervisees as they do not, in these instances, usually have the contract to go in there and work with the transference to resolve it psychotherapeutically.

It is frequently essential that the transference be effectively minimised or resolved before doing developmentally needed replacement work. If it is not resolved, the attempted replacement work could be damaging or, more likely, ineffective because it will not penetrate the shell of fixed expectations in which the patient is still caught. The Gouldings (1978) minimise the transference by externalising the internal dialogue (rather than inviting dialogue with the therapist), using gestalt techniques, Adult–Adult contracts (working alliance), and analysing games.

Resolving the Transference

To resolve it, the therapist may allow the transference to develop, to become fully alive and yet be experienced as something alien to here-and-now reality. Then the therapist may invite the patient to test reality through the use of his or her senses. 'When you were little, it is true that no one listened to you or paid you attention. Is that still true now? Look around the room, what do you see? People, yes. Are they looking at you? Do they seem to be listening? Are they paying attention to you? How can you tell?' At other times, or with other patients, the therapist must encourage resolution of the transference through successful mastery of the Child ego state's developmental tasks.

In achieving such resolution the therapist uses experiencing, collecting evidence, analysing, confronting, recognising where the transference originates and why, cognitive understanding, emotional catharsis, and moving from reliving to remembering with the affective charge removed. The therapist also fosters the patient's skills in spotting transference reactions in future relationships, and coaches patients to either avoid situations that echo the original unmet needs or to be skilful in dealing with them – and knowing the difference between the two. The therapist helps the patient develop reality testing – identifying the kind of people to whom the patient had repeatedly been attracted, and helping the patient to change his or her attractiveness patterns. The therapist encourages the patient to have new experiences with real relationships and real people, to begin to trust and expect such relationships, and to know what to do when something goes wrong. Any resolution of the transference is inevitably healing, as past damage usually resulted from an absence of a true and genuine, contactful relationship.

The following example illustrates a transferential situation that was resolved towards the end of the patient's therapy. The patient, who had a history of somatising and a tendency to hypochondriasis and feeling victimised, used to get most of her strokes or recognition for ways in which she was incompetent, incapacitated, or inadequate. Although she had made great gains in therapy, some of the old patterns lingered, and it was difficult for her to relate to new people as a healthy person without inviting them to see her in the first instance as 'an individual who suffers'.

This is how she describes her experience:

> In a psychotherapy group one member asks about how I got paralysed when I was twenty. Pleased to have the opportunity to tell my story again, I commence with tears in my eyes. The psychotherapist intervenes by stopping this. I protest: 'I am only telling what happened'. The psychotherapist reiterates that I should not continue with this tale of drudgery and misery, which had been told many times before. I scream at the psychotherapist, 'I hate you!', glaring at her with all the rage I can muster. The psychotherapist then stops an interaction with someone else on the far side of the room and comes over slowly to sit cross-legged, about a yard in front of me, in a receptive, open posture. I say, 'I feel very, very angry with you'. The psychotherapist says, 'What would your mother do now?' I reply, 'What a stupid question! My mother would hit me and then send me to my room. She would never let me speak to her like this'. The psychotherapist continues looking steadily at me with what I can only describe as compassionate concern. Then she reached out her hands to me, palms upwards, without touching me, and I dissolved into tears as I realised that I can show my anger at her without being punished or rejected the way I had been in the past.

The patient chose for herself to respond in a self-reparative way. Another example is Georgina, who continued to believe that her own needs could not be met without detriment to others, just as her archaic baby needs had not been met. In a group situation, the therapist chose to hold Georgina while she howled in pain over her unmet needs. Simultaneously, the therapist encouraged Georgina to experience a contradictory here-and-now reality – that the therapist was perfectly able to take care of herself, of Georgina's needs, and of the needs of the other group members for the duration of the group. In assessing the capacity of such an intervention, the therapist needs to ask, 'Does Georgina still believe that her needs cannot be met, or how attached is Georgina still to the transferential distortion?' Only when the patient has resolved the pervasive transferential expectation is it advisable to do repair work, which needs to be firmly based in here-and-now reality with the patient taking full adult responsibility for requesting the repair work.

Management and Use of Countertransference Phenomena in Transactional Analysis

One hopes that therapists who use transactional analysis will have resolved most of the major ways in which their own pathology (or scripts) might interfere with their work with patients. However, as few of us resolve all of our script issues completely, it is important that we at least understand ourselves enough to be able to skilfully identify and counteract our own pathological patterns, especially countertransferential responses based on unresolved issues from our own past.

Berne (1972) himself saw transference and countertransference reactions in the form of stimulus–response transactional patterns (Figure 10.1).

Indeed Berne (1966) saw *interpretation* as one of the eight major categories of psychotherapeutic operations, which he listed among the basic techniques of psychotherapy as the prototype of a crossed transaction. For example, in a case where a patient asks for help, the

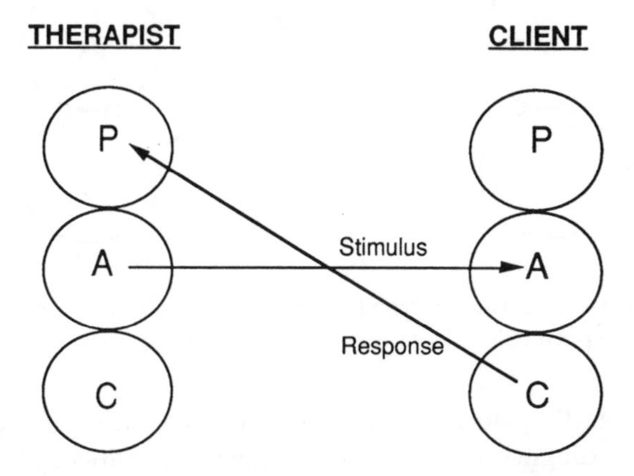

Figure 10.1. Crossed transaction type I representing the common form of transference reaction as it occurs in psychotherapy. P = Parent; A = Adult; C = Child. (Reproduced, with permission, from Berne, 1972, p. 16.)

patient responds with a Child or Parent reaction to the therapist's interpretation which takes the form of a question directed to the patient's Adult. The patient expects a Parent-to-Child response to his or her request for help or assistance. Instead, the therapist invites the patient into integrated Adult thinking about the historical roots of the way in which the request was made, for example, 'Did you have to suffer more than your sisters, and wait for someone to notice you in your family?' The therapist's question or interpretation is experienced as a crossed transaction, because the response is unexpected and contrary to what the patient expected according to his or her history. Traditional psychoanalysis concentrates primarily on this particular form of transaction.

Berne represented countertransference by crossed transaction type II, where an Adult-to-Adult stimulus such as a question from the patient, for example, receives a patronising or pompous Parent or Child response inappropriate to the situation, and is influenced by the therapist's own past agendas (Figure 10.2).

In the design of both Figures 10.1 and 10.2, Berne showed an intuitive understanding of the interdependence of transference and countertransference. These phenomena constitute an interactional field created by recurrent stimulus–response pairs within the relationship.

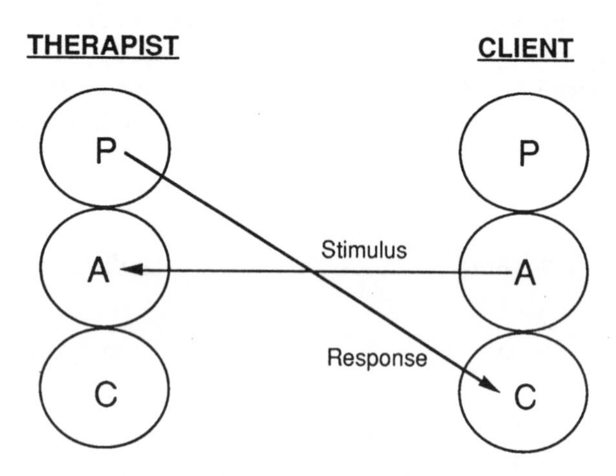

Figure 10.2. Crossed transaction type II. P = Parent; A = Adult; C = Child. (Reproduced, with permission, from Berne, 1972, p. 16.)

As was shown earlier, Berne also recognised the value of the therapist (or the person diagnosing ego states) paying attention to his or her own emotional responses, when he underlined the value of social diagnosis of ego states. For example, a therapist may consider a situation as follows: 'How do I feel towards Joan when she offers to help me? If I feel slightly scared that she may not be able to keep her promise, but so grateful that she is offering that I do not want to offend her, my emotional Parental reaction to her Child ego state may help confirm a diagnostic hypothesis that she is relating to me from a Child ego state.' (This also needs to be corroborated by a behavioural, historical and subjective or phenomenologically reported fit.)

Interactional Field Transference and Countertransference

It is clear that as early as 1955, Berne (1977) was encouraging therapists to use their own intuition to sense and diagnose Child ego states, and in 1961 he elaborated on this to include subjective social responses in order to diagnose any one of the ego state categories. This is similar to what has been termed *reactive psychotherapist countertransference* (see Chapter 9).

In the last chapter I developed this perspective, clearly anticipated by Berne, to offer a theoretical map which can be used to discriminate between:

1. What the patient brings to the relationship (proactive transference).
2. What the therapist brings (proactive countertransference or therapist transference – pathological).
3. What the therapist reacts to in the patient (reactive countertransference – inductive).
4. What the patient reacts to as a result of what the therapist brings (patient countertransference or reactive transference).

Any of these may form the basis for facilitative or destructive psychotherapeutic outcomes.

Therefore, because the meaning of a transaction lies in the communicative space between the dialoguing partners, it is postulated that a circular interaction serves as the dynamic field for what is called *parallel process*.

It is well known that therapists often behave in supervision in the same way the patient behaves in therapy. Thus, if a patient experiences a sense of helplessness and leans on the psychotherapist, the therapist may feel the same helplessness as he or she leans on the supervisor, thus acting out in supervision a transient identification with the patient. This is called *parallel process* in supervision and *parallel process phenomenon* in treatment (Moldawsky, 1980, p. 131).

M.J.G. Doehrman (in Hess, 1980, p. 132) investigated this parallel process by conducting clinical interviews of patients, psychotherapists, and supervisors over a period of time. She concluded that the usual understanding goes only half the way. Rather, the supervisor stirs the psychotherapist, who then acts out with his or her patients. Thus, parallel process is not reflective alone – it works in both directions. This discovery has just begun to find its way into supervisors' work. It speaks to the complexity of the patient–psychotherapist–supervisor interactions and encourages a humbleness in supervisors.

As discussed in the previous chapter, particularly with regard to reactive patient countertransference, patients may be responding to therapists' induced material. In the same way, supervisees may be part of a ***projective identification process*** initiated by supervisors, outside the conscious awareness of either. Hypnotists are very familiar with such phenomena and, as Conway and Clarkson (1987) discussed, there are many situations where hypnotic inductions occur in every day life. Who is hypnotising whom becomes a question. What is clear is that this complex interactional process occurs in what Langs (1976) called the ***bipersonal field***.

Of course, therapists ask, 'How do I know if it is my issue or the supervisee's issue?' A good rule of thumb is to begin by assuming that it is the therapist's responsibility. This is most useful, because maximum change can be brought about in the part of the system for which therapists are 100% responsible – that is, in themselves.

I propose that parallel process be conceptualised as a way to describe the pattern of the patient–psychotherapist transference/countertransference relationship or the interpersonal pattern of the dyadic therapeutic relationship (Figure 10.3).

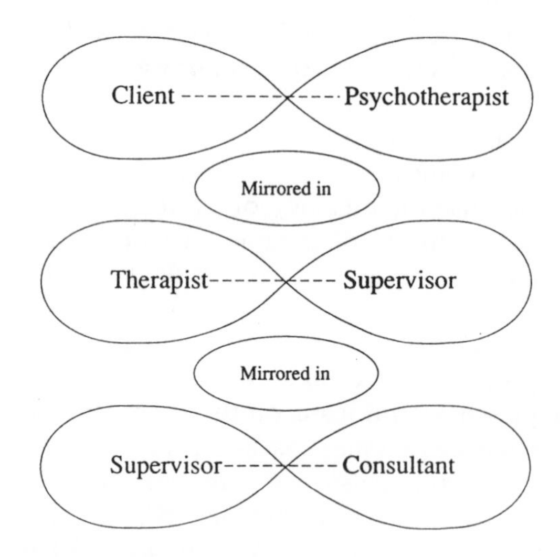

Figure 10.3 Parallel process.

Thus the categories and types previously discussed in the last chapter can be seen as the raw material for identifying parallel processes in terms of the interdependent field between patient and psychotherapist. Each category makes either the ***patient*** or the ***therapist*** the focus of attention in order to facilitate exploration, understanding and intervention design at a particular moment in the therapeutic/supervisory process. However, it must be clear that such division is intrinsically arbitrary and never 'correct' or 'provable'. Patient and therapist processes often interact out of awareness (unconsciously) in ways that may be mutually or differentially influencing each other 'hypnotically' (Conway and Clarkson, 1987).

Specifically, parallel process is the interactional field of the therapist/patient field replicated in the therapist/supervisor field. Any combination of patient and therapist reactions to each other thus forms a dynamic field which is manifested in the supervisory relationship and variously referred to as parallel process (Figure 10.4).

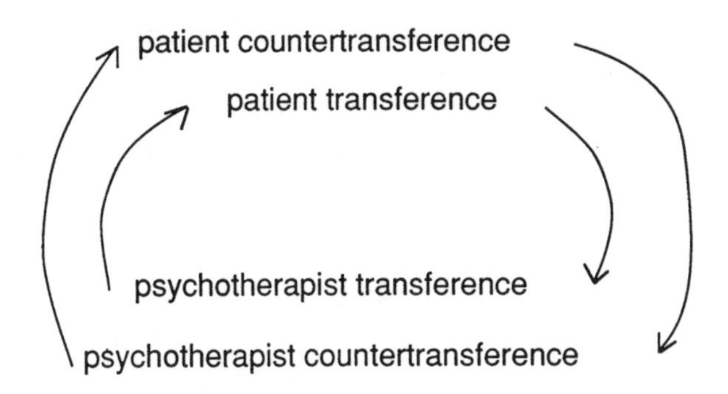

Figure 10.4 The interactional field in context.

Understanding the shape and nature of the parallel process is not only useful when it gets in the way of supervision, but also for prevention, understanding, learning and relief.

It seems more accurately representative of the complexity of the patient/therapist field to represent the different forces in it in a circular dynamic relationship to one another. As we know from physics, the idea that the observer can remain neutral and not influence the observational field is quite disproved (Zohar, 1990). Similarly, it seems obvious that we cannot unequivocally lay the responsibility on the patient for transferring 'onto the psychotherapist', *as if* that particular transference could happen with any therapist. Equally it appears clinically correct that, for many therapists, patients present problems *as if* they are acutely aware of the vulnerable areas or developmental tasks of the therapist, and sometimes even work in some strange kind of tandem. Often, as the trainee becomes more in touch with their negative transference in therapy, so the trainee's patients become more willing to express anger and disappointment to the trainee. To seek *first causes* in such a complex, dynamically interactive situation seems to be futile. It is more fruitful to recognise the co-occurrence of such phenomena and their prevalence in many clinical teaching situations. Perhaps it may even be beneficial to consider Jung's (1972, p. 36) concept of synchronicity (acausal connecting principle) so that our models may serve our ends instead of forcing our experiences to fit our perceptual prejudices or existing cognitive categories.

Because most of these processes are also at the same time unconscious (or out of awareness) and extremely complex, it may be useful to think about the parallel process as being a fractal of the field, that is, as representing (even though in minute form) the structure of the larger whole (Gleick, 1988). No matter how small the size to which it is reduced, the essential features of the field will remain present and available for inspection. Following these analogies of fractals or even holons, it is more possible to subject the dynamic interactional transference/countertransference field to investigation. However, it is important to avoid assigning first causes to either patient or therapist, or trying to prioritise a particular transference reaction before a particular countertransference reaction in a sequence.

It is interesting to consider the possibility that a therapist draws to himself or herself the kind of patients who are most useful for the therapist's development. There is growing and disturbing evidence from modern physics that unidirectional causality is a highly dubious notion in explaining physical (or psychological) events. In fact, it seems increasingly possible that everything is connected with everything else.

Herbert (1985) cites the work of John Bell, a theoretical physicist, as follows:

> Despite physicists' traditional rejection of non-local interactions, ...Bell maintains that the world is filled with innumerable non-local influences. Furthermore these unmediated connections are present not only in rare and exotic circumstances, but underlie all the events of everyday life. Non-local connections are ubiquitous because reality itself is non-local.
>
> (Herbert, 1985, pp. 214–215)

Implications for Psychotherapy and Supervision

In the absence of proof of causality and directionality, it may be more useful and more congruent with the present state of our knowledge to assume that the phenomena of transference and countertransference are interconnected in ways which we do not yet understand. Mutual hypnotic inductions (Conway and Clarkson, 1987) (which I understand as similar to projective identification from either or both the patient and psychotherapist) deserve intensive and long-term research, yet the clinical field is probably one of the very last that will open itself to rigorous scientific analysis, even supposing that we had the tools with which to do the studies.

It is certainly more pragmatic to place the emphasis on those areas where it is possible to achieve the *maximum leverage* or *most efficient* resolution. For this a simple figure–ground gestalt model may be useful. When the therapist is actively engaging in the therapeutic relationship with the patient, he or she can assume that most of the dynamics are contributed by the patient, and develop interventions from such a frame of reference. In other words, *at the moment of therapeutic engagement in the relationship*, it may be most useful to consider that patient transference and the therapist reactive countertransference are most likely to provide the richest and most accurate options for intervention.

On the other hand, when the therapist is doing self-supervision, the field most available for intervention is that of the therapist. Therefore, it may be most fruitful to consider hypothetically that most of the phenomena in the field are being caused by the therapist's proactive transference and the patient's reactive countertransference. Let us then assume that the therapist's unresolved conflicts, confusions and deficits are completely at cause in the therapy. Of course, it cannot be proven that either of these positions is accurate, or even likely. Clinical supervisory evidence, however, bears out that frequent alterations between these two viewpoints, with the emphasis on where the smallest intervention is likely to lead to the largest degree of shift in the problem, are exceptionally useful and empowering for both the patient and psychotherapist.

Conclusion

This chapter is intended to offer the therapist in training, as well as the experienced clinician and supervisor, one possible map by means of which to understand parallel process in psychotherapy, counselling and the supervision of both. This is a way of discriminating between different types of transferential and countertransferential phenomena in order to facilitate teaching and supervision. A map is suggested for the analysis of the concepts of transference, countertransferences, patient countertransference and understanding the notion of parallel process. It is not intended to be a comprehensive review of the literature on transference, countertransference or parallel process, but a practical guide which may stimulate readers to investigate this fascinating area further.

An understanding of parallel process is invited, which is achieved by analysing the constituent parts of the interactional field of the therapeutic relationship. Although these are ultimately conceived of as interacting as an inseparable systemic whole, for the sake of discussion four categories of transferential phenomena have been delineated: what the patient brings to the relationship (proactive transference); what the therapist brings (proactive countertransference or therapist transference); what the therapist reacts to in the patient (reactive countertransference), and what the patient reacts to as a result of what the therapist brings (countertransference or reactive transference). Any of these may form the basis for facilitative or destructive psychotherapeutic outcomes.

References

BERNE, E. (1966). *Principles of Group Treatment.* New York: Grove Press.

BERNE, E. (1968). *Games People Play.* Harmondsworth, Middx: Penguin. (Originally published 1964.)

BERNE, E. (1972). *What Do You Say After You Say Hello?* New York: Grove Press.

BERNE, E. (1975). *Transactional Analysis in Psychotherapy.* London: Souvenir. (Originally published 1961.)

BERNE, E. (1977). Primal images and primal judgment. In: P. McCormick (Ed.), *Intuition and Ego States,* pp. 67–97. San Francisco: TA Press. (Original work entitled *Intuition IV: Primal Images and Primal Judgment*, published 1955.)

CONWAY, A. and CLARKSON, P. (1987). Everyday hypnotic inductions. *Transactional Analysis Journal,* **17** (2), 17–23.

FREUD, A. (1937). *Ego and the Mechanisms of Defence* (C. Baines, trans.). London: Hogarth Press.

FREUD, S. (1973). Recommendations to physicians practising psycho-analysis. In: J. Strachey (Ed.), *The Standard Edition of the Complete Psychological Works of Sigmund Freud*, Vol. 12, pp. 109–120. London: Hogarth Press. (Originally published 1912.)

GLEICK, J. (1988). *Chaos: Making a New Science.* London: Heinemann.

GOULDING, M.M. and GOULDING, R.L. (1978). *The Power is in the Patient* (P. McCormick, Ed.). San Francisco: TA Press.

HERBERT, N. (1985). *Quantum Reality: Beyond the New Physics.* London: Anchor Press/Doubleday.

HESS, A.K. (Ed.) (1980). *Psychotherapy Supervision: Theory, Research and Practice.* New York: John Wiley.

JUNG, C.G. (1972). *Synchronicity: An Acausal Connecting Principle* (R.F.C. Hull, trans.). London: Routledge and Kegan Paul. (Originally published 1952)

KERNBERG, O. (1982). Self, ego, affects, drives. *Journal of the American Psychoanalytic Association,* **30**, 893–917.

LANGS, R. (1976). *The Bipersonal Field.* New York: Jason Aronson.

MASTERSON, J.F. (1985). *The Real Self: A Developmental, Self and Object Relations Approach.* New York: Brunner/Mazel.

MOISO, C. (1985). Ego states and transference. *Transactional Analysis Journal,* 15 (3), 194–201.

MOLDAWSKY, S. (1980). Psychoanalytic psychotherapy supervision. In: A.K. Hess (Ed.), *Psychotherapy Supervision: Theory, Research and Practice,* pp. 126–135. New York: Wiley.

NOVELLINO, M. (1984). Self-analysis of transference in integrative transactional analysis. *Transactional Analysis Journal,* **14** (1), 63–67.

ROBINSON, W.L. (1974). Conscious competency: The mark of a competent instructor. *Personnel Journal,* **53**, 538–539.

SCHIFF, J.L. with SCHIFF, A.W. MELLOR, K., SCHIFF, E., SCHIFF,S., RICHMAN, D., FISHMAN, J., WOLZ, L., FISHMAN, C. and MOMB, D. (1975). *Cathexis Reader: Transactional Analysis Treatment of Psychosis.* New York: Harper and Row.

ZOHAR, D. (1990). *The Quantum Self.* London: Bloomsbury.

Part V
New Perspectives

Chapter 11
New Perspectives in Counselling and Psychotherapy (or Adrift in a Sea of Change)

Introduction

I have now been an individual and group psychotherapist and an organisational consultant and supervisor for more than two decades. What drew me to psychotherapy in the first instance was my interest in the possibilities and limitations of change within people, within systems such as schools and organisations, and within nations.

Although I have studied a great many wise and brilliant teachings, the most enduring wisdom has been from a sage of 500 BC – Heraclitus. Heraclitus postulated that the only thing in life of which we can be sure, is change. Everything is in a constant state of flux. According to Heraclitus, the human experience is one of continuously trying to make meaning from the ever-recurring, cycling interplay between things staying the same and things changing – or 'The cycle is the experiential reconciliation of permanence and regeneration' (Guerriere, 1980, p. 88). This perpetual motion between stasis and change, between certainty and doubt, illumination and confusion, hope and realisation is most descriptive of my own process over these years. Instead of a linear incremental increase in my knowledge or skills, I have experienced developments as well as the disintegration of previous developments, new structures arising from the waste products of the old, leaps from unknowing to understanding and back again.

This cyclic nature of change has certainly been my experience as I have held on to raft after raft of certainty or scientific truth or conviction about values over these years. Repeatedly I have realised that as soon as I felt that I had fully grasped or understood a particular facet of what it meant to be human, the current would shift and I would have to reconsider. For example, I remember at a sociology lecture in my late teens that I vehemently objected to the idea that the individual can

---

Based on two conference addresses: New Perspectives in Supervision, delivered at the UK Supervision Conference 1991, and The Counselling Psychologist at Work, delivered at the British Psychological Society's Counselling Psychology Conference, 1991.

be defined in terms of his membership of different groups. Yet nowadays I am frequently convinced of exactly this point which I was so passionately contesting then.

I am currently persuaded of the essential truth in the statement which I retained from some now forgotten book that 'we are our others'. Of course, human beings are formed largely by the influence of significant others and the collective influences generated by others such as church, entertainment, state, culture and education. At the moment from a systems view, I am also very impressed by the extent to which individuals can be conceived of as the effects of the people who surround them at any particular time. On reading some so-called postmodern authors who concentrate on de-centring of the subject (Kvale, 1990; Lather, 1990), I can certainly encompass the idea that I do not exist separately from other people. Anthropological discoveries (languages without a term for 'self') and historical perspectives (the anonymity of medieval or aboriginal artists) also suggest that the notion of the individual is but one possible perspective, and not even a necessary one.

There was a time when I considered any attempt at diagnosis a violation of my clients' unique individuality, and necessarily an impediment to genuine relationship with them. There have also been times when I realised that only through the medium of a diagnostic description of my patient could I usefully access the experience and wisdom of other, more experienced and perhaps more effective colleagues in working with certain issues. As discussed in Chapter 2, I now look at these as interchanging relationships between figure and ground – either or both useful for particular people at particular times.

The desire for an unchanging certainty is a very common human experience. It is based in the well-documented need of the child for a certain amount of structure, ritual, predictability and thus physical and emotional security. In adulthood, the desire for certainty becomes more abstract but appears to come from a still-childlike wish that there is an answer that we *can* know. Knowing this right answer, our scientific uncertainties, moral ambiguities, and existential anxiety would cease. Life, if one is open to it, seems to have a habit of upsetting the conceptual apple cart just as soon as we have it fully laden.

My personal experience and my personal interest has thus centred around the subject of change. Of all subjects, it seems the most fruitful and useful for human beings because there is so much that needs changing in our world – not least of all ourselves. Paradoxically, it has also been said that the more things change, the more they stay the same. Furthermore, from another perspective, nothing needs to be changed, because anything, if left static, will inevitably change – frequently into its opposite. Interestingly, the Greek root of stasis means riot, argument, dispute – a connotation which again, within itself, enfolds a sense of dynamic and even oppositional action. So, however it is approached, I still believe that the notion of changing (or not) is one of the most interesting, ubiquitous, and potentially fertile subjects in the whole world.

A pre-Christian Greek word for change is 'metanoia', meaning a turning around or transformation, as explained more extensively in Chapter 4. Sam Keen (1985), an existential psychotherapist, also defines metanoia as the opposite of paranoia, and akin to 'repentance, a re-owning of the shadow, turning around...away from the persona and toward the self' (pp. 146–147). For Laing and Esterson (1972), 'metanoia is dialectical rationality, a praxis of reconciliation and dynamic unity, an enterprise of continual and continuing reappraisal and renewal, constantly bringing forth new experience with deepening understanding and wholeness' (p. 63). Senge (1990) defines metanoia as 'a shift of mind.... For the Greeks, it meant a fundamental shift or change, or more literally transcendence' (p. 13).

In this sense, when I named the METANOIA Psychotherapy Training Institute, and the associated charity, METANOIA Education for Living, I meant metanoia both as a field of study of human and organisational change, but also as a prayer. It is an emblem of hope that in our world we could find the capacity to make the turnabout from racial injustice, the transcendence of the apparently insuperable division between communism and capitalism, and the liberation of people from oppressive regimes as well as from their own self-oppression. This could be through abuse inflicted by parental figures, society's rejection reinforced by self-oppression of homosexual men and women, or the painful remnants of educational trauma which I encountered time and time again as a teacher of adults.

As a psychotherapist I am concerned with the personal metanoias that people can make in their convictions, feelings and experiences about their own capacities, relationships, and resources. I know that in the intimate confines of the individual therapeutic relationship the world *out there* can seem very remote. Indeed some psychotherapeutic schools believe that any material extraneous to the transference is not relevant to the process of personal change or even insight. This is another issue in which I have found myself making a volte-face. If modern science continues (as I will explain further later) to underline the indivisibility of the part from the whole, the observer from the field, the individual from his or her planetary connectedness, it may be an absurdity to work with the individual in psychotherapy. I am not suggesting that this statement is true; I do, however, believe that the assumptions underlying individual psychotherapy are largely unquestioned and unchallenged, culturally and ideologically determined and perhaps even mistaken. It certainly flies in the face of massively accumulating perspectives which, if taken seriously, must affect our thinking about individual psychotherapy, if not actually our practice.

In my opinion, a serious, unremitting concern with the changes which are affecting our world on a much broader canvas of history and universal consciousness can only be ignored at the peril of the individual, whether civilian or patient. However the attempt to do this, in addition to the daily work of healing, can seem overwhelming. It has simply become impossible to keep up with the new developments even in one's field of specialisation. The information explosion in the world, the way in which word processors have led to multitudes of books inundating potential readers, the statistics that show that we are exposed to thousands of advertising messages in a single day, has led to what O'Hara (1991) calls 'sensory and psychic overload...between multiple, often competing realities' (p. 71).

Yet I believe some sincere attempt to salute these realities in our conceptual environment must be made, and it must be made by counsellors and psychotherapists because the implications affect our work most profoundly. Yet the bulk of psychotherapeutic writing does not refer to or contextualise itself within the collective cultural, conceptual, scientific, and moral storms of our turbulent times. One of the reasons that psychotherapists may metaphorically retreat to the enclosed chamber of the consulting room, insulating themselves (as far as they can) from these cross-currents is because of this experience or anticipation of the sheer impossibility of managing or making a kind of enduring sense of the world and a natural and understandable reluctance to 'ride the waves of change'. Erv Polster (1992) once told me that he thought the human mind is a simplification machine, it likes to have hard categories and simple moral dilemmas. This chapter is therefore an exercise against simplification and in favour of complexity. It does not mean for me that simple is necessarily better or worse than complex – essentially, both should have a place in the thoughts and action that are our practice. Perhaps because of its very nature, complexity is more comfortable in avoidance than in encounter, as I experienced most vividly in grappling with the themes I address here.

I have had tremendous difficulty in completing this discussion. I believe my process has mirrored the content that I have attempted to garner in one reasonably small, linear, paper-shaped space. For the reasons mentioned above, I have often felt overpowered with the scope of what cries out to be said, the vast amount of words and images that may be necessary even to indicate the nature of the problems and the sheer enormity of the task I had set myself. Yet I wanted to expire conceptually in the attempt. I know that I have not achieved my goals, but I hope to have indicated some of the directions for others to follow – or to avoid! Therefore, in this chapter, I am not attempting to be comprehensively accurate in any way. I aim to share with the reader some of my experiences, emphases, and questions only in the hope that the reader may find him- or herself stimulated to consider the impact of at least some, if not all, of these upon the practice of counselling, psychotherapy, organisational consultancy, as well as training and supervision in these fields.

I will focus on an arbitrarily selected number of issues under two headings: changes in our conceptual environment, and changes in our world. I will draw out some implications of these for changes in psychology and psychotherapy. If I can inspire psychotherapists, counsellors and psychologists to reconsider what we think we know or ought to know about human beings and psychology, then my purpose will be accomplished.

Changes in Our Cultural Field

Our times are characterised by a proliferation of our awareness of different cultures – not only because of television, but also because of the increasing internationalism of our neighbourhoods, our political and economic alliances, for example, the formation of the European Community. There has also been an analogous multiplication of cultural idioms between and even within any one cultural group, as witness the coexistence of 'high and low art forms' in literature. The radio serial, the comic strip and the detective novel straddle the conventional cultural categories, and confuse traditional hierarchies and categories.

O'Hara (1991) is one of a number of theoreticians of the cultural climate of our time who have used the term *post-modernism* to describe the current, most prevalent phenomena in literature, art and architecture. Although there is much debate about whether the term is useful, adequately defined, or even meaningful, it does encapsulate a generation's attempt to name the condition of fragmented conceptual realities that characterises our time (Connor, 1989). And naming (a nominative level operation) is a basic but important step towards understanding, as we see in our clients, who may move from reporting 'Daddy messing about' to 'Daddy raping me'.

Post-modernism is but one of the names that has been used to describe collectively a number of different strands of development in art, architecture, literature and other fields – lately even psychology. It is viewed by some as the emerging cultural tradition that reflects upon, interprets and experiences the manifestations of our Western culture at this time, although others, by definition, would disagree.

So people have different understandings, or argue with the concepts of post-modernism, constructivism, post-structuralism or radical perspectivism. Nevertheless, many of the fine minds of our time are engaged in grappling with an exponentially changing conceptual and cultural world, and these are some of the terms and concomitant conceptual worlds that have emerged from this struggle. Once, there was a hope that we could find an answer, for example that research would progressively lead towards the truth. Current issues of the *Journal of Clinical Psychology* (1992a, b) seem still unquestionably to assume this paradigm. It appears as if the very fundamental assumptions of a positivistic science have not yet buckled under the onslaught of the tidal wave of philosophical, scientific and moral questioning which characterises much of the current North American and European intellectual climate.

Now, according to Lyotard (1989, p. 34), the 'meta-narrative' has collapsed. There is no longer one story or even the hope of one *grand* story. The ideal used to be that we could build our knowledge piece by piece based on previous research. As Gergen (1990) points out, 'we do not improve our knowledge of the world through systematic study...so much as shift our way of seeing the world' (p. 27). 'There is today an advance of a multi-method approach, including qualitative, interactive and contextual methods' (Kvale, 1990, p. 52).

Gergen (1990) is one of the first psychologists to address the issues of post-modern consciousness. He claims that psychologists and society are being brought closer together by 'demystifying the grand narrative of modernism' (p. 33). The grand narrative can be understood as the expectation that there is an ultimate story behind all human experience which, when found, would precipitate Utopia or, at the very least, enlightenment. Such a grand narrative was the hope of the enlightenment project of the Renaissance. It was encapsulated in the conviction that somehow human beings could find an ultimate answer or solution to the dilemmas of human existence, whether it be in religion, communism, or the final findings of a positivistic science. The world has, however, become more complex than even Da Vinci imagined. New technology and discoveries have meant that we have more realities to contend with. New, more complex, technological language has proliferated, with which we seek to explain it all, but fail repeatedly.

> We live in a world in which the authority of previous guides has apparently crumbled. They have become fragments, bits of a particular archive (of Western Europe, of the white male voice), part of a local history that once involved the presumption (and power) to speak in the name of the 'world'.
>
> (B. Boradori in Chambers, 1990, p. 82)

We have seen ideological dream after ideological dream flower, and fail to solve the monumental problems facing our world – the impending destruction of the planet, the millions of people dying of hunger and disease, the rise of fundamentalism of an extreme degree. There is a profound sense in which we have become disillusioned, and yet many lack the energetic, courageous despair of existentialists such as Kierkegaard. Although they largely conform to the externals, the young seem to listen to authorities now with a built-in scepticism. At the same time there is a 74% increase in suicides among young men in the UK alone in the last 10 years (Pepinster, 1992).

Thus the criticism of our culture can be read in such statistics as well as in the post-modern movement. Whereas modernism tended to be both upper class and eurocentric, the ideas of post-modernism are characterised by the presence of *the other* – many different cultures find a voice, and the places of women and minority groups become of significant interest.

> Postmodern consciousness...by demystifying the grand narrative of modernism, attempts to bring psychologists and society closer together. Not only is technology placed in the service of values to which one is committed; more importantly, the psychologist is encouraged to join in forms of valuation advocacy and to develop new intelligibilities that present new options to the culture. There is no promise of utopias here, but the possibility of active and engaged participation in cultural process is significantly enhanced.
>
> (Gergen, 1990, p. 33)

The powerful *collective* nature of psychotherapy, whether or not it is conducted in individual or group settings, is, however, frequently avoided or minimised in much of psychotherapy training and practice. Many of us conduct psychotherapy as if the individual is genuinely totally responsible for his or her life choices. Although I had substantial training and experience in other orientations, I became an existential psychotherapist when I discovered Frankl's (1992) remarkable book *Man's Search for Meaning*. This book was the result of three years he spent as a prisoner in four different German concentration camps where people appeared to have lost all possibilities of choosing or influencing their own destiny or their own choices. According to Frankl the last of the human freedoms is the ability to 'choose one's attitude in a given set of circumstances' (p. iii).

I used Frankl to support my belief that, as human beings, we are completely responsible for our reactions to life's exigencies. Although this still appears to me to be fundamentally true, I have become much more humble and compassionate towards the enormous influence of collective forces on individual psychotherapy. The impact of class, race, gender, culture and current world events such as acts of terrorism, the death of major figures such as John Lennon, and the divorces of the royal family in the UK, can be minimised if there is an over-emphasis on individual responsibility. Sometimes it seems as if the internal fantasy or transferential life of the patient/client were the only reality relevant to the conduct of psychotherapy, counselling or psychoanalysis, yet time after time I discover that that is not true at all for the unique individual.

As my skills, knowledge, and experience have grown, so has my humility. In particular, life has impressed upon me the limits of what is possible when my focus is only on the microcosms of my professional domains. The whole background – historical, sociological, perhaps even astrological, of any individual – impinges on and interpenetrates my therapeutic and consulting work more and more.

It seems true and real to me that the individual has many more choices than those of which they are usually aware – and that, above all, it is vital to keep reviewing them, as the choices may change. A large percentage of our adult clients come to us with problems possibly caused by the continuing beliefs of (for example) their one-time three-year-old self or unfortunate suckling experiences. At the same time, it seems equally true that the individual is limited in awareness as well as in choice by collective factors which exceed our worst imaginings. It has been my experience that the disavowal as well as the attribution of individual responsibility can become oppressive. For example an open marriage may be an imposed freedom, not a genuine choice of both partners but an unwilling acquiescence by one in the hope that this will retain the other's love. A client's freedom and consequent responsibility to abandon abusive family ties varies, as we know, from circumstance to circumstance.

Of course relatively few of the limits are absolutely impossible to overcome. People continue to liberate themselves with 'amazing grace' from the constraints of heredity, history, class and conditioning. However, this kind of freedom cannot be imposed, for it can be claimed or owned by the individual alone. Although still unaware that there are genuine, other options, the 16-year-old unmarried Irish mother has her scope for individual choice and responsibility enormously reduced by her cultural, ideological and religious environment. Any psychotherapy that minimises the monumental collective pressures under which we all live is ultimately bound for disablement and despair. I believe it is only to this extent that we can carve out our degrees of freedom, even as we are appalled by an increasing awareness of our culturally and ideologically limiting conditioning.

If, on the other hand, one feels responsible for everything, it can be incapacitating. The decentring of confluence, of losing your identity to the perceived priority of others, is just as disempowering as the crusading feeling that everything depends on you. For example, a woman in our culture invites detrimental consequences if she sits in a certain way, for example, with her legs apart, like a man. I refer readers to the book called *Let's Take Back Our Space* by Wex (1979), which chillingly demonstrates with hundreds of photographs of men and women from different classes, statuses and ages, the 'invisible corsets' and behavioural bondage to which women in our culture are subjected. Wolf, in her book *The Beauty Myth* (1990), also explores the influence of collective conditioning. She points out that today's ideal female body image can only be maintained on the same number of calories that was considered starvation rations during the German occupation in Holland. This means that most women are consistently confronted with images that imply that they have somehow fallen short of the ideal due to their hunger – for food, for life, for freedom? Wolf points out that more than 14 women have died from the liposuction operation, where living tissue is sucked out of a woman's body so she may achieve the socially desired shape, yet there has been no outcry about this.

Bly (1990) in *Iron John* and other authors of the new 'men's movement', for example, Keen (1992), have also drawn attention to the cultural constraints and imposed handicaps which face men collectively in our culture.

I now believe that an undue emphasis is sometimes placed on the relative proportions of individual responsibility and freedom within the grand constraints of collective influences. These appear to me to be equally if not more potent. Even where we perhaps can refuse to be passive smokers, we cannot choose *not* to breathe the polluted air in which we live. Perhaps therefore such collective or environmental forces are the more dangerous, because we can be so unaware of their influence and effects. Collective messages, hypnotic suggestions and ideological descriptions are so ubiquitously embedded in our culture, our advertisements, our television serials, that they become largely unknown to us. Every dawning awareness of some prejudice of mine is accompanied by an unease about the many I probably still hold (not intentionally but in inadvertent blindness).

In the same vein, how many pictures do we see of older women in our society? How many Christmas cards with black faces? If I hadn't personally seen these cards and experienced the shock of recognising that I had never seen them before, I might still not have known the extent to which the absence of these images has permeated the collective psyche, and mine in particular. The influence of the media, whether a crime is reported to be committed by a black person or not, or whether a woman is 21 or 81, whether the house is worth £79 000 or £750 000, is omnipresent in shaping and even determining the collective psyche. A friend commented that she was watching the news on television about the riots in Los Angeles in spring 1992, and was surprised to hear the newscaster making the point that 'blacks, Koreans, and even whites...were on the streets' as if to say that it was surprising that whites were joining in the fray. Perhaps the therapeutic task is to find the balance between personal autonomy and a contribution to the collective good, always questioning the messages we think we send or receive. 'For sense here lies not in the separate fates of individualised identities and isolated accounts, but in the interconnected weaving together of the stories, languages, differences and bodies in which we are caught' (Chambers, 1990, p. 110).

Another influential strand of post-modernist thinking is the breakdown of the division between *high* and *low* culture; comic books and detective novels, for example, become novelistic paradigms accessible to human beings of all classes, educational background and diversity of interests. For example, the post-modernist novel by Umberto Eco, *The Name Of The Rose* (1983) has now been made into a film. I can see similar manifestations in the world of psychology – an integration of so-called high and low culture.

Popular varieties of psychology such as expounded by Rowe (1983), Skynner and Cleese (1983), the agony columns of magazines and television programmes on sexual problems and family difficulties, together with scientists such as Hawking (1988), make the underlying questions of psychology, the universe and creation familiar to all instead of to a closed circle of scientists. More and more academic or clinical psychologists seem to be willing to write for a less psychologically educated public, or to appear on television or radio programmes where their audiences consist of people primarily seeking entertainment. Perhaps the attention span of the modern viewer, which is notoriously short, is a factor in the prevalence of this type of mass psychological education. Of course, it also frequently suffers from over-generalisation, simplification, de-contextualisation and other disadvantages that accrue when knowledge is cut loose from its moorings. This does not mean, however, that I do not think this is important.

Ten years ago I was asked why counselling was so unpopular in Britain. Even at the time, I said to the interviewer that there was a false perception that the British are not interested in counselling, because almost every person that I ever met in this country was genuinely and sincerely interested in personality, human behaviour, communication and the solving of life's problems. Even the enduring popularity of so-called soap operas supports this belief. If, somehow, psychotherapy and counselling had not reached those people, it was because the professionals had not yet found a way of speaking or communicating with the very large numbers of people who are desperate for the information available to the affluent, the educated and the pretentious.

In the current intellectual climate, it is thought that philosophical and epistemological questioning is undermining the very foundations of the modern world (O'Hara, 1991). A thoroughgoing, radical perspectivism is a characteristic feature of post-modernist thinking and gaining credence as a viewpoint elsewhere. Radical perspectivism sees all attempts at philosophical or ideological foundations as potentially valuable. However, they are each reflections of particular perspectives, which have no justification except by recourse to other, equally subjective perspectives. Critical questions are asked regarding the possibility or the viability of the search for or the adherence to any one particular view of the person, psychology or the world. The importance of opening new vistas for study is pre-eminent, along with an appropriately questioning and critical attitude to established views or accepted opinions.

The idea that there may be a *depth* psychology as opposed to another psychology which is not deep and may therefore be less valuable or less true, is being thoroughly re-thought. Chambers (1990) points out that a 'surface' psychology may have equally viable potential. This is consistent with a Perlsian idea that gestalt is the psychology of the obvious on the one hand, and the concepts from chaos theory discussed next, which also support the notion that all that is relevant is already present on the surface – that the whole is present and fully encoded in the phenomenon as it manifests itself.

The implications of this may lie in the rethinking of 'depth' psychology. 'The surface is everything, appearance is being and therefore the whole dialectic between "appearance" and "reality", between "surface" and "depth", so central to the Kantian and enlightenment traditions, collapses at a stroke' (Chambers, 1990, p. 94).

This is a strong image, but needs to be carefully considered in context. There does appear now to be an increasing concern with theoretical as opposed to empirical issues in psychology and psychotherapy, as witness the inception of a new journal on theory in psychology. Whereas post-modernism has been particularly associated with architecture and literature, and only recently been broached in psychotherapy, constructivism has been influential in the helping professions for some decades. Constructivism posits that what we know is determined by our ideas – it is a perspective we constructed or invented in our heads, therefore we can never know an external reality, we can only have perspectives or views on that reality determined by what we know already. Constructivism developed in contrast to realism – stating that knowledge can be discovered by people in an objective way as reality exists outside a particular individual perspective. The concept that the relationship is fundamental to effective psychotherapy (see Chapter 2), and maybe to all of life, may be seen in this sense as *co-constructivism*. Speed (1991) outlines co-constructivism as follows:

> Co-constructivism offers an alternative to realism, constructivism and social constructionism. By co-constructivism is meant the view that what we know arises in a relationship between the knower and the known (see Speed, 1984). It takes for granted that a structured reality exists but recognises that that reality is constructed or mediated in the sense that different aspects are highlighted according to ideas that people individually or in groups have about it.
>
> (p. 410)

Changes in Our Scientific Context

Another important change in our conceptual environment is, of course, in the area of science, particularly quantum dynamics and human systems. The scientific context is particularly concerned with quantum dynamics in human systems on the one hand, and chaos theory on the other. Zohar (1990) describes the process in modern physics thus:

> Quantum field theory takes us even further beyond Newton's dead and silent universe, giving us a vivid picture of the dynamic flux which lies at the heart of an indeterminate being. Here, even those particles which do manifest themselves as individual beings do so only briefly.... [It gives a] graphic picture of the emergence and return, or the beginning and ceasing, of individual subatomic particles at the quantum level of reality [which] holds out deep implications of our way of looking at the nature and function of individual personalities or the survival of the individual self.
>
> (p. 13)

The new physics (though being already almost an octogenarian, it is not so new) has hardly been addressed in any of the major systems of psychotherapy. There is only an occasional paper in Jungian and gestalt journals. The implications of quantum physics for psychology are potentially enormous. For example, the Cartesian dualism between mind and matter is called into question in a radical and fundamental sense. Such a dualism has virtually been transcended in modern physics. It has already potentially invalidated the classical or positivist ideal of an objective description of nature; the goal of traditional academic psychology.

As in post-modernism, the new physics makes it untenable to consider an objective or value-free scientific approach. It also postulates the coexistence of apparently contradictory views of reality, for example, in the words of Sir William Bragg, 'Elementary particles seem to be waves on Mondays, Wednesdays and Fridays, and particles on Tuesdays, Thursdays and Saturdays' (in Zohar, 1990, p. 10).

The whole idea of unidirectional causality (that past conditions cause future conditions) is thus up for rethinking. For example, many of our psychological theories are based on the idea that early childhood influences affect adult life choices and patterns. However, if we consider the human being as a quantum system, such an idea of past causes may become quite invalid and unhelpful in effecting changes for the future. It is equally possible, according to the new paradigms, that we live in a teleological universe where the future is determining the present. I do not think we should rule out the possibility of a Copernican revolution in psychotherapy and I do think we should pay attention to the almost automatic knee-jerk mental reflex by which we may reject such revolutionary and 'upsetting' ideas.

Quantum dynamics in human systems

Quantum physics is 'the physics of that tiny micro-world within the atom, it describes the inner workings of everything we see, and at least physically, are' (Zohar, 1990, p. 4). Quantum physics is also an invitation for the psychologist to think about possibilities.

There are aspects of the so-called quantum physics that operate, according to some theorists, only at certain quantum levels. Others (such as the controversial author Zohar) believe that human beings also operate on psyche and soma levels (or many more), and that these constitute quantum systems. Their smooth interaction is health – on all levels and quantum dynamics.

> The whole world of matter, including our own bodies, is made up of atoms and their even smaller components, and the laws which govern these tiny bits of basic reality spill over into our daily lives. A single photon, or 'particle' of light, affects the sensitivity of the optic nerve. The uncertainty principle that rules the behaviour of electrons plays a role in the build-up of genetic mistakes that contribute to the ageing process and the development of certain cancers, and the process of evolution itself is thought to be similarly influenced.
>
> (Zohar, 1990, p. 4)

Playwrights and novelists have long exploited this fractal effect, by which the whole is fully present in any fragment of it (Atlas, 1992).

In common with some art forms, psychotherapy is the art and craft of promoting growth and/or healing in human beings. However, our most usual paradigm for psychotherapy is that of client and therapist in a one-to-one, individual relationship. Group psychotherapy or even community therapy is less popularised. Even from biology, new information and new models for human behaviour, particularly the relationship between individuals and the community, are being discovered and developed. Studies of slime moulds (Elliott and Williams, 1991) are being used as analogies to human communities. Cellular slime moulds are a group of soil inhabitants which live as single-celled amoebae. When conditions are adverse, however, they aggregate to form a cellular collective based on mutual communication, specialisation of tasks, and coordination.

As in post-modernism, the notion of the individual as separate from others, as an aspect of received consciousness, may bite the dust and what remains are the encodings of life in terms of relationships. Zohar (1990), for example, doubts that this perspective has yet been adequately addressed. 'Klein, like Freud, Sartre and Heidegger, has no model for genuine two-way relationship of the sort that leads to intimacy. None can discriminate between the way we relate to other people and the way we might relate to a machine because for them all both machines and people share the quality of being objects (Zohar, 1990, p. 113).

Interestingly, as Rogers (1986) pointed out in the 1960s, an emphasis on groups, genuine encounter and mutuality of relationships tends to be construed by right-wing governments and right-wing climates as revolutionary and subversive. This is, of course, not unusual as the group is the most powerful fulcrum for individual or social change. It is the family or cultural group that sometimes appears to create most benefit or to do most damage. It is the group that scapegoats the Jew, the crowd that crucifies Christ, and the mob that lynches a black man in Alabama. It is also a feature of the time at which I am writing that right-wing governments and neo-fascist or fundamentalist groups are in the ascendant in Asia, Africa and Europe.

There are then the questions of causality and acausality. Unidirectional causality is a highly dubious notion in explaining physical (or psychological) illness. This also has remarkable implications for parallel process in the transference/countertransference field, as the encoding of a relational, mutual hypnotically induced field between therapist and client. It becomes very difficult, if not impossible, to determine whether the client, frightened of being harshly judged by the therapist, seeks out a therapist who judges him- or herself harshly, or interacts with such a therapist in such a way that brings about, or at least obviates, the resolution of a similar pattern in the client. How come sometimes our clients bring us the very problems that we now need to deal with in our own personal work? We have all noticed occasions when, after dealing with, say, a parent symbolically in therapy, the real life parent changes. Much is unexplained.

After much analysis of separate parts, relativity and quantum mechanics, scientists have been brought to the inescapable acceptance that the world cannot be analysed into separate and independently existing parts. Each part involves all the others in some way, contains or enfolds them (Bohm, 1985). The implications of this, taken seriously, could herald the end of empiricism or, at the very least, give equal weight to other possible perspectives such as phenomenology.

> Freudian psychoanalysis, too, largely influenced by Descartes and Newton and in turn so responsible for the way so many ordinary people see themselves, has no conceptual framework for interpersonal relationships.... As the author of the *Dictionary of Psychoanalysis* puts it 'This is because psychoanalysis is a psychology of the individual and therefore discusses objects and relationships only from the point of view of a single subject'.
>
> (Rycroft, 1968, p. 101, in Zohar, 1990, p. 112)

The fact that the observer is always part of the field has remarkable implications for psychotherapy and supervision. For example, in Chapters 9 and 10, I explained how parallel process can be seen as the encoding of a mutual, hypnotically induced field of the relationship between psychotherapist and patient, replicated in the supervisor–

supervisee field. I question whether a traditionally understood causality limits and restrains rather than enhances our understanding of and effectiveness in the therapeutic and supervisory relationship.

In particular, the new physics underlines the vitality of the relationship field and its crucial importance for psychotherapy of the future.

> Epistemologically, the things we see (people, objects etc.) exist only in relationship and, when analysed microscopically, they too are best viewed as relationships. It is no secret in physics (Capra, 1975; 1978) that the closer we analyse some 'thing' the less it appears as a thing and the more it appears as a dynamic process (things in relationship). Consequently, relationships become a primary source of our knowledge of the world. This can be taken to the ontological extreme by stating that things do not exist...that, in fact, things ultimately *are* relationships.
>
> (Cottone, 1988, p. 360)

Chaos theory at large in psychotherapy?

As well as quantum changes in large systems, the other scientific area of fascinating implications of interest for psychologists and psychotherapists, is chaos theory.

> The first Chaos theorists...had an eye for pattern, especially pattern that appeared on different scales at the same time. They had a taste for randomness and complexity, for jagged edges and sudden leaps. Believers in chaos speculate about determinism and free will, about evolution, about the nature of conscious intelligence. They feel that they are turning back a trend in science toward reductionism, the analysis of systems in terms of their constituent parts...they believe that they are looking for the whole.
>
> (Gleick, 1989, p. 5)

This raises many questions for psychotherapy and psychology. For example, can there be a representative sample if every part encodes the whole, and the macrocosm is infinitely replicated in every microscopic aspect?

The word 'fractal' was coined by Mandelbrot (1974) to describe the phenomenon of a repeating pattern – elements of the whole are repeated in every fragment, and spiral off each other towards creative evolution. 'Above all, fractal meant self-similar. Self-similarity is symmetry across scale. It implies recursion, pattern inside of pattern' (Gleick, 1989, p. 103).

This, again, is true of our life and belief systems – psychotherapists know that you can go on repeating certain patterns of belief to infinity too, such as habitual self-deception, or letting addictive habits become the very meaning of life. 'When we try to pick out anything by itself, we find it hitched to everything else in the Universe.... The whole wilderness is unity and interrelation is alive and familiar' (Muir in Wolfe, 1951, p. 123). It is not that chaos is without order – it is that it *is* order, with its own nature and in a new dimension. Bohm (1985) has addressed this whole-making tendency in his thought-provoking book, *The Implicate Order*. I also find illumination in the holism theory of Smuts (1987), the South African philosopher-general who was developing similar ideas well before Bohm or the chaos theorists.

> The final net result is that this is a whole-making universe, that it is the fundamental character of this universe to be active in the production of wholes, of ever more complete and advanced wholes, and that the Evolution of the universe, inorganic and organic, is nothing but the record of this whole-making activity in its progressive development.
>
> (Smuts, 1987, p. 326)

The whole penetrates each of its parts; it is one universe. 'God conceived it as a unique, living being, and its intelligible Model is itself a whole' (Chenu, 1957, p. 6).

> In science as in life, it is well known that a chain of events can have a point of crisis that could magnify small changes. But chaos means that such points were everywhere. They were pervasive. In systems like the weather, sensitive dependence on initial conditions was an inescapable consequence of the way small scales intertwined with large.
>
> (Gleick, 1989, p. 23)

If it is true that there is such an incredible consequence of initial conditions, what does this mean about our understanding of the psychotherapeutic process? This may dictate a shift in clinical approaches to the treatment of psychiatric disorders, for example, A. Mandell (in Briggs and Peat, 1990, p. 168) questions traditional models for treating human beings – these most unstable, dynamic, infinitely multidimensional, choice- and meaning-making organisms – with linear and reductionist models. Simple systems give rise to complex behaviour. Complex systems give rise to simple behaviour. The laws of complexity hold universally. Should this not shake or at least rumble the accepted psychological paradigms? 'Is it possible that mathematical pathology, i.e. chaos is health? And that mathematical health, which is the predictability and differentiability of this kind of a structure, is disease?' (Gleick, 1989, p. 298).

Chaos scientists have discovered that predictability and regularity can be a sign of illness – the only time the heartbeat, for example, is truly regular is just before a coronary. In psychology, too, there has often been a preoccupation with homeostasis, equilibrium, adaptation. Exploration of disequilibrium, disruption and disturbance has but rarely been conceived of as healthy or creative. Yet creativity happens at far from equilibrium conditions, often needing the stimulus of deadlines, emotional turmoil or a change of setting to flourish. All these themes we are considering can have a massive impact on theory, practice and research in all the human disciplines, but not least in psychology, psychotherapy, supervision and organisational work.

Potentially the impact of these developments on these fields must be disturbing, disorientating and perhaps even precipitate disequilibrium. It certainly seems important to me that some of us are willing to have our own theoretical experiences and our philosophical constructions challenged by these new and provocative models, conceptions and developments. It is possible that under such stimulus, creativity in psychology can continue to evolve disruptively rather than dogmatically. Gergen (1990), for example, encourages the construction of new and more practical forms of theory as one of the most important tasks of the psychology of the future. Ford, self-proclaimed evangelist of chaos, sees the excitement in the prospect of disequilibrium conditions in organisations: 'Dynamics freed at last from the shackles of order and predictability.... Systems liberated to randomly explore their every dynamical possibility.... Exciting variety, richness of choice, a cornucopia of opportunity' (1986, p. 114–115).

> Until recently, such phenomena as the volatility of weather systems, the fluctuation of the stock market, or the random firing of neurons in the brain were considered too 'noisy' and complex to be probed by science.... [Chaos theory is] turning our perception of the world on its head; and...discoveries in mathematics, biology, and physics...are heralding a revolution more profound than the one responsible for producing the atomic bomb. With practical applications ranging from the control of traffic flow and the development of artificial intelligence to the treatment of heart attacks and schizophrenia, chaos promises to be an increasingly rewarding area of inquiry – of interest to everyone.
>
> (Briggs and Peat, 1990, back cover)

Like quantum physics, chaos theory highlights the importance of relationships. In this way, chaos theory has shown us that everything and potentially everybody is related in a kind of dance. Everything is in this sense connected with everything else and any separation is therefore theoretical rather than actual. Along with these fundamental and mind-changing developments in our relationship with our conceptual environment, there are changes in our actual world relationships.

Our Changing World

The development of technology and communications has led to a situation where 'For the first time...all humanity has the technological means to sit round the same planetary hearth and listen to each other's stories' (O'Hara, 1991, p. 73). The ecological connectedness of our world has been dramatically brought to our attention by the way in which, for example, the damage to the ozone layer can affect people in all parts of the world. In the same way, the fallout of Chernobyl can affect sheep in Wales. According to chaos theory (Gleick, 1989), even the fluttering of a butterfly's wings in South America can affect weather conditions in Europe.

There are many thinkers whose work more and more supports the notion that the earth is a whole. One of the most ingenious of these is Lovelock (1989), who postulates the idea that the life of the earth functions as a single organism which actually defines and maintains conditions necessary for its survival. It has become famous as the 'Gaia' hypothesis.

It can no longer be said that one part of the planet can be said to exist separately from any other part. Our planet is moaning from the assault of pollution in the seas, the deforestation in South America, and the extinction of rare and beautiful species of animals, all of which add up to the equivalent for the planet of cancer in a body. For too long man has attempted to control nature, as opposed to connecting or co-operating with nature and yet, according to Rinzler (1984): 'Our human malaise of disconnection from natural sensation, our symptoms of violence on all levels, our lack of compassion for our home, the earth, our incomprehension of the connectedness among all the things of the earth, of the universe, are curable – if we are willing' (p. 236).

Metanoia in large systems

Another important aspect of our changing world is some extraordinary turnarounds or metanoias in large systems. I am particularly interested in the process of change and learning how to become more proficient at facilitating changes. Subsequently it has been my privilege to witness several large-scale systems in the process of massive changes. My peculiar sensitivity to this field of study made me particularly grateful for the opportunity of studying and experiencing at least three nations undergoing a metanoia or a turnaround. These provided me with an enormous rich and fertile field experiment. It was idiosyncratically, empathically, and collectively that I engaged with the structure and dynamics of these learning experiences. I imagine that my struggle intellectually to understand, emotionally to resonate, and pragmatically to apply what I am learning, will continue for the rest of my life. Of course my hope is that some of what I learn on the macrocosmic scale may usefully fertilise the work of organisational, group, and of course, individual therapy.

The Berlin Wall

When I heard on 11 November 1989 that the Berlin Wall was being demolished I booked the first possible flight to see just what would be happening in Berlin when the celebrations began. I expressed some of it in a poem called 'The Opening of the Wall' (see Appendix I).

The willingness to surrender the previous frame of reference is vital for effective change. 'No precise figures are yet available but when the Berlin Wall fell, several East German soldiers chose to commit suicide. Rather than attempt to make the painful transition to a new reality where those who yesterday were the 'enemy' today become the 'friend', some guards preferred the strange safety of death' (Clarkson in George, 1990, p. 14).

South Africa revisited

I had been a voluntary exile from South Africa since after 1976 when black schoolchildren were being killed in increasing numbers for protesting against the injustices of the South African 'Bantu' education system. I would no longer live a normal life in an abnormal society, in a situation where my very existence was a cause for guilt. After the lifting of the state of emergency in South Africa in 1990, I returned to work for a while and to be educated again in my country of birth (see Appendix I). I spent some time in Imbali, the black township where the worst violence was happening between blacks and blacks at the time, and adolescent corpses were being picked up from rubbish dumps before breakfast. I worked with the architects of apartheid and on interracial communication as well as in higher education staff healing in community counselling projects. I found that 'Unbelievably...there is an astonishing level of compassion, love and tolerance still left. They call it *ubuntu* – which means fellow human feeling – and it is because of this that she still feels tremendous hope that the horrendous problems that are South Africa can progress towards peace' (Clarkson, 1990, p. 11).

The second Russian revolution

For some years we had been planning to go to Russia on the invitation of gestalt and transactional analysis communities in (what is once again called) St Petersburg and Murmansk, inside the Arctic circle. On the morning of Monday, 19 August 1991 when we started the workshop, and were still considering how to focus or energise the group, the second Russian revolution broke out. I was deeply moved and impressed by this, the third major experience at this scale and intensity (see Appendix I).

There was to be another experience when I was invited to speak on metanoia and Physis at the international psychotherapy conference in Zagreb in September 1989 but, in this particular case, the war intervened to such an extent that the conference was cancelled. I have only been able to work with a few, very special people from the former Yugoslavia who have come to Britain to study change processes. Hopefully they will then go back to their war-torn country and help in whatever way they can.

At the same time as these incredible breakdowns between artificial divisions: communism and capitalism, black and white beaches, west and east of the Wall, there has been a swing towards right-wing governments in Europe, enormous increases in bureaucratic control for everything from psychotherapy to cheese, a rise in numbers of people associated with fundamentalist Christianity, as well as the powerful march of Islam and a growth in the scope and sophistication of international terrorism.

More nations are dividing and sub-dividing into separate sections, such as the break-up of the Soviet Union, Czechoslovakia and Yugoslavia. On the other hand there is a coming together of nations, such as the establishment of the European Community and the establishment of many worldwide networks such as the Worldwide Fund for Nature. At its heart is first a desire to belong, which is common to all humanity. That achieved, the security of belonging then frees up energy to assist others.

However complex and overwhelming it is to try to make sense from these vividly contrasting and frequently perplexing changes, several things seem to be clear to me. Firstly, whatever changes are accomplished in the world, which are experienced as solutions at a particular time, they contain within them the seeds of the future problems for the very same situation. Secondly, our Utopian dreams of final solutions need to be relinquished. We need to become skilful in living in a world in which constant change has become the norm. Thirdly, we are all responsible. Because of the dynamic interconnectedness of our one world, there is no way in which some of us can claim to be innocent bystanders in respect of any injustice or pain in any part of the rest of our world.

Temporary Conclusions

The conceptual changes in our psychosocial and cultural environment mentioned here, constitute some of the strands of our current psychosocial *Zeitgeist*. Much that I say here is arguable, hopefully all of it, but I invite the reader to think and grapple with the consequences of certain developing currents in our scientific and cultural world, and their impact on counselling, psychotherapy and supervision. I cannot do justice to these perspectives. These brief words are meant merely to introduce these themes into the field of psychotherapy, where unfortunately they are more conspicuous by their absence. What I believe is needed now is serious and thorough-going concern with the impact they may have, or already are having, on the collective psyche of our time.

The Perlsian idea (Perls, 1969) that we are *response-able* (p. 65) has been a guiding value for me in my work with individuals and organisations. This idea of individual freedom of choice was also very compelling to me as a person. It remains so. However, I have become more and more convinced that we are not only creatures of our genes and of our families of origin. We are also, to an inconceivable extent, the creatures of our schools, our churches, our health systems, the entertainments to which we are exposed, our laws, our politics, our climate and – who knows – even our stars. Jung wondered about the influence of astrology on psychology and I, for one, am by no means certain that he was misguided in this. An ancient saying claims that 'As above, so below'. The individual may indeed be embedded in the collective or the collective may be viewed coherently as the individual WRIT LARGE. 'These planets...(Uranus, Neptune and Pluto)...are termed "transpersonal" and address our awareness of collective experience, ie. the "body of mankind" – our collective body and soul. ...Pluto in Scorpio [until 1995] is a symbol which beautifully mirrors this new awareness of our capacity for potential collective self-destruction and collective self-transformation' (Costello, 1991).

My PhD in 1974 was concerned with the overlap area between personality, psychophysiology, and environmental factors. My *naïveté* in expecting sufficiently to penetrate to the core truths of this interacting field is amazing to me now. My passion for exploring these interfaces has, however, remained intact. For example, I see that individual psychologies appear to be replicated in larger systems. Personality patterns and problems similar to, but larger than, individuals, can be recognised in macroscopic configurations in large-scale systems such as groups and organisations.

The personal qualities I find essential are:

1. Personal experience of change, particularly the dark night of the soul, which seems to be an essential requirement for any creative breakthrough, whether in art, in psychotherapy or in national change.
2. The willingness to do it again and again, that the nature of the change experience is cyclic or resembles that of a spiral, and we need to enter the void again and again if we are to merge more fully and completely.
3. Positive attitude to change, an investment in evolution, willingness to bear the disintegrating and fragmenting forces without incapacitating ourselves.

I believe that counselling, psychology and all their associated disciplines need to take on the challenges of the new contexts – not to be learnt by rote, but to be held at the mind as a constant resource, otherwise they may become a symptom of those conditions which called them into being. Can it be that the other professions have not fully responded to the call of our time, as no-one else, including any established church, seems fully to have answered it? A discipline such as psychology in its particular British shape does not appear to be responding to the fragmentation and chaotic complexity of our post-modern era, which is moving at exponentially increasing speeds. The problems facing the world on a macroscopic level, as well as psychologists on a microscopic level, have become too complex for psychologists or counsellors to have unbridled faith in singular solutions, or to insist on imposing such singular solutions on their trainees or colleagues. We must learn to listen to each other, no matter what our differences of opinion or seniority. There are three requirements for all associated helping professions: that we be willing to move with our times; we move with our art/science; and move with each other.

In the turbulent and troubled psychological waters at the end of this century, communication may become more important than certainty, effectiveness more important than positivistic elegance for its own sake, and intellectual and moral questioning of our basic assumptions more important than adherence to a single way of integration.

Another strand of this incredibly rich tapestry of changing paradigms and collapsing realities is the momentous event that Macpherson reported happening in April 1992: 'a robot spacecraft "heard" the very birth pangs of the creation of the universe from almost unimaginable depths of space and time' (p. 17).

Evidence has now been found that galaxies and stars, and ultimately humans therefore, condensed from a violent explosive fog of radiation and elementary particles more than 14 thousand million years ago. The universe was thus born from an infinitesimal point – out of nothingness. Even as the boundaries of our knowledge expand in this way, many more scientists are acknowledging some form of ultimate consciousness which can be understood as God. I like to think of this as Physis (Murray, 1955). First named by the pre-Socratic Greeks, it is defined as a generalised creative force of Nature which eternally strives to make things grow and to make growing things more perfect. It was conceived of as the *healing* factor in illness, the *energetic* motive for *evolution*, and the driving force of *creativity* in the individual and collective psyche.

P. Davies (in Macpherson, 1992), concerning the Big Bang evidence, suggests that there is a purpose and design to the universe and that we, as intelligent and conscious human beings, are necessary to the functioning of the universe. Maybe we are more intelligent than we know in continuing to try to make sense and meaning of a seemingly chaotic universe – often with too few or too many clues. And maybe this is why we continue to try to make sense and meaning of our own lives, and live them to a fulfilment that goes beyond the mere satisfaction of physiological, even psychological needs, but that reaches towards the transcendent, the transpersonal, the ultimate wholeness. I believe that psychology, counselling, psychotherapy, supervision and organisational work needs also to acknowledge the final mysteries – the end of our knowledge and the beginning of nothingness.

References

ATLAS, J. (1992). Vogue arts: books, review of Nicholson Baker's *Vox*, *Vogue* (March 1992). London: Condé Nast.

BLY, R. (1990). *Iron John: A Book About Men.* Shaftesbury: Element.

BOHM, D. (1985) *Wholeness and the Implicate Order.* London: Ark Paperbacks. (Originally published 1980.)

BRIGGS, J. and PEAT, F.D. (1990). *Turbulent Mirror.* New York: Harper and Row. (Originally published 1989.)

CAPRA, F. (1975). *The Tao of Physics.* Toronto: Bantam.

CAPRA, F. (1978). *The Turning Point: Science, Society and the Rising Culture.* Toronto: Bantam.

CHAMBERS, I. (1990). *Border Dialogues: Journeys in Postmodernity.* London: Routledge.

CHENU, M.D. (1957). *Nature, Man and Society in the Twelfth Century.* Chicago: Chicago University Press.

CLARKSON, P. (1990). Despair before change, *Counselling News* (March 1991), 11.

CONNOR, S. (1989). *Postmodernist Culture.* Oxford: Basil Blackwell.

COSTELLO, D. (1991). Our changing world: signs on the path through 1992. *Elfin Astrological Journal* (Tokyo, Japan), **10** (2), 16–19.

COTTONE, R.R. (1988). Epistemological and ontological issues in counselling: implications of social systems theory. *Counselling Psychology Quarterly,* **1** (4), 357–365.

ECO, U. (1983). *The Name of the Rose.* London: Secker and Warburg.

ELLIOTT, S. and WILLIAMS, K.L. (1991). Modelling people using cellular slime moulds. *Australian Natural History,* **23** (8), 609–616.

FORD, J. (1986). Book reviews. *International Journal of Theoretical Physics,* **25** (1), 113–115.

FRANKL, V. (1992). *Man's Search for Meaning.* London: Hodder and Stoughton. (Originally published 1946.)

GEORGE, E. (1990). Shortwave: heard in the global village (interview with P. Clarkson). *Wave,* (Autumn 1990), 14.

GERGEN, K.J. (1990). Towards a postmodern psychology. *The Humanistic Psychologist,* **18**, Spring , 23–34.

GLEICK, J. (1989). *Chaos: Making a New Science.* London: Heinemann. (Originally published 1988.)

GUERRIERE, D. (1980). Physis, Sophia, Psyche. In: J. Sallis and K. Maly (Eds), *Heraclitean Fragments: A Companion Volume to the Heidegger/Fink Seminar on Heraclitus,* pp. 87–134. Tuscaloosa, AL: University of Alabama Press.

HAWKING, S. (1988). *A Brief History of Time: From the Big Bang to Black Holes.* London: Bantam.

Journal of Clinical Psychology (1992a) **48** (1).

Journal of Clinical Psychology (1992b) **48** (2).

KEEN, S. (1985). *The Passionate Life.* London: Gateway.

KEEN, S. (1992). *Fire in the Belly: On Being a Man.* London: Piatkus.

KVALE, S. (1990). Postmodern psychology: a contradictio in adjecto? *The Humanistic Psychologist,* **18**, 35–52.

LAING, R.D. and ESTERSON, A. (1972). *Leaves of Spring.* Harmondsworth, Middx: Penguin.

LATHER, P. (1990). Postmodernism and the human sciences. *The Humanistic Psychologist,* **18**, 64–84.

LOVELOCK, J. (1989). *Gaia: A New Look at Life on Earth.* Oxford: Oxford University Press. (Originally published 1979.)

LYOTARD, J-F. (1989). *The Postmodern Condition: A Report on Knowledge.* Manchester: Manchester University Press. (Originally published 1979.)

MACPHERSON, A. (1992). Does this give God his P45? *Mail on Sunday,* 26 April, p. 17.

MANDELBROT, B.B. (1974). *The Fractal Geometry of Nature.* New York: Freeman.

MURRAY, G. (1955). *Five Stages of Greek Religion.* New York: Doubleday Anchor.

O'HARA, M. (1991). Horizons of reality: demystifying postmodernism (book review). *Networker,* Jul/Aug, 71–74.

PEPINSTER, C. (1992). Lost generation. *Time Out,* (1135), 13. London: Time Out Publications.

PERLS, F. S. (1969). *Gestalt Therapy Verbatim.* Moab, UT: Real People Press.

RINZLER, D. (1984). Human disconnection and the murder of the earth. *Transactional Analysis Journal,* **14** (4), 231–236.

ROGERS, C.R. (1986). *Client-centred Therapy: Its Current Practice, Implications and Theory.* London: Constable. (Originally published 1951.)

ROWE, D. (1983). *Depression: The Way Out of Your Prison.* London: Routledge and Kegan Paul.

RYCROFT, C. (1968). *A Critical Dictionary of Psychoanalysis.* London: Thomas Nelson.

SENGE, P.M. (1990). *The Fifth Discipline – The Art and Practice of the Learning Organization.* New York: Doubleday.

SKYNNER, R. and CLEESE, J. (1983). *Families and How to Survive Them.* London: Methuen.

SMUTS, J.C. (1987). *Holism and Evolution.* Cape Town, RSA: N and S Press. (Originally published 1926.)

SPEED, B. (1984). How really real is real? *Family Process,* **23**, 511–520.

SPEED, B. (1991). Reality exists OK?: An argument against constructivism and social constructionism. *Journal of Family Therapy,* **13**, 395–410.

WEX, M. (1979). *Let's Take Back Our Space.* (Alba, P. and Garlick, V., Eds, English ed). (Albert, J. and Schultz S., trans.). Hamburg: Frauenliteraturverlag Hermine Fees.

WOLF, N. (1990). *The Beauty Myth.* London: Chatto and Windus.

WOLFE, L. M. (1951). *John Muir: Son of the Wilderness.* New York: Houghton Mifflin.

ZOHAR, D. (1990). *The Quantum Self.* London: Bloomsbury.

Appendix I
The Opening of the Wall; End of Voluntary South African Exile, October 1990; Moscow Morning, August 1991

The Opening of the Wall

There was such rejoicing in the air
and such exuberance in people's eyes and hands and feet
many were laughing and crying or stoic and shining
and many came to welcome them and to get drunk on freedom
and through the people-lined womb of Checkpoint Charlie – what a happy name –
they came with their lovers to share a first kiss of free soil
two medical students with tears and stars on their faces
and a photograph of a wall and a photograph of a house – for all my life I have
woken up every morning seeing that wall in front of my house
For all my life

With the help of the policemen and the lights and the champagne they came with
their babies and their children – look my child – this is a moment of such
magnitude that you will hardly be able to bear it in your heart when you
remember in years to come no matter what happens next
and the blond baby sat on his father's shoulders and yawned while
the welcomers clapped and shouted and kept spilling into the road to
greet the drivers of the tired unsensual cars and the megaphone
instruction hovered between repression and chaos became a chant to free the
road, to make free the road, let them through, *fahrbahn frei, fahrbahn frei,*
fahrbahn frei

At the same time the schizophrenic danced and the waiting people looked
at him in sympathy and tolerance and did not burn him in a concentration
camp even though he whirled around in a slow motion dance of his own and
followed no sense nor made no sense that we could see but that
he said he was waiting for his mother who had never come before

---

From Clarkson, P. (1990). The opening of the Wall. *Self and Society,* **18**, 28–30, with permission.

and we crowded together as if there were no differences between us
the young and the old, the natives of the soil and the visitors, the one
journalist who said to the other that there were enough pictures to go round and
the guards and we were willing them on – no matter how sane they were – with
every step they took towards us
As if they needed it

An old woman came and showed what she had bought for the hundred marks
she got from the bank which was open even late at night even on Sunday in a
queue that was twenty-one years and thousands of patient people long –
a black polyester dress, bananas and chocolate for her granddaughter
since her husband was long dead and she was going home east even though
she was dumpily lovely because that was her home what a day she had had
and she would like some coffee and yes to beer and brandy and she had never
even tasted Coca-Cola before – she drank it all, it was one o'clock in the
morning and she had nowhere to sleep and no desire
I can sleep again another time

After seeing candles and flowers and wreaths and names of men who had died
and people remembering people crying and people dying – the sadder lonelier
dates of the *unbekannt* – the unknown dead (they say a child drowned in the
canal because to save her would have been death too)

Standing on a lookout post seventy people thick and tightly pressed against each
other because of the warmth of Potsdammerplatz as with
implacable efficiency the mines were cleared in the so-called death zone and
fences were built before the walls were knocked down and that left a passage
for people to walk through as though nothing was wrong
And hardly any rubble was left at all

Even though young men testosterone high and brave in a way they had felt
before climbed the walls and borrowed the hammers and chipped away at the
wall to look out through the holes through the graffiti through the arms of Allied
soldiers who were more than a bit puzzled that they had ended up defending the
wall from demolition by their own people?
There is a huge golden angel commemorating another war not far from the
Brandenburg gate which was constructed using the mouths of cannons who
might be surveying all this and another statue screaming for peace –
it is whispered that some eastern guards committed suicide rather than
protect those they had hunted before

If we are all connected to each other on this our planet Gaia of the one soul the
healing of this scar across the face of a city making separation between good
and bad, sheep or goats, either depending on which side you stood, one that
was right and another that was wrong while never yet truly cruelly seeing their

deepest flaws through the eyes of each other, this is our healing too. While my
shadow was where I was not what comforts lies the sickness unto death of the
nuclear bomb

But now the breaking of the wall in a city becomes the breaking of a wall in the
world soul with the line dividing good and evil going through the middle of
every heart

Liberty is no longer the opposite of oppression, no, liberty can be oppressive
and the oppressor liberating – what devastation to certainty, what a challenge to
despair, when people can come and go and nothing remains but that we take
responsibility for our choices and pay the price? And maybe as we begin to let
down the walls in our hearts, the sins which so long have disfigured our faces
can begin to constellate forgiveness for our own past crimes and a hope that we
would do somewhat better tomorrow.... I heard someone say having looked
my brother in the eyes I cannot want to kill him any more even though
I may hate him for taking my job

If a change is irrevocable, it cannot be unchanged, but it can change again.
In the nights of fear or despair to remember that change is possible. Even for
you. This commentator says this, that commentator says that. Does it
really matter? Will people from now on not have to pay for their choices?
Did you dream of one truth? And did you really expect one act to solve the world?
If the world was solved, how would we need each other?
After the change is made, the turning point turned, did you really think
the problems would be over? No, no, the problems are only just
beginning, maybe the worst ones.

The individual soul and the world soul echo each other indivisible and
synchronously connected in time chaotically connected in space
Are some less brainwashed than others just because the conditioning comes
brightly coloured and with images of golden screwdrivers hawking death on
billboards and in neon with jokes on a flickering screen with prices clearly
marked when cheap, but studiously hidden when you've got so much you don't
show how much you care. If that wall stands for anything it stands for
limitation, for the acceptance and protection of a frontier of imagination, a point
which beyond you do not think. Once love opposed death and now?
And what now?

Petrūska Clarkson

Berlin, 11 November 1989

End of Voluntary South African Exile, October 1990

Why come back now?
Why end the chosen exile, even speak the language
Help even the people who (on grounds of autonomy) resent the confession
(of a churchman on their behalf) of the 'sin' of apartheid?

Because they let the grey old black man out of prison
Because they ended the state of emergency
Because the whole 'European' laager is trembling
With the proof of toilets where black and white shit all come out brown.

No enough is not enough,
A colleague of many years says to a woman who thought she was a friend:
'I hate all whites' and she shudders in disbelief, betrayal, fear
I thought we were friends and that you trusted me all these years

It cannot ever be enough because the legacy is too ancient
The hatred's putrefied, the envy corrosive, the terror real
She is frightened that they will take her house away and
Keep her dogs on chains in the backyard when they finally win.

How would they know?
The ones who didn't know of her good works and her blanched
Devotion to their cause but saw only her face as she boarded their bus
And they were very angry at all the people they could not reach?

The houses have barbed wire round the fencing
The jacarandas and hibiscus bloom, the swimming pools gleam
Every house has a sign saying 'immediate armed response to alarm'
As he opens the iron ' rape gate' the man says: 'Welcome to our prison'.

Haloes of fire encircle the heads of the guilty as well as the innocent
Brains explode when they 'necklace' a person with petrol-soaked tyres.
A white man 'practices' how to cut the throat of a black taxi-driver and then after
A chase, a bullet and he claims it was a political crime.

Rumour has it that young children are killed to make 'medicine' for
The warriors to protect them from bullets (since they prefer knives).
A starved and chained white child was found in a dogkennel in suburbia
He barked and moved on all fours *as if* his real mother was a female dog.

Honour and honour and honour to all those who are prepared
For the generations it must take to unravel this particular part of
The human hell which suffers not only from its own particular cruelty,
But also from the ills of all the rest of our pathetically heroic human race.

Petrūska Clarkson, 1990

Moscow Morning, August 1991

The hum and the pulse and the noise of big city
Reminiscent of Johannesburg and New York
Alive with the human concerns of millions of beings
Standing in lines for food, spending money like dreams
Craving dollars, singing songs and making sculptures
Having tea and discussing weather, making love
Learning about healing from magicians or scientists
The hiss of speeding cars on scarred wet tarmac
The bite in the air with an edge of fear
The pity of it wasted isolated done

The anger of it, the despair and the righteousness
The dream, the intention that humans were perfectible
Even the good and the bad and the ugly.
There are puddles around the biers of carnations and dahlias
Cigarettes, sweets and drinks for the dead as the living
Protect the bypass from traffic until sufficient time has elapsed?
Even a fluffy toy dog is cuddled among the tributes of flowers
Which are important to the Russian people no matter what happens
A one-legged man stands guard over the memory of his friend
His tears are bitter gashes in his face
These are no ignorant natives no –
These are the sons and daughters
Of Tchaikovsky, Dostoevsky, Tolstoy, Gogol,
Rachmaninoff, Shakarov, Romanov.
These are the peasants of splendour
The people with soul in their eyes and their hearts
Who made barricades from magnificent rubble
Tore down the statues, dyed the road in blood and rain
A martyr shielded Hope from the peephole of a tank
A soldier refused to obey just like decades before
Stuck carnations – for real – into his gun and smiled
Wearing jeans and making music and choosing again
Another solution to become another problem
Endlessly life spins us in the eternal flux and every time
People believe that this time we have it right
And of course we have, for now.

Petrūska Clarkson, August 1991

Appendix II Post-modernist versus Modernist Terms

A setting out of terms in which post-modernism may be seen as opposed to modernism rather than a reformulation of it (Hassan, 1982, pp.267–268). No doubt, other conceptual problems lurk in the matter of postmodernism. Such problems, however, can not finally inhibit the intellectual imagination... Yet the dichotomies this table represents remain insecure, equivocal. For differences shift, defer, even collapse; concepts in any one vertical column are not at all equivalent; and inversions and exceptions, in both modernism and post-modernism, abound.

Modernism	**Post-modernism**
Romanticism/symbolism	'Pataphysics'/Dadaism
Form (conjunctive/closed)	Antiform (disjunctive/open)
Purpose	Play
Design	Chance
Heirarchy	Anarchy
Mastery/logos	Exhaustion/Silence
Art object/finished work	Process/performance/happening
Distance	Participation
Creation/totalisation	Decreation/deconstruction
Synthesis	Antithesis
Presence	Absence
Centring	Dispersal
Semantics	Rhetoric
Genre/boundary	Text/intertext
Paradigm	Syntagm
Hypotaxis	Parataxis
Metaphor	Metonymy
Selection	Combination
Root/depth	Rhizome/surface
Interpretation/reading	Against interpretation/misreading
Signified	Signifier
Lisible (readerly)	*Scriptible* (writerly)
Narrative/*grand histoire*	Antinarrative/*petit histoire*
Master code	Idiolect
Symptom	Desire
Genital/phallic	Polymorphous/androgynous
Paranoia	Schizophrenia
God the Father	The Holy Ghost
Origin/cause	Difference–difference/trace
Metaphysics	Irony
Determinacy	Indeterminacy
Transcendence	Immanence

Reproduced from Hassan, I. (1982). *The Dismemberment of Orpheus: Toward a Postmodern Literature.* Madison, WI: University of Wisconson Press, with permission.

Author Index

Subject Index